Challenge Authority

Memoir of a Baby Boomer

Tom Garrison

Challenge Authority

Address all inquiries to Tom Garrison at:
challengeauthority78@yahoo.com

Visit the Challenge Authority Facebook page
Your comments are welcome.

Published by CreateSpace Independent Publishing Platform

First Edition
St. George, Utah
Copyright 2014
ISBN 978-1494798246

Challenge Authority
Memoir of a Baby Boomer
Contents

Dedication   6

Introduction   7

Chapter One
January 18, 1952—Summer 1970: The Groundwork

    Introduction   13

    The Original Hanging Chads Caper   19

    Pinball Wizard   21

    Canal Water Skiing   23

    Americans Won't Do That Type of Work   25

    Who Are the Brain Police?   29

    Don't Disrespect the Varsity Letter   31

    Against the Vietnam War? Sure.   32
    Against the Country? Nope.

    Feel a Draft?   34

Chapter Two
Fall 1970—Fall 1980: College and First Marriage

    Introduction   41

    A Concern for Quality   44

    Damn, They Were Right   47

    Little Politics   52

A Night at the Opera   57

Antiwar Work and Nonviolence   59

Sly and the Family Stone   65
Smoking Head Concert

The Chair of Power   67

Road Trip   69

Chapter Three
Winter 1981—Fall 1989: Intense Leftist Political Activity

Introduction   73

Divorce and the Great Santa   75
Barbara Man Shortage of 1981

Defeat the Devil: Diablo Canyon   78
Nuclear Power Plant

New Job, New Love, New Life   87

War Resisters League   92
And War Tax Resistance

Justice Prevails!   98

Santa Barbara Tenants Union   103

Go Reds, Smash State   107

Storming the Gates of Santa Barbara City Hall   117

Gays and Lesbians   130

Peace and Freedom Party   132

Socialists as Party Animals   138

Self-defense and the Left   141

Chapter Four
Winter 1990—Winter 2000: The Questioning Years

Introduction   143

Scared? I Ain't Scared of Nuthin!   146
(Well, Maybe a Few Things.)

Great Expectations   152

I am Somebody   155

Lucy the Vibes Monitoring Cat   157

Guide to Political Videos   161

Desert Rats   164

Illegal Immigration: The Third Rail   168
of Leftist Politics

Dad's Death—Do I Have Cirrhosis of the Soul?   176

Why I Left the Left   178

Chapter Five
Spring 2000—Fall 2013: Risk Taking

Introduction   192

Me? I Work for the Government   194

Look Out Donald Trump,   201
Here Comes Tom and Deb

Is There Anything More Annoying   206
Than a Family Christmas Letter?

Sonya Deserved Better   215

Can I Make Up My Incompletes?   218

Hell in the 'Hood   220

Those Who Can Do, Those Who Can't Write   225

Timeline: Personal and Historical   231

Another Book by Tom Garrison   260

Dedication

This memoir is dedicated to my wonderful wife Deb Looker. Thanks for all the editing, suggestions, and general good cheer as I struggled to put this book together. You now know more about my life than is probably good for either of us.

Introduction

The Baby Boomer generation (estimated at around 75 million) became politically active in the 1960s and 1970s, leaving its' mark on society. The sheer size of this human tsunami rolled through American society and fueled the continuing Civil Rights, Gay Rights, and Women's Movements and agitation against war. It also coincided with (caused?) loosening social mores, the sexual revolution, widespread recreational drug use, political correctness, identity politics, diminishment of personal responsibility, and excesses in many areas.

In addition, the leftist portion of my generation shouldered two burdens—work for a more egalitarian and just society without succumbing to a group rights/identity politics/political correctness that negates the bedrock of individual rights on which our country was founded and flourished. There is no disputing the first goal has met much success while the latter has, unfortunately, become entrenched in political life and discourse.

In his book *Popular Government in America* (1968), Dr. Charles S. Hyneman argues that a stable popular government rests on three social requisites: (1) a commitment to and provision for *individual and group autonomy* (freedom); (2) a commitment to *equality*; and (3) *commonalty*—a common mind on the objectives and methods of government. To complicate matters, these social requisites are often in conflict. A nation cannot achieve these ideals in equal measure—it is a dynamic interaction.

For example, government that promotes equality by legalizing closed union shops (a worker must join the union as a condition of employment) may ostensibly enhance equality among the employees. However, it certainly and sharply reduces the individual employees' autonomy or freedom. The individual cannot bargain with the employer; they must join the union as a requirement of employment; their mandatory dues may fund political candidates with which they disagree; and so on.

As classical liberal economist and Nobel Laureate Friedrich A. Hayek (1948) noted:

> There is all the difference in the world between treating people equally and attempting to make them equal.

While the first is the condition of a free society, the second means as De Tocqueville describes it, "a new form of servitude."

My first four decades, the emphasis was upon increasing the commitment to equality. At the time I believed it was necessary. However, beginning in the mid-1990s I saw the pendulum swing so far toward equality that autonomy/freedom became threatened. This trend also greatly contributed to a lessening of commonalty. As limited government becomes only a hazy memory, our country has become sharply divided on objectives and methods of government.

The 1960s mantra of "Challenge Authority" was the basis of my political activism. What exactly does "challenge authority" mean? Certainly more than disobeying your parents as a kid. Or calling the police "pigs." Those are juvenile acts of rebellion. Challenging authority is not an attention getting ploy to display your courage or smarts or just for the sake of a good fight. A key component is resisting the temptation to act impulsively. In short, it's okay to break certain rules. But know why the rule exists, and have a good reason for breaking it.

In a serious political context, challenging authority does not have to be negative, especially when done with a clear purpose. Challenging authority is a form of nonviolent direct action. You must know what you want to accomplish—hence the need for focus, confidence, and hard facts. A legal/moral/ethical foundation is a prerequisite for such disciplined non-conformity.

Actively challenging the status quo has always been the first step in important societal change. The Women's Movement began with women challenging the dominant paradigm that women were unfit or unable to accomplish certain tasks. The modern Civil Rights struggle began with people such as Rosa Parks refusing to accept second class citizenship. As Mahatma Gandhi notes:

Without an active expression of it, non-violence, to my mind is meaningless (Merton 1964, 36).

In the United States we are fortunate that these challenges don't generally result in bloody confrontations. As I write, American still have the ability to nonviolently challenge the government and other institutions of authority.

However, challenging the status quo does require an informed citizenry. It does little good to agitate for change when no one cares or knows about your actions. Voltaire probably expressed it best when he said:

> So long as the people do not care to exercise their freedom, those who wish to tyrannize will do so; for tyrants are active and ardent, and will devote themselves in the name of any number of gods, religious and otherwise, to put shackles upon sleeping men ("Selected Political Writings of Voltaire" 2013).

The title *Challenge Authority: Memoir of a Baby Boomer* tells it all. Each of the five chapters contains at least a couple of challenge authority stories. In most cases I still believe my challenge, or at least questioning authority, was justified and the correct path. However, a few times my challenging authority was a dismal failure, often due to my immaturity and lack of experience.

In Chapter One I questioned the rule, while in high school, of disallowing the wearing of an earned varsity letter on anything other than a letter jacket. Pretty trivial, but it indicates my mindset. Upon turning 18, I began a 2 ½ battle with the Selective Service System (The Draft). I could have been permanently deferred from the outset, bad eyesight that did not meet military standards, and I knew this. But my struggle against the most coercive arm of the government took precedent.

In the 1970s, Chapter Two, I got married to my high school sweetheart in 1972. Her parents didn't much like me, and believed the marriage would not last. They were right. I now believe my desire to challenge their authority and prove them wrong was at least as strong as my love for their daughter. But it was not all self-centered activity. In my senior year in college (1973-74) I challenged my professors, all decent people and some were friends, to equalize the structural power somewhat and let the student, me, sit in their plush swivel "chair of power" behind the imposing desk while they took the hard-backed small student chair. We discussed the reasoning, and they all went along. I'm not sure the partial role reversal made much difference, but it was a worthwhile exercise for me and them.

The eighties (Chapter Three)—what a decade. I ended graduate school, found a job I held for 18 years, got married to my still sweetie, and was a whirling dervish of political activity. I was arrested, with nearly 2,000 other protesters for blockading Diablo Canyon Nuclear Power Plant in an attempt to prevent it going online. Deb and I challenged our last landlord in court over a cleaning deposit and won. I co-founded the Santa Barbara Chapter of the Socialist Party as a vehicle to challenge the prevailing capitalist system. Electoral politics beckoned and I twice ran openly as a socialist for Santa Barbara City Council. And more. I'm exhausted just thinking of the enormous amount of energy my comrades and I put into nonviolently challenging the political establishment.

The 1990s (Chapter Four) Deb and I shifted from intense political activity to more personal concerns. I still took a few risks. A big one was writing a couple letters to the editor and an opinion essay about illegal immigration that were published in local newspapers. I openly opposed the prevailing leftist position of basically supporting an open door policy for illegal immigrants. That cost a few friendships. Other actions were more personal. How about challenging my fears? I got my ear pierced (I have a fear of holes in my body) and bungee jumped out of a hot air balloon (I'm not a big fan of heights). Several hikes Deb and I went on included walking along exposed trails on the sides of cliffs. By the middle of the decade we had drifted away from socialism and flirted with libertarianism. At the end of the 1990s we were registered libertarians.

Since 2000 (Chapter Five) a few cases of risk taking have dominated our lives. In 2000 I quit my job of 18 years to begin a new career in a totally different field as a real property appraiser in the Santa Barbara County Assessor's Office. A bit of my challenging authority personality came out during this job (in 2006) via my infamous "No Carrots, No Sticks" email to top management. In it I criticized their inability to reward self-motivated, productive employees (me and some others) and to punish unmotivated, unproductive, "just putting in my time" employees. Of course, mandatory union membership was a contributing factor. In 2005, Deb and I challenged prevailing wisdom by producing the first of our annual Christmas letters that were creative and funny while informing the reader of our activities. Hard to believe, but true. We ended the decade by saying good-bye to Santa Barbara and moving to St.

George, Utah. We knew no one in Utah and I quit my well-paying job to make the move.

While important, politics is not everything. I have found that a life solely devoted to political activity is an impoverished life. I enjoyed, and continue to enjoy, sports. I was a good high school athlete, and since enjoy participating in softball, basketball, and bowling. Since 1982 I've had an enthusiastic spouse who shares in my crazy adventures. We both enjoy gardening, sports, politics, and exploring/hiking the most remote places we can find in the great American southwest.

Most memoirs such as mine utilize some original documents, but ultimately rely on analysis from afar, removed from the daily grind of life and the concomitant emotional highs and lows and laughter. My story is grounded in that daily life. The analysis is not years or decades removed from events. The stories are based on years of correspondence to and from me; my published articles; articles published about me; decades of journals; poems; photographs; other written material; and my, hopefully not too faulty, memory. The point is that this history is based on original material; it is not edited to suit any agenda. The events and ideas are discussed in their historical context as we Baby Boomers lived it. The raw analysis and emotion of planning a city council campaign is presented, not what an outside observer (or even a participant) chooses to focus on in some distant future. In short this is history as lived and perceived by the participants as it was happening.

While I doubt most Baby Boomers experienced politics as intensely as I, virtually every member of my generation went through at least some of what I experienced. I changed from a bright, hard-working yet insecure youth, to assertive democratic socialist political activist, to a more secure, mature, and happy middle-aged libertarian.

Every Baby Boomer, and anyone interested in recent history from the ground level can share the experience of my book on both a rational and deeply emotional level. If you were not there (there being that state of "in the zone" focus on your activity), this is a chance to vicariously experience the intensity, and if you were there you can reminisce about the "old days."

This book was occasionally painful to write—difficult memories. I spent hours reading original documents—much of it my letters and journals from decades ago. I'd like to think I'm a fairly normal guy within one standard deviation of the norm for emotional development. That may have been a bit of a stretch in my 20s (the 1970s). Later in life, I think I achieved that elusive emotional "normal" status.

I have a strong desire to be truthful in my stories, yet not lower the hurtful bomb on unsuspecting friends and acquaintances who knew me over the decades. This desire provided a strong motivation to constantly examine my own feelings, thoughts, and behavior. Given the blessing of perspective (it does help to be decades removed from my most pain causing behavior) I was all too often not the person I'd now like to think I was. That's my burden.

A person needs three things to be happy: someone to love; something to do; and something to look forward to. I deeply love my wife Deb. She has been there more than half my life.

Regarding something to do, this retirement gig is nothing if not busy—basketball each week, hiking each month, house chores, gardening, volunteer work, and slipping in a little writing when I have time.

I look forward to exploring new areas in the southwest with Deb and writing about our newest adventure. I look forward to chuckling when Deb comes up with a witticism. And I look forward to this book becoming a bestseller. I am nothing if not positive.

References

Hayek, Friedrich A. 1948. *Individualism and Economic Order*. Chicago: University of Chicago Press.

Hyneman, Charles S. 1968. *Popular Government in America*. New York: Atherton Press.

Merton, Thomas. 1964. *Gandhi on Non-Violence*. New York: New Directions.

"Selected Political Writings of Voltaire" website. 2013. Last modification unknown.
http://www.constitution.org/volt/volt.htm.

Chapter One
January 18, 1952—Summer 1970
The Groundwork

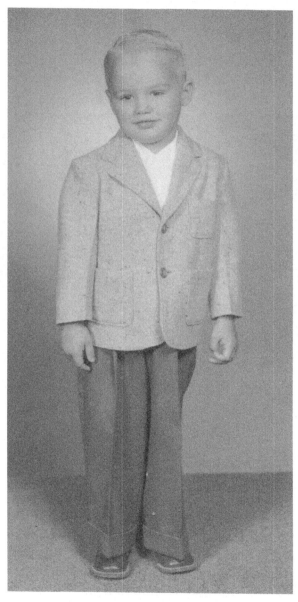

Me styling at three years old.

Introduction

I am the youngest of four children (three boys and one girl) to two Dust Bowl Okies who migrated to the Central Valley in California. My mother, Nell, was memorialized in a famous Merle Haggard (Haggard 1969) song "Okie from Muskogee" released in 1969. Well, maybe Merle was not singing about my mom, but she is an Okie from Muskogee.

My parents were fairly apolitical, with Republican leanings. My father, "Tommy" to his friends, was a hay loader and small-time entrepreneur.

Mom and dad, circa 1945

What's a hay loader? If you ever lived in or have driven through a farming area, you probably saw alfalfa fields. A hay bailer traverses the field, cutting the alfalfa and compressing it into large rectangular bales (about four by three by two feet) bound by wire. The hay bales were stacked, 15 feet or so high, near the fields. My father's job entailed the use of a Rube Goldberg-type car engine-based contraption (that he built) on the bed of his pick-up to move bales from the stack to 18-wheel trucks. It went like this: he stuck a long steel J-shaped spike on the end of a steel cable in a hay bale; the steel cable ran through a pulley at the top of a long A-frame; rev the engine with a cord to the gas intake; lift the bale from the stack to the truck bed; the truck driver grabs the bale with hand hooks and moves into place; move the pick-up when necessary. Four or five jobs a day, sometimes at night, wasn't unusual; hundreds of hay bales moved. A lot of physical labor, not much fun, but enough remuneration to support a family of six in the 1950s and 1960s.

As kids he would occasionally take some of us, never four at once (we couldn't all fit in the cab of a pick-up), to a job site to "help." Help usually consisted of chasing lizards, fetching water or a soda, and generally making a nuisance of ourselves.

The siblings: (left to right) Ted, Kathy, me, and Jim, circa late 1950s

Of all my siblings, I'm the only one who inherited my dad's tinkering/mechanical abilities. Not to be too harsh, but my two older brothers did well changing a light bulb without getting electrocuted. In my teens I disassembled a neighbor's non-working lawn mower; reassembled it; and amazingly it worked. I carried this interest and ability into adulthood. It served me well in fixing bikes and cars and maintaining and repairing an eighty-year old house that my future wife Deb and I owned for 25 years in Santa Barbara.

Dad also owned half interest in the local Foster's Freeze burger joint. Conveniently located just down our street, it played a pivotal role in my nutritional upbringing. He also occasionally supplemented his income at the poker game in the back room of the Shafter Motel. Only years later did I learn that he won much more often than not.

As was the norm in those days, my mom was a homemaker. I don't recall her being a great cook. She made up for it by having a good heart, of which I too often took advantage. For some transgression it would be "go to your room." No time limit, and within 15 minutes she would be there saying I could go outside if I promised to be good. Sure, I was a kid and kids don't take such promises too seriously. I believe this leniency on the part of mom, was partially attributable to a "been there, done that" feeling since I was the last of the brood. In contemporary parlance, I was a free range kid (Skenazy 2009). I got used to bugs, rocks, cuts and scrapes without constant supervision. I would make it mostly on my own, or not make it at all—and for that I'm grateful.

While mom was a bit too lenient in parenting, my father balanced the equation. Ever been spanked with a belt? Didn't really hurt much, but made a bit of a psychic impression. Don't do the deed if you can't take the punishment. Today this would be labeled child abuse. As the spankee, I disagree. If my father had been socialized in later, gentler times perhaps he would have given me a "time out." However, there are wrong behaviors and consequences for those behaviors. That is an essential lesson for anyone, especially a child, to learn. It's called personal responsibility and is the basis of any just and stable civilization.

We lived in a three bedroom, one bath, 1,500 or so square foot house—fairly crowded with six people and a collection of animals. Both parents loved animals. Our family always had at least one cat and usually a dog. At various times rabbits, hamsters, and horned toads joined the menagerie. My siblings and I carried on the family tradition of rescuing cats and dogs. There have been only a couple of very short periods that my life was not shared with an "animal companion."

What is more apropos for a Baby Boomer than growing up in a small town in a rural area? Not exactly "Leave it to Beaver", but like the Beaver I was a mischievous kid. Not a bad child, but one with an abundance of energy and curiosity—if I was born decades later I would undoubtedly have been a Ritalin kid. I'm sure in my somewhat rebellious teenage years my parents secretly wished, at least once or twice, that I would run away. I fooled them and hung around.

It was a great opportunity being raised in a small farming community—Shafter, California—in the southern end of the Central Valley. The town was established as a loading dock alongside the Santa Fe Railroad. Beginning in 1914 property was sold and the town incorporated in 1938. It was named after General William Rufus Shafter who commanded US troops in Cuba during the Spanish-American War ("Shafter, California" 2013).

The town was surrounded by miles of fields—mostly cotton, potatoes, and alfalfa—in which to roam on my bike (and later cars) with my buddies. I'd bet all the parents were relieved with us spending most our waking hours outside, we'd be annoying someone other than them. Shafter is 18 miles northwest of Bakersfield, the commercial hub of the southern San Joaquin Valley. There is an old joke about small towns: a real small town meant that you didn't have to use the turn signals on your car, because anybody behind you already knew where you were going. Not quite true, but close enough.

During my years there, 1952 to 1969, the community was 95+% white. Looking at my grade and high school yearbooks reveals few black or brown faces. Even with the Civil Rights Movement gathering steam at this time, I don't recall racial epithets and racism being part of the cultural mix.

The town's population of about 4,500 in the 1950s meant one school system; those in your age cohort accompanied you from elementary through high school. Of course, once the hormones kicked in, dating presented a problem. You had sat in the same classes with most of the people you knew since kindergarten. Like an extended family, everyone knew just about everything about everyone. It made for close friendships, but boy-girl relationships felt a little like dating your sister.

As a youngster, my family and it seemed as if the town as a whole was not politically interested or involved to any large degree. Reflecting back, it's obvious that for the adults this was a function of a particular social milieu—a small, white farming community. Very few 1950s version of uber-liberals would find many kindred spirits in a conservative farm community. Additionally, the political lines were much softer in those days—politics had not evolved into a blood sport. After all, who could get terribly excited about "I like Ike" or Adali Stevenson.

That all changed as the Baby Boomers hit their teenage years in the 1960s. Change and challenges to authority where everywhere—the Civil Rights Movement; the anti-Vietnam War and Anti-Draft Movements; the nascent Women's Movement; rock 'n roll; hippies; and, of course, drugs, especially marijuana.

The oddity is my attraction to politics from an early age—perhaps some long dormant recessive political gene coming to fore. I was a political animal. Unfortunately, shyness was part of the mix. I seldom spoke in class, other than wisecracks. I was active, always involved in sports, loved to read just about anything (my older siblings textbooks and the baseball cards found on the back of cereal boxes being favorites), and enjoyed learning and did well in school. But the shyness prevented me from participating in school politics as an insider. I was, however, very active outsider as I entered my teenage years. By the summer of my 18th year I was a draft counselor, a "job" I continued for several years.

References

Haggard, Merle. 1969. "Okie from Muskogee (song)." Song co-written and sung by Merle Haggard. Wikipedia. Last modified September 26, 2013. http://en.wikipedia.org/wiki/Okie_from_Muskogee_(song).

Skenazy, Lenore. 2009. *Free-Range Kids; How to Raise Safe, Self-Reliant Children (Without Going Nuts With Worry)*. New York: Jossey-Bass.

"Shafter, California." 2013. Wikipedia. Last modified April 29, 2013. http://en.wikipedia.org/wiki/Shafter,_California.

The Original Hanging Chads Caper

Most people never heard of a chad, or hanging chad, until the contentious 2000 presidential election. Remember the disputed results in Florida due to the use of punch card ballots in the Sunshine State? A chad refers to paper fragments created when holes are punched in paper, cardstock, or similar materials and the material is not cleanly cut ("Chad" 2013). The result is a "hanging chad"—a bit of paper linking the larger material to the punched out part. Anyone using a hole punch has undoubtedly created a few hanging chads.

Being a small town, Shafter had only one elementary school—Richland School. The courageous teachers handled the local rug rats from kindergarten through eighth grade. Most all the kids purchased the school lunch. Each week you bought a school lunch card of fairly flimsy cardstock, printed with five squares for five meals. Then it cost three bucks or so. Exiting the lunch line with your nutritious meal, you handed your lunch card to the "lunch card lady" who punched out one of the squares with a hand-held hole punch, creating a chad.

Gap-tooth, squinty-eyed six year old 1st grader (1958-59)—me.

Occasionally, just like in Florida in 2000, the hole was not cleanly punched and the circular dot of paper (the hanging chad) remained attached to the lunch card. Being an enterprising fellow even at a young age, I slightly moistened any hanging chad and did my best to reinsert it in its hole; smuched the chad around so it—kind of—appeared the square was not punched. Some of my attempts to reinsert the chad resembled a child's effort (imagine that), while others were a piece of art.

Holding my breath I presented my doctored lunch card the next day and hoped the lunch card lady would repunch the altered square. Alas, her hawk eyes almost always avoided my repaired square and she moved to the next one. However, occasionally to my delight, I snuck one past her.

If you can do this over a couple of months at some point you collect five days of free lunches. When your parents gave you money to purchase the next weekly lunch card, you pocketed the cash instead. It was the original hanging chads caper.

References

"Chad (paper)." 2013. Wikipedia. Last modified May 7, 2013. http://en.wikipedia.org/wiki/Chad_(paper).

Pinball Wizard

My dad was a small-time entrepreneur and owned half of the local Foster's Freeze burger joint. Conveniently located just down our street, it played a pivotal role in my nutritional upbringing. Along with sustenance, I learned some valuable lessons at Foster's Freeze; among the most important was don't get caught.

Like most such places, Foster's Freeze had a small enclosed dining area. The joint was a hangout for local kids from grade school age to teenagers. One attraction was the pinball machine. That machine was the beginning of my love affair with pinball. She (all pinball machines are female) was an electro-mechanical wonder with a colorful board and blinking lights. It was almost as if she were calling me, "Tommy, come and play me. Can you earn a replay?"

Put the silver sphere in play, work the flippers, rack up the points—adolescent nirvana.

After hours of play, my buddies and I were pretty good. But pretty good does not earn a replay after every paid game. (Maybe after every tenth game.) What we needed was an edge, a way to level the playing field. Wait a minute, level the playing field. Hmmm. The playing field is literally at a slight slant. If it was more level the ball would move a bit slower, increasing your chances of achieving perfect timing on those fairly rare but crucial tipping the ball from the end of one flipper to the other flipper shots. And, of course, also giving a few milliseconds more time to line up routine flipper strokes.

What a breakthrough. Shove some folded paper napkins under the front two legs and a more level field ensued. There was a tradeoff, however. The more level machine tilted easily. You had to be careful with your bumps while flipping. Sure we were cheating, but we earned more free games so somehow that made it okay.

Of course, one day the manager noticed the stacks of folded paper napkins under the front legs of the machine. From then on it was a cat and mouse game. The manager would periodically check the dining area to see if we were cheating and, if possible, we would quickly remove the offending napkins. Sure enough one day I was caught in the act of altering the machine and was banned from the establishment for two weeks. My parents were not happy, but somehow I survived.

21

Was it a coincidence that one of the best rock bands from this era, The Who, came out with their hit "Pinball Wizard" in 1969? Or that the single was part of the rock opera album *Tommy*. It had to be named Tommy and feature a pinball wizard? Come on. Okay, I wasn't deaf, dumb, and blind, but I was a pinball wizard. That song was written for me ("Pinball Wizard" 1969A; "Pinball Wizard" 1969B).

References

"Pinball Wizard." 1969A. Song by The Who. Written by Pete Townshend and released in 1969. Wikipedia. Last modified September 6, 2013.
http://en.wikipedia.org/wiki/Pinball_Wizard.

"Pinball Wizard" Lyrics—The Who. 1969B. Sing365.com website. Last modification unknown.
http://www.sing365.com/music/lyric.nsf/Pinball-Wizard-lyrics-The-Who/214479A85C625AEE48256977002CE1D3.

Canal Water Skiing

California has the nation's most irrigation-intensive agriculture. Over decades Californians, often with federal assistance, created an extensive irrigation canal infrastructure. Most of the thousands of miles of irrigation canals are located in the Central Valley. Mention California and most folks think of sunny beaches, movie stars, and goofy politicians. But agriculture is the economic backbone of the state; it produces about 25 percent of the nation's food supply ("Central Valley Project" 2013).

Entering teenage years, Shafter boys thought of three things: obtaining a driver's license, getting the girl, and water skiing. The first and third sometimes led to the second. Water skiing was a bit of problem since there are few close-by lakes and the need for a boat. However the good folks in government and their agribusiness allies helped us out. Through the magic of unanticipated consequences, they provided miles of easily accessible, albeit narrow, waterways in which to water ski.

Many of the major irrigation canals crisscrossing the southern Central Valley are 20 to 25 feet across, eight to ten feet deep at their deepest, and, best of all, have dirt roads on each bank. Upon someone in your group getting a driver's license, we all piled in the wreck of a car they finagled from their parents and went canal water skiing.

Here is how it goes. Have the skier on the far side of the canal; tie a tow line to the car bumper and throw the line to the skier; yell at the idiot, excuse me the skier, to get ready; and then drive as fast as possible on a very narrow dirt road with a four feet embankment on one side and a water canal on the other. Every mile or so a large diameter standpipe juts a few feet above the water line. Add some alcohol and real water skiing commences. This is not some sissy sport on a peaceful lake. This takes courage, partially due to the risk of bodily damage and it was illegal. But you can't find a better way to beat the 95+ degree summer heat in the southern Central Valley.

Several things can happen. The car can veer off the dirt road, doesn't happen often. The skier falls and forgets to let go of the tow line. This occasionally occurs and results in dirt burns, seldom real damage. The skier manages to weave back and forth, kicking up huge rooster tails until smashing into a standpipe—never happened. Or, best of all, the skier completes the run, releases the tow line, cruises to the dirt bank, and steps out of the skis onto dry land without anything other than their lower legs getting wet. That is a "ten" run.

Canal water skiing was a potentially dangerous, albeit useful rite of passage. I never heard of anyone dying or being gravely injured doing this sport. Sure there were some bumps and bruises, the price of showing you had guts. In addition, canal water skiing engendered camaraderie and was a nonviolent method for young guys, and some gals, to gain a modicum of respect.

References

"Central Valley Project." 2013. Wikipedia. Last modified October 6, 2013.
http://en.wikipedia.org/wiki/Central_Valley_Project.

Americans Won't Do That Type of Work

"American won't do that type of work." In the last two decades or so, I've heard that phrase from elected officials, political pundits and activists, and read it as the theme of many articles. I don't believe the validity of that statement. It acts as a cover for people who want to justify the invasion of illegal aliens who supposedly will do the work Americans won't. Of course, open border advocates never consider that a flood of low-skilled workers puts downward pressure on wages in those jobs for which they do have necessary skills—agricultural work, low level service work in restaurants, and so on. If millions of illegal aliens were not doing those entry level jobs, the scarcity of labor would inevitably push up wages. Those jobs would then be more attractive for Americans.

In any case, at least one American—me—did those low skilled jobs for several years. I took pride in my work and was a good employee.

In the summer of 1966 I was 14-years old and looking forward to entering high school. Coming from a working class family, it wasn't a question of working or not, but when I would begin. It was summer, school was out, and I looked for a job. In Shafter, most high school-age guys worked in agriculture or the packing plants or "sheds." Being totally unskilled I began my search at the minor leagues of packing sheds, the onion sheds.

Onion and the more numerous potato packing plants were built alongside railroad tracks, a necessary location for moving the produce. Both applied the division of labor concept to sort, package, and begin transportation of the vegetables. Large trucks dumped the onions/potatoes into a huge bin; conveyor belts carried the produce to a washing area; sorting, usually by women, was next (prime, seconds, and lousy grades); and then on to a packing area. For onions, the majority were guided into 50 pound bags; for potatoes, 50 or 100 pounds depending on the order.

Wide conveyor belts hummed carrying their produce. Dividers along the belt diverted onions/potatoes into several openings or stations where they fell into burlap bags. The "front" received the bulk of the produce and higher per hour wages; the "side" had a more relaxed pace and less pay. A man at each station (no women worked the front line), the "jigger," filled the bag; moved it to a scale; and quickly attached another bag to four hooks. The sewer weighted the bag, adding or subtracting a few onions/potatoes to reach 50 or 100 pounds. He then placed a paper shim advertising the shed's name in the bag, sewed it up with half hitches on each end ("ear") with three stitches in the middle, and nudged it onto another conveyor belt that took it to the "trucker." My buddy, Jim, a big guy usually worked as a trucker. The trucker loaded the bags onto hand carts, five to a cart. He then "trucked" the bags to a semi-truck or railroad boxcar for transportation. It took a hell of a lot of bags to fill a boxcar.

Repeat that process for hours in a cacophony of industrial squeaks, whirrs, and moans reverberating off the sheet metal walls and roof. Most times the line was evenly paced and work was steady but not overwhelming. But a few times a day several trucks in a row would dump loads—quick time. This is where you earned your money. The bags would fill in less than ten seconds. The sewer had to adjust the weight, sew the bag, and place it on the belt to the trucker every few seconds. Do that for 30 to 45 minutes without falling behind. Worse than failing to draw to an inside straight was shutting down the line because you were overwhelmed. Not only was it embarrassing, if you did it often enough you could be demoted to the much slower "side" line at reduced pay.

My first job was as a "jigger." I quickly learned the basics and practiced sewing whenever possible. I usually worked the slower "side" but had a few stints with the big boys on the "front." Sewers had the highest status in the sheds—they had to know how to quickly and tightly sew a bag without jabbing themselves too many times with the cat claw sharp six inch long steel needle.

The sheds were no place for sissies, even the women working as sorters were tough. High school teenagers worked alongside rough looking men with tattoos. This was decades before every mother's son, and many daughters, was covered in tats—back then it meant something. Although I was no stranger to alcohol, breaks at the sheds were instructive. A game of craps and half pints of cheap whiskey were often prominent at lunch. I'm sure I took an occasional sip, but had enough sense to steer clear of the crap games. Money was too hard to come by to lose in a game of chance.

My mother, with a kind heart, brought me a sack lunch on one of my first days. A nice gesture that, being a teenager, pissed me off. Nothing quite as embarrassing as having your mom calling your name, looking for your while your high school friends and the lumpen proletariat milled about. I always bought or brought a lunch after that.

The onion and potato harvest season lasted only a few weeks each year. For the time I worked there I carried the onion fragrance, no matter how many showers I took—it was part of the job description. That side of the town also smelled of freshly cut onion for a few weeks. Potatoes weren't so bad. My first year I earned $104.26. The government took $14.60 in income taxes and $4.38 in FICA taxes.

In following years I moved up to the major leagues and worked the potato sheds, mostly as a sewer. Upon the completion of the harvest, I found work moving sprinkler irrigation pipes in the fields.

Moving pipe was a job. You and one other guy out in the fields before the sun made its appearance. Unhooking 40-foot lengths of three or four inch diameter pipe, move them a few rows, and putting them back together. Over and over and over until you finished a huge field. Mind numbing, back breaking. But the worst was working with wet, muddy pants and shoes for invariably water would slosh out a pipe onto your clothes.

In subsequent years I spent some post-onion/potato harvest time picking peaches. Like my other forays into the teenage work world, this provided much exercise and little money. The theory was that you fetch the peach, it ain't coming to you. You were given a large canvas sack with a strap that went over your neck. The sack was open at the bottom. On the bottom were two snap hooks. You folded the sack so the snap hooks attached to rings sewn into the top third of the bag. Then the fun began. Wrestle an eight foot long tripod ladder in a peach orchard so you were strategically positioned to pick as many peaches as you could reach—my long arms helped. Of course, a picker wanted to move the ladder as seldom as possible, so there was a lot of reaching for those last few fruits. Throughout the day, you would occasionally hear loud swearing and a thump—another picker straining for that last peach falling off their ladder. If memory serves, I spent a fair amount of time on the ground after a fall throwing eye darts at the just out of reach peach.

That sounds like a fun day. The torture part needs mentioning. All this was done in usually 95+ degree summer heat wearing long sleeve shirts. You did not want to come down with a bad case of peach fuzz itches—hence the long sleeves.

My second summer I grossed $348.20. I continued working the sheds, moving irrigation pipe, and picking fruit through high school. My earnings topped out at $541.36 in 1969.

Sure it was hard work, so what. We Baby Boomers were young and physically up to the challenge. In the 1960s the nanny state as we know it now was only a liberal dream. To a degree unheard of now, people had to earn their own way. Many people then, and now, work hard. My co-workers in these manual labor jobs, as far as I could tell, were all citizens. Americans did do that type of work.

Who Are the Brain Police?

No Baby Boomer memoir is complete without a drug story. The summer I was 15, 1967, the kids in my age cohort discovered marijuana. Actually some discovered it a little earlier and some never did (the pot smokers never trusted the latter).

One of my first experiences with smoking pot took place that summer. In July and August the average daytime temperature runs in the high 90s. Being a small town, we rode our bikes everywhere. Somehow a couple of buddies and I scored some reefer. The safest place to partake was in the country, never far away. After doing the deed, it seemed a great idea to cool off. Back on the bikes to Rick's house. His parents had true air conditioning, not just some cranky swamp cooler on the roof. We wobbled along on our bikes admiring the world. Somehow we managed to infiltrate his room without being spotted by parental units.

What to do? Not long before, the Mothers of Invention (creatively driven by Frank Zappa) released their debut album, *Freak Out!* ("Who Are the Brain Police?" 1966A; "Who Are the Brain Police" 1966B). Being very hip teenagers, we had a copy of said album. Put on the album, lay back, and let the Mothers mess with your mind. It would not be too far off the mark to say that this was one of those experiences that feel as if you had fallen down Alice's rabbit hole.

Frank begins teasing about brain police and melted plastic and chrome. Is my face melting? Brain police? Nooo, don't need any police in my brain. Then the refrain hits "I think I'm gonna die ... I think I'm gonna die ..." What? Don't do that. I'm young and healthy and NOT gonna die.

Although it would be years before I read Aldous Huxley's *The Doors of Perception*, (Huxley 1954) this experience certainly qualifies as a perceptional door opener. Three guys chilled in a small room with the temperature outside rivaling the sun's surface listening to music that would quickly break an Al-Qaeda sleeper agent. Throw in some Mary Jane and doors to new, strange perceptions begin to open.

References

Huxley, Aldous. 1954. *The Doors of Perception.* New York: Harper & Row.

"Who Are the Brain Police?" 1966A. Wikipedia. Last modified September 29, 2013.
http://en.wikipedia.org/wiki/Who_Are_the_Brain_Police%3F.

"Who Are The Brain Police?" 1966B. Zappa Wiki Kawaka. Last modified May 25, 2011.
http://wiki.killuglyradio.com/wiki/Who_Are_The_Brain_Polic e%3F.

Don't Disrespect the Varsity Letter

In the spring of my sophomore year, 1968, I earned a varsity letter in track for my pole vaulting ability. I was proud of it; few sophomores earned a varsity letter.

That fall, the beginning of my junior year, I wore my varsity letter sewn on a corduroy jacket, part of my "uniform." I did not want a letter jacket. Even though I was a jock, that was not my crowd. Besides, the jackets were an extravagant expense for a working class family.

This did not go over too well. Shafter High had a letterman's club, the arbiters of decorum for sports lettermen (and women). It seems as if I had made a grievous faux pas. Within a couple of days of first wearing my letter, I was confronted by several upper class lettermen. "You can't disrespect the letter by sewing it on that ratty coat." What? I stood my ground, we argued, and postured. Threats of pounding (them on me) emerged.

Luckily for my tormentors, for I would have torn them up, a teacher intervened. We took it to the principle. According to him, the letterman's club had the right to insist that letters be only worn on letterman's jackets—it was some rule. My argument that I had earned the letter and had the right to wear it on whatever apparel I wanted fell on deaf ears.

While this episode certainly alienated me even more from the conventional jock crowd, it did not dampen my enthusiasm for sports. My last year and a half of high school I attended West High School in Bakersfield. I was on the track team and earned a varsity letter each year.

Against the Vietnam War? Sure.
Against the Country? Nope.

October 15, 1969 and I was walking in Los Angles in my first major anti-war demonstration—The Moratorium to End the War in Vietnam ("Moratorium to End the War in Vietnam" 2013). I had attended demonstrations in Bakersfield, but they never amounted to much, a few dozen people at most. And the reception was mixed at best.

Here in LA it was heady times for the anti-war movement. Millions of Americans took part around the country, an estimated 10,000 in Los Angeles. All kinds of people carrying signs—teachers, students, ethnic and racial groups, workers, socialists, and so on. This is what people power is about I thought, my kind of place. These were the first major demonstrations against the Nixon administration's handling of the war. A Gallup poll that month revealed 58% of respondents said US entry into the war was a mistake ("Opposition to the U.S. involvement in the Vietnam War" 2013).

Then the chants began. "Ho, Ho, Ho Chi Minh, the NLF is gonna win." Okay, the NLF was the National Liberation Front (South Vietnamese communists) and Ho Chi Minh the leader of North Vietnam.

Shit, here I am all geared up to end the war and many of my fellow demonstrators were shouting that slogan. I was staunchly against the war, but not a communist sympathizer. Sure I wanted the US out of Vietnam, but even at the tender age of 17 I knew that communism was not a people-empowering ideology. Couldn't both sides just let the South Vietnamese decide their own fate?

Could I be an anti-war activist and not a communist sympathizer? Of course. The vast majority of the scores of anti-war folks I met as an activist through the next few decades were socialists or liberals, but not reds.

I do wish my fellow protesters that day had focused more on US withdrawal rather than a NLF victory.

References

"Moratorium to End the War in Vietnam." 2013. Wikipedia. Last modified September 14, 2013.

http://en.wikipedia.org/wiki/Moratorium_to_End_the_War_in_Vietnam.

"Opposition to the U.S. involvement in the Vietnam War." 2013. Wikipedia. Last modified October 12, 2013. http://en.wikipedia.org/wiki/Opposition_to_the_U.S._involvem ent_in_the_Vietnam_War

Feel a Draft?

January 18, 1970, my 18th birthday and a real milestone. The trappings of being a full citizen were within reach. Hadn't I contributed to society through my summer jobs for several years and paid my share of taxes. What else? How about voting?

In 1970 the voting age for most states, including California, was 21. Three more years before I, and millions of others in their late teens, were enfranchised. Bummer. But little did we, or anyone, know that within six months the voting age would be lowered to 18. On June 22, 1970, President Richard Nixon—the very embodiment of evil for many Baby Boomers—did a domestic version of going to China and signed an extension of the Voting Rights Act of 1965 lowering the voting age to 18. Within a little over another year, on July 1, 1971, the 26th Amendment to the US Constitution was ratified. This amendment barred the states or federal government from setting a voting age higher than 18 ("Twenty-sixth Amendment to the United State Constitution" 2013).

Nixon's action effectively ended the argument made by many young men that they could fight and die for their country (via The Draft) but not vote for the leaders who prosecuted the war.

Speaking of The Draft, the last chore for birthday 18 was registering with the Selective Service System (The Draft). While it seems unthinkable today, all men upon reaching their 18th birthday not only had to register within 30 days, but they could actually be conscripted (i.e., forced) into the military. Women did not, and still do not, face this burden—where the hell were the feminists when we males needed them?

I dutifully went down to the local Selective Service System (SSS) office and registered one day after my birthday. Having studied the SSS laws a bit (within six months I became a volunteer draft counselor), I knew my responsibility and rights. That day was the beginning of a titanic, but quiet to virtually the rest of the world, 2 ½ year battle between me and the most coercive arm of the federal government. What other government agency could throw you in jail for years for NOT doing something—either not registering for The Draft or refusing to join the military if conscripted.

Sounds a bit much to our present day sensibilities? Nope. Here is what is written in tiny type on the back of each draft card.

34

The law requires you to have this certificate in your personal possession at all times and to surrender it upon entering active duty in the Armed Forces.

The law requires you to notify your local board in writing within 10 days after it occurs, (1) of every change in your address, physical condition and occupational (including student), marital, family, dependency and military status, and (2) of any other fact which might change your classification.

Any person who alters, forges, knowingly destroys, knowingly mutilates or in any manner changes this certificate or who, for the purpose of false identification or representation, has in his possession a certificate of another or who delivers his certificate to another to be used for such purpose, may be fined not to exceed $10,000 or be imprisoned for not more than 5 years, or both (Selective Service System 1970).

Thus, a young man could be imprisoned for FIVE years and fined up to $10,000 (back in the 1970s) for destroying his draft card.

Being a vocal high school anti-war activist, I got involved in draft counseling with the Kern County Draft Information Service, organized about a year before, in the summer of 1970. Kern County was not exactly a hotbed of anti-war feelings. On December 19, 1971, the local newspaper, *The Bakersfield Californian*, ran a lengthy article titled "County Has Little Vocal War Protest."

There has been neither vocal antiwar nor antidraft movements in Kern County. Little evidence exists that in late 1971 either one is on the verge of surfacing.

Yet there are persons who oppose the draft and who believe young men facing military conscription aren't properly informed of their rights under the Selective Service laws....

Tom Garrison is a 19-year old political science major at Cal State Bakersfield and a volunteer draft counselor for 18 months.

Most who seek his services "want to stay out of the army" by their first admission.

"I'm just an average American youth" he says in response to how he would characterize himself. "I'm concerned about helping other kids."

Has he been successful? "It's hard to measure," he answers matter-of-factly. "Most don't come back."

A West High graduate, Garrison became upset several years ago when the school refused to allow equal time for rebuttal to an Army captain's presentation.

Although the Selective Service has prepared a draft rights curriculum for use in high schools, it has not been implemented in Kern County (Kearns 1971).

This was a fair article. It was a lonely struggle against The Draft and the Vietnam War. At times it seemed to be me—a budding agnostic—and a few local Quakers and assorted liberal odd balls. The local hippy contingent was content to stay stoned and seldom got involved in politics. Their activism, such as it was, seemed rooted in slogans, not rigorous analysis.

Draft-age young people, although not in great numbers, are still taking advantage of counseling offered by the Kern County Draft Information Service. Counselor Tom Garrison, far right, a Cal State Bakersfield student, "raps" with Gene Traver, Ron Antongiovanni and Steve Bispo. KCDIS spokesmen, who are unable to say if their two-year efforts are successful, contend the group exists not to "magically" exempt persons from military service but more realistically to inform registrants of rights under the Selective Service Act.—(Californian Photo)

Me, far right in photo, doing some draft counseling, December 1971.

My lifelong distrust of self-identified "hippies" was a result of their generally apolitical nature. Of course that generalization has tons of exceptions. But, again in general, most hippy types might do some sporadic political action but very few had the staying power (perhaps being stoned so often had something to do with that) for long-term political campaigns.

On the surface this may seem odd for someone such as me. During the 1970s I pretty much looked the part of a hippy—long hair and jeans and I occasionally smoked pot. The former were simply outward manifestations of the youth culture (like most youth I was slave to fashion) and the latter was a sometimes weekend thing. It would have been unlikely to graduate magna cum laude (3.64 GPA) from a rigorous state college in pre-grade inflation days while being stoned very often.

Upon entering college in the fall of 1970, one of the first things I did after getting oriented to college life was to organize the Cal State Bakersfield Draft Information Service. It was useful work, I may have helped a few young men. It certainly came in handy with my personal struggle with The Draft.

On March 11, 1970 while still in high school I filed Form 150 and several reference letters with my local draft board. Form 150 is filed by those claiming conscientious objector (CO) status. That is, they are conscientiously opposed to participation in war, but are prepared to perform civilian alternative service if drafted. Since I was not a member of a recognized pacifist church such as the Quakers (or even a member of any church) my request was denied. At that time a CO had to oppose participation in war due to religious training and belief.

While I attended Bible School and church (Congregational, Southern Baptist, and later Unitarian Universalist) as a child and teen, my attendance was spotty as was my growing uncertainty as to the existence of God. Since I was well schooled in the SSS laws, I knew my claim, especially in conservative Kern County, had the proverbial snowballs chance in hell of being approved.

I was right and classified as 1-A—registrant available for military service.

On August 5, 1971, I finally won a lottery. Unfortunately it was for The Draft. On this date the SSS held a lottery for men born in 1952 (including me). My birthday came up with number 51, a low number (out of 365). The highest lottery number called for this group was 95; all men assigned that lottery number or lower and classified 1-A were called to report for a pre-induction physical. That would be me. There were 94,092 inducted in 1971 and 49,514 men inducted in 1972 ("Results from Lottery Drawing—Vietnam Era, 1972." 2013).

During my struggle with the SSS I could have applied for, and would have been granted, a 2-S student deferment for college students making progress toward a degree. Although these deferments were discontinued in December 1971, that would have carried me through the first two years.

I had a bout of conscientiousness (after all, I was a conscientious objector) and knew this was not for me. It simply was not fair that someone like me who somehow could put a few grey matter cells together and receive a deferment from The Draft for a few years while some poor smuck who could not or lacked the money or ambition to attend college would most likely be snatched up by The Draft like a poor mouse in the clutches of a hawk. A student deferment would certainly have made my life easier, but was wrong.

Beginning with my 18th birthday and for the next 2 ½ years I filed various appeals at the local and state levels; appeared in person before the Draft Board; and generally made a legal pest of myself. Although I did get the SSS State Director to reopen my classification on May 31, 1972, nothing came of it. Why? Because I was called for a pre-induction physical on June 13, 1972.

What a day. About 5:00 am I joined about three dozen other poor souls and boarded the bus that transported us to the pre-induction physical site in Fresno, a pleasant two hour drive up the Central Valley. Since I was a seasoned draft counselor, I took the liberty of discussing various aspects of The Draft and the upcoming physical inspection with my bus mates. Some were receptive, most didn't much care and accepted their fate.

Arriving around 7:30 we herded into the austere facility. Marine Corps Captain B.C. Wilson greeted us warmly (not) and the process began. Prodded, poked, and mentally tested. All the while I surreptitiously advised some guys on the law and physical standards. Captain Wilson did not appreciate that and let me know in front of the assembled group. Nothing gets the juices flowing like being called a cowardly shit by a Marine in uniform. Hey, I was simply helping young American men understand their rights under the law.

But in my heart of hearts, I knew he might have been right. I certainly did not want to die in some jungle in what was essentially a foreign civil war. I was also not too excited about killing in those circumstances. It's not like the Viet Cong were any direct threat to America. I had no problem with personal self-defense. Was this war simply an extension of a nation's self-defense? Ultimately no.

The pre-induction physical forced me to play my trump card. I didn't want to, I believed I was a legitimate conscientious objector and the battle over the past two plus years was interesting. But I knew since this struggle began I would never pass the physical exam—my poor eyesight was well beyond the standard established by law. What army wants a soldier who would have a hell of a time distinguishing friend from foe at more than ten feet if they lost their glasses? Clearly not the US military. On July 6, 1972, I received my final draft card and was reclassified 4-F, not qualified for military service.

Within less than a year, January 27, 1973, the draft was but a fond memory. An all-volunteer armed forces was created. On June 30, 1973 the last man to be inducted via the draft entered the army ("Induction Statistics" 2013).

References

"Conscription in the United States." 2013. Wikipedia. Last modified October 20, 2013. http://en.wikipedia.org/wiki/Conscription_in_the_United_States.

"Induction Statistics." 2013. Selective Service System, History and Records. Last modified May 28, 2003. http://www.sss.gov/induct.htm.

Kearns, Jr., Owen. 1971. "County Has Little Vocal War Protest. *The Bakersfield Californian*. December 19.

"Results from Lottery Drawing—Vietnam Era, 1972." 2013. Selective Service System, History and Records. Last modified June 18, 2009. http://www.sss.gov/LOTTER3.HTM.

"Selective Service System." 1970. My Selective Service System registration certificate (draft card).

"Selective Service System." 2013. Wikipedia. Last modified October 12, 2013.
http://en.wikipedia.org/wiki/Selective_Service_System.

"Twenty-sixth Amendment to the United State Constitution." 2013. Wikipedia. Last modified October 15, 2013. http://en.wikipedia.org/wiki/Twenty-sixth_Amendment_to_the_United_States_Constitution.

Chapter Two
Fall 1970—Fall 1980
College and First Marriage

Introduction

To borrow from Charles Dickens, this was a decade of great expectations ("Dickens" 1861). While my adventures in the 1970s don't quite approach those of Pip, they are similar in that it was a period of change. Being an overachiever in endeavors such as academics and sports, I expected a lot from myself. As is generally the case, the results were mixed. Too bad I can't be good at everything. Some experiences—higher education—totally met my expectations; others—having a good marriage—were to put it kindly, sub-optimal.

I began my higher education journey as a fairly shy hayseed from a small town, Shafter, northwest of Bakersfield in the Central Valley. One might think "sure that will take care of four years." No, thrown in a Master's Degree and almost Doctorate and the decade flew by.

I was a good student, hell I was a great student. I knew I wanted to study political science and then become a lawyer and help change "the system." By the time I graduated with my BA in political science in 1974, several professors, some who became lifelong friends, disabused me of the notion of law school. "Tom, you'll be bored to death in law school and the system is damn hard to change. You'll do much better in graduate school."

My expectations about higher education were surpassed. I enjoyed college and learning everything I could about politics. I was a teaching assistant, teaching fellow, and taught a few of my own classes for several years and loved it. Nothing quite like giving a lecture and seeing some undergraduates' face light up in understanding Robert A. Dahl's polyarchy as a descriptor of American politics (Dahl 1971). Like John Travolta was born to dance in *Saturday Night Fever*, I was born to teach (*Saturday Night Fever* 1977). Alas, as with disco, that idea crashed by the end of the decade.

41

Along the way, I began to dabble in real world politics. First as the campaign manager for a local city council candidate in 1973—we lost. Later in the late 1970s I became heavily involved in graduate student politics at UC Santa Barbara. Wow, something more interesting than studying politics was putting all that book learning into practice in the real world.

As good as I was at intellectual endeavors, I was just about as bad regarding my primary relationship. Funny, I got better in school as I gained experience and knowledge (my GPA increased from 3.65 as an undergraduate; to 3.74 for my master's degree; to 3.97 in my PhD program—this was well before the advent of grade inflation).

Especially frustrating was the fact that I formed several lifelong friendships during this decade with professors and fellow students. They seemed to think I was a decent fellow.

The problem of disparate results may lie in another slice of my character—stubbornness or sometimes misused will power. Sticking with an intellectual endeavor greatly increases the chance of success and has fairly immediate payoffs—you understand a new concept, your report is quality work, you ace a test. Thomas A. Edison, no slouch in the realm of success, is famously quoted for saying, "Success is ten percent inspiration and 90 percent perspiration" ("Edison" 2013). While I may have had occasional inspiration, I certainly possessed perspiration.

Stubbornness, or will power, served me well in intellectual pursuits, or even physical activities such as sports. But as I gained experience and knowledge about my spouse and marriage the relationship deteriorated. Stubbornness and a desire to excel can create a volatile mixture—a recipe for excellence or disaster.

Excellence because coupling knowledge and experience gained over time (with a bit of native intelligence) with a strong desire to stick with a project and success looms. This was certainly within my grasp when dealing with facts, theories, and tangible things.

But when dealing with another person on an intimate level, the misused will power becomes a tool for control, for "helping" them to become a better person. In other words, a disaster.

Regarding the lack of success in my primary relationship I must agree with Ben Franklin, "We are all born ignorant, but one must work hard to remain stupid" ("Franklin" 2013). At least in this decade, I worked pretty hard to remain stupid in one major area of my life. But there is hope, in the 1980s—perhaps a bit more mature—I found the love of my life. We are still together.

References

Dahl, Robert A. 1956. *A Preface to Democratic Theory*. Chicago: University of Chicago Press.

Dahl, Robert A. 1971. *Polyarchy*. New Haven, CT: Yale University Press.

"Dickens," Charles. 1861. *Great Expectations*. Wikipedia. Last modified October 4, 2013. http://en.wikipedia.org/wiki/Great_Expectations.

"Edison," Thomas Alva. 2013. Quote from thinkexist.com website. Last modification unknown. http://thinkexist.com/quotation/success_is-percent_inspiration_and-percent/252431.html.

"Franklin," Benjamin. 2013. Quote from thinkexist.com website. Last modification unknown. http://thinkexist.com/quotation/we_are_all_born_ignorant-but_one_must_work_hard/326829.html.

Saturday Night Fever. 1977. Directed by John Badham. Wikipedia. Last modified October 21, 2013. http://en.wikipedia.org/wiki/Saturday_Night_Fever.

A Concern for Quality

Like many Baby Boomers, especially those from California, I flirted with Zen Buddhism and meditation. Other than the standard Zen texts—*The Way of Zen* by Alan Watts (1959), *The Three Pillars of Zen* by Philip Kapleau (1967), *Zen Mind, Beginners Mind* by Shunryu Suzuki (1970), *Essays in Zen Buddhism* by D. T. Suzuki (1949), and others—I was most taken by Robert Pirsig's *Zen and the Art of Motorcycle Maintenance: An Inquiry into Values* which came out in 1974. Among other things, Pirsig explores the idea of "quality." While left undefined, Pirsig's thesis is that to truly experience life one must embrace and apply quality as best fits the situation. In other words, embrace the hereness and oneness of any endeavor. Be one with your activity.

I began the BA program in Political Science at California State College, Bakersfield in September 1970. The school opened that fall; I was in the first freshman class. New facilities and young enthusiastic professors—perfect for a country boy eager to learn. My education was financed with student loans, grants, work-study, and my wife's employment (after our marriage in 1972). My parents, divorced by then, could not afford to pay for my college education. Being from a working class family I expected to work. I worked every summer at hard physical labor since I was 14—no big deal.

My first college work-study job, lasting two years including summers, was working on the grounds crew. Basically this involved yard work on a massive scale. The campus was large and on former agricultural land, so plants grew well. Because it was a new campus there was plenty of work—planting and maintaining trees, shrubs, lawns, and flowers; pruning; endlessly sweeping acres of concrete; cleaning up messes the privileged sons and daughters attending college thoughtlessly left us; weeding and hoeing; and so forth.

Located in the southern Central Valley, Bakersfield got a bit warm in the summer, not quite the 10,000 degree Fahrenheit temperature of the sun's photosphere, but often above 100. One summer day in 1972, Mr. Tony, an older black guy who was a fulltime member of the crew, and I found ourselves hoeing and raking a new flower bed.

"Tom, what are you doing with that leaf rake?"

"Ummm, raking?"

"Boy, use your eyes and notice what you are doing," Mr. Tony told me. "Use the rake with the teeth down to gather rocks and leaves. Then turn it over to smooth out the dirt once you've finished gathering the big stuff. It makes a pattern of fine lines. Nice, huh?"

"Okay, it does look pretty good once you finish," I stammered.

"And notice how this bed is contoured. Don't just apply the finishing touch side to side or up and down. Allow your rake to follow the contours of the ground."

Now I thought I was as good as the next guy at leaf rake raking. Mr. Tony made it clear that proper raking involved more than slopping the dirt around gathering up rocks and leaves. You must use both sides of the rake; teeth down for gathering large debris, teeth up for smoothing the dirt in aesthetically pleasing patterns following the planting area contours. Although *The Karate Kid* movie was more than a decade from being released, this was a gardening equivalent to "wax on, wax off." (*The Karate Kid* 1984) Following his advice, my raking—and more importantly my attitude toward raking—improved. As Shunryu Suzuki (1970) notes in *Zen Mind, Beginner's Mind*, "The trying to do something in itself is enlightenment" (P. 122). Cool, my becoming a raking master was a bit of enlightenment.

As much as anyone I've ever met, Mr. Tony epitomized a Zen-like approach to his work—a concern for quality, no matter how seemingly mundane the chore. Whether applied to motorcycle maintenance, raking, or rocket science the hereness and oneness with the task should be constant. Do the best you can while being conscious of the activity.

At the time of my gardening lesson, Pirsig's book had not been published and I had only approached Zen in a dilettantish manner. Only in retrospect did my raking take on meaning as a quality-creating experience.

In the mid- to late-'70s I dove into Zen and meditation. Being the budding intellectual I took to the former like a starving man grabs a Big Mac. The more classical approaches to Zen supplemented Pirsig's contemporary discussion. As a 20-something American male and raised in the 1950s and '60s I had to moderate my "if I only study and try hard enough I too can attain enlightenment" attitude. (This was well before political correctness raised its ugly head. Most people, as did I, believed that hard work, some innate abilities, and being

45

responsible for your behavior could lead to success.) The Zen masters, and probably Mr. Tony, would caution me to not push for enlightenment, but open yourself to the experience—enlightenment would come, or not. Unfortunately for me, it seems as if the "or not" option prevailed.

The meditation part was a bit tough; it seems as if quieting my mind was a task for the ages. Zen masters preach a beginner's mind, allow the experience—any experience—to wash over you. Do not become attached to any one emotion or stimuli. Easy to say, try doing it. More than anything, a beginner's mind seemed boring. I was raised in a noisy culture where action was paramount—a rock 'n roll type of guy. Perhaps that explains my adopting the Rolling Stones as my official meditation music—hardly the tunes for beginner's mind (but certainly full of energy).

In any case, I studied the basic Zen lessons. Unfortunately, my mind and spirit were like a sieve regarding the precepts of Zen, a sieve with two foot holes. I caught the large concepts but the more subtle ideas like stilling one's mind escaped me. I have, however, maintained a decades-long appreciation for, and attempt to emulate, Mr. Tony's approach to raking.

Since that lesson, I try to lead a life wherein I approach every task as one demanding my full attention and concern for quality. Some days are better than others.

References

Kapleau, Philip. 1967. *The Three Pillars of Zen*. New York: Beacon Press.

The Karate Kid. 1984. Written by Robert Mark Kamen, directed by John G. Avildsen. Distributed by Columbia Pictures.

Pirsig, Robert M. 1974. *Zen and the Art of Motorcycle Maintenance*. New York: Bantam Books.

Suzuki, D. T. 1949. *Essays in Zen Buddhism*. New York: Grove Press.

Suzuki, Shunryu. 1970. *Zen Mind, Beginner's Mind*. New York: John Weatherhill, Inc.

Watts, Alan W. 1959. *The Way of Zen*. New York: The New American Library.

Damn, They Were Right

Franklin D. Roosevelt rightly called December 7, 1941 a day that would live in infamy. That was the day of the Japanese sneak attack on Pearl Harbor, Hawaii ushering in open US participation in World War II.

While not quite as important to world history, my day of infamy was June 24, 1972—the date of my first wedding. We were young, Lori 18 and me an ancient 20. Ours was the first wedding at California State College, Bakersfield—the setting a wonderfully green sweeping lawn near a pond.

Wedding reception, June 24, 1972

We met in high school during my senior year (1969-70), Lori was a sophomore. I first dated her older sister, but was soon attracted to her younger sibling—the very cute Lori.

For the next two years we exclusively dated each other—we were in love. While some friends were a bit skeptical of the

47

relationship, Lori's parents were often openly hostile. They sometimes made it difficult for us to be together. Of course, my all too often aggressive attitude and behavior toward them did not help. For example, Lori's parents, being conservative in a conservative town, were not fond of my long hair and liberal politics. Well, I would show them. I wrote up a sort of "petition" that said "in my opinion, Tom's hair is not too long" and asked just about every person I met if they thought my hair was too long. If they thought not, I got them to sign my petition. When I presented her parents with the petition, they were not too impressed. Public opinion be damned.

In retrospect, Lori and I were very different people and should have never married. The old adage that opposites attract is true for subatomic particles, but in my experience not for people. Those with whom I most enjoy always have at least some interests and personal characteristics similar to mine. You do not have to be clones, but shared interests make for shared enthusiasm.

For example, I was the budding intellectual, very intense, and interested in politics; Lori much more relaxed about education and politics. At one point prior to getting hitched, Lori's mom asked if the coming gap in our education levels would be a problem. Of course not. We would always communicate and learn from each other. Silly me. During our entire marriage I was in undergraduate or graduate school. Lori occasionally took college level classes in Bakersfield and Davis and earned a two year degree from Santa Barbara City College in the late 1970s. As time passed, we had less and less to discuss. Why couldn't she just understand the importance of multivariate regression analysis? Lori mostly wanted to live life; I wanted that but throughout our marriage was stuck in studying politics. Her mom was right.

I was, and still am, very organized with my time and things. Not so much so as to alphabetize the small bottles and cans in the spice rack, but enough to alphabetize the record collection. For some reason, no matter how much I complained Lori would not get with the program.

My wanting to mold her into a better person (well, at least someone more to my liking) might have a teensy bit to do with the relationship not working. What's wrong with badgering your spouse to improve herself, read more, laugh more (in the later years neither of us laughed much around each other, probably because there was little to laugh about), be more "touchy-feely"/playful and not so tightly controlled. It is beyond me why anyone would resist and become resentful simply due to my good intentions.

Me and Lori, December 1977.

Moving to Santa Barbara, California in 1976 for my doctorate program in political science was the death knell. I took classes, studied for PhD exams, researched and wrote about half of my dissertation, taught and did paid research, got heavily involved in Graduate Student Association politics, shamelessly flirted with undergraduate women (I was a teaching assistant for two years), and had a short-lived affair with a grad student (not in my department, I wasn't totally stupid) friend. Lori attended the local community college and by 1979 had a night time job running a huge printing press at a local print shop. We certainly had a lot of quality face time—not. Well over half the married couples we knew in which at least one was a grad student got divorced while I attended UC Santa Barbara.

Up until the late 1970s, when it became clear even to me that our relationship was not working, I never failed, or even did poorly, at anything—I was good at sports, did excellent in college, was a good teacher, could disassemble and reassemble a bicycle (and it worked), pretty good at public speaking, had several good friends. But the marriage was troubled and I was too stubborn to admit it and too egocentric to do anything of real value to save it. For me, like the ill-fated Apollo 13 astronauts, failure was not an option.

Lori, 1979.

Lori and I were the victims of those twin scourges that visit most youth—raging hormones coupled with excessive stupidity. Not much to do about the former, the latter was a function of a paucity of life experience and general immaturity on my part. It is testament to inertia and my stubbornness that we lasted as long as we did. Evidently she spent a few years not much liking me. I didn't much like her either. We put up with each other for no good reason other than my inability to admit failure. The relationship clearly exceeded its expiration date. Not much to brag about.

Perhaps the only positive to survive this relationship (besides learning what not to do in a marriage) was an excellent four-bean salad recipe I got from one of Lori's relatives. That salad finds its way to potlucks and our dinner table even today.

While I would like to place the blame on Lori for the failed marriage, to borrow a phrase from Richard Nixon during his Watergate phase, "… that would be wrong." ("My Favorite Nixon Quote" 1997) We jointly share responsibility, neither of was emotionally ready for a deeply committed partnership. Nor were we right for each other.

Before we married, a fair number of people said the marriage would not last. They were right.

References

"My Favorite Nixon Quote" website. 1997. Last modification unknown. http://www.jimloy.com/history/nixon.htm

Little Politics

I am clearly a political animal. At the age of 20 I got my first taste of electoral politics. I had been doing volunteer draft counseling with the Kern County Draft Information Service since the summer of 1970. It was there I met another volunteer counselor, Jim Leek, a 26 year-old electronics firm manager and UC Berkeley graduate in chemistry. Except for college, he was a lifelong Bakersfield resident. In late fall 1972 Jim decided to run for the Seventh Ward City Council seat. Being friends and me such a political animal, I volunteered and became his campaign manager. I wanted to experience electoral politics at the local level and wasn't too busy except for attending college full time, recently getting married, working part-time, and volunteering as a draft counselor.

We duly created a few large plywood campaign signs, printed a basic flyer, and assembled a large group precinct walkers (i.e., me, Jim, our spouses, and a couple of friends). Jim was the liberal in a three candidate race, an uphill battle in conservative Bakersfield. We walked precincts, talked with potential voters, and generated a groundswell of support—the latter not so much.

Election day was February 27, 1973, and the turnout was low, 30.4% or 1,359 voters. Jim finished third out of three candidates and received 171 votes (12.6%) (*The Bakersfield Californian* 1973).

Later that year I conducted an extensive survey research project analyzing the voting in that election for a political science class at California State College, Bakersfield. Not surprisingly most voters could not correctly identify Jim's liberal ideology. Our campaign had little money and received very little media attention, he was a first-time candidate, and we were running against a longtime powerful incumbent (who won with almost 53% of the vote in a three person race).

The next few election cycles I supported local, statewide, and national candidates through precinct work and donating money. Nothing very intense. But fast forward a few years and I once again entered the electoral fray in a different arena.

In the fall of 1976 I entered the PhD program in political science at UC Santa Barbara. As one might expect, most of my time was spent with class work, preparing for doctoral exams, teaching and grading papers, researching my dissertation, and tending to a rocky marriage. That was not enough.

Within a couple of years I was heavily involved in graduate student politics via the Graduate Students Association (GSA). My first position was political science representative to the GSA Council (its governing body). The GSA's main functions were to liaison between the university administration and graduate students and lobby at the state level. Graduate student politics clearly follows Sayre's law: "In any dispute the intensity of feeling is inversely proportional to the value of the issues at stake," and its corollary "That is why academic politics are so bitter" ("Sayer's law" 2013).

At the first (October) GSA Council meeting of the 1978 school year I proposed a motion to oppose Proposition 6 (Briggs Initiative) that was appearing on the November ballot. The vote was unanimous (Yep 1978). The Briggs Initiative allowed any gay or lesbian teacher to be fired for simply being gay or lesbian. The Initiative lost in the November 7 general election 58% to 42%. This was the first political stance ever taken by the GSA. But not its last.

I was on a roll and at the next monthly meeting I authored a resolution stating:

> The GSA Council shall decide, on an ad hoc basis which issues are suitable for consideration. This will include, but not be limited to, taking stands on particular political issues by a majority vote.

My allies and I pointed out that by its nature the GSA was a political organization and we were only moving to recognize an already extant state. The debate was intense, but the good guys (me and my cohorts) won in a landslide ten to nine vote (Letter to Editor 1978). While resting on my laurels at this point was an option, I was only getting warmed up.

At the March 2, 1979 meeting I introduced a slate of candidates for the Executive Committee that ran the daily operations of GSA and was the real center of power. The election was scheduled for April. For months I had been organizing a graduate student political party—the People Opposed to Oppressive Politics (POOP) Party (Togut 1979). There really wasn't any oppressive politics but I loved the name. POOP had a platform and gathered endorsements from 42 grad students. (Given campus-wide grad student apathy, the latter was a show of strong support.) We also proposed that the GSA add another office to the five-person Executive Committee, a press secretary. This was quickly approved. After all, it had been established that GSA was a political organization and any real political group needed a press secretary.

The GSA Executive Committee election was held on April 19. The POOP Party slate won all six offices. I was elected as Vice President for Academic Affairs—the only candidate to not win unanimously, even though I ran unopposed (Brent 1979). Political rabble rouses are not loved by all.

The steamroller continued at the May meeting when the GSA Council, upon the advice of the Executive Committee and at my urging, unanimously adopted a resolution supporting and urging all students to support the Coors boycott. The charge against Coors, in general terms, was that they engaged in unfair labor practices at their breweries. Another stunning victory for symbolic politics. Didn't mean much to me personally since I did not drink beer.

That fall (1979) GSA unveiled the initial issue of UC Santa Barbara's first ever grad student newsletter—*The Monthly Planet* (*The Monthly Planet* 1979). I was co-editor, contributed several articles, and wrote an advice column, "Ask Dr. Zhivago," in which I made up the questions and answers. It was a quarterly publication and lasted until April 1980.

At our January 1980 meeting, I once again mounted my soapbox and the GSA Council unanimously (19 to 0) endorsed the Nestle products boycott. The January 25, 1980 *Daily Nexus* (UC Santa Barbara's student newspaper) reported on this and quoted me as saying "They sell a powdered milk formula in parts of the world where clean water is unavailable, illiterate mothers can't read the instructions on the label, and family incomes may be so low that 20-80 percent of the entire family income is spent on the infant" (Conley 1980). Sounds like something I would say.

Later that month, January 31, I represented the GSA at an anti-draft rally in Storke Plaza, the largest open air meeting area on campus. More than 500 people attended. This rally was sparked by rumors that The Draft was to be reestablished as part of our government's response to the recent (December 1979) Soviet introduction of a substantial number of regular army troops into pro-Soviet Afghanistan to fight a growing US-sponsored guerrilla movement. Part of the February 1, 1980 *Daily Nexus* reporting on the rally reads:

> "Well it's back," said Tom Garrison of the Graduate Students Association, encouraging the audience to be idealistic and question government authority. Several other speakers urged this type of questioning.
>
> Garrison told students to visualize what it would be like to kill another person. He said war reduces men to meat whose function is to "kill other individuals, people you don't know." He concluded his speech with a quote from Plato, "Only the dead know the end of war" ("Anti-Draft Rally Attracts Crowd" 1980).

Other than the newsletter, this was my last major GSA activity.

For almost a decade I studied politics. Except for Jim Leek's campaign in 1973 and the last couple of years of UC Santa Barbara grad school politics I only experienced the rough and tumble of real world politics through reading and discussions, not good for a political animal. But I had a taste now and the 1980s beckoned; a chance to apply theory and practice in a big way.

References

"Anti-Draft Rally Attracts Crowd." 1980. *Daily Nexus*. February 1.

The Bakersfield Californian. 1973. "Rees defeated; Rucker, Strong vie in runoff." *The Bakersfield Californian*. February 28.

Brent, Kim. 1979. "GSA Elects Officers, Discuss Graduate Requirement Change." *Daily Nexus*. April 24.

Conley, Bill. 1980. "GSA Concerned About Jarvis II." *Daily Nexus*. January 25.

Letter to editor. 1978. "Expanded Horizon." Letter to the editor authored by Tom Garrison, Gayle Olson, Fred Young, Kevin R. McCauley, and Bee Hanson. *Daily Nexus*. November 17.

The Monthly Planet. 1979. UC Santa Barbara Graduate Students Association Newsletter. Vol. 1, No. 1. October 1979.

"Sayer's law." 2013. Wikipedia. Last modified October 16, 2013. http://en.wikipedia.org/wiki/Sayre%27s_Law.

Togut, Michelle. 1979. "GSA Asks Council for Vote on Proposed Constitutional Changes." *Daily Nexus.* March 2.

Yep, Richard. 1978. "GSA Takes a Political Stand Against Briggs Initiative." *Daily Nexus.* October 17.

A Night at the Opera

I was in the first class to enter the newly created California State College, Bakersfield in the fall of 1970. Born and raised in the southern Central Valley to a working class family, my exposure to "high" culture was rather limited. But I was eager to learn and open to new experiences.

Gene Clark, me, and Charles McCall, Summer 1975

Fortunately, Dr. Charles McCall and Dr. Gene Clark in the Political Science Department and Dr. Bill Hanson in Sociology seemed to take a liking to me. They not only encouraged me academically, but took it upon themselves to expose me to the more refined aspects of our culture.

In my junior year (1972-73) Charles (Dr. McCall then), took me and my first wife Lori to an Italian opera in Los Angeles. I'm glad the opportunity arose. What other 21 year-old could spend an evening soaking up Puccini with their political science professor? Who cares if we didn't understand a word of the Italian opera, Lori and I were in the big leagues.

Unbelievably enough, I don't like opera. I prefer the modern version of musical theater—Mick Jagger prancing around like a goof belting out "Sympathy for the Devil." But knowing that my teachers wanted me to have more than an academic education meant a lot.

Although the opera did not, and does not, interest me much, I must thank Charles for sparking my interest in other areas. For example, since my days as an undergraduate, and encouraged by Charles, reading science fiction has been a major interest of mine. I well remember feeling guilty for reading a couple more pages of a John Brunner novel when I should have studied a few more minutes for my exams in graduate school.

Or magic. While I will never approach the prestidigitation abilities of Charles, I have become a very amateur magician over the years. Charles encouraged this interest and even taught me a couple of tricks. On another road trip with Charles we took in the famous Magic Castle in Los Angeles.

Years later, after wife number one left (she wasn't much for magic), Deb (wife number two) and I developed an entire magic routine. We memorized the patter and performed at various social (and some political) functions in the 1980s and '90s. We were not that good, but it was a hell of a lot of fun. To this day I'll still show a new acquaintance the pencil trick.

Me showing the pencil trick to UC Santa Barbara grad
student friend Ilene, Fall 1976.

I was a lucky guy. Several professors helped provide me with a first rate liberal arts education and grounding in political science. Along with the extras such as science fiction and magic, my life has been fuller for knowing these people. Thanks.

Antiwar Work and Nonviolence

Due to my personal struggle with The Draft, being a volunteer draft counselor, and general dislike of organized violence I read everything I could about the theory and practice of nonviolence. This included the well-known names Mohandas K. Gandhi, Henry David Thoreau, Dr. Martin Luther King, Jr., and others. However, I gained the most insight from those who analyzed and chronicled various nonviolent political actions. The most influential include Clarence Case's *Non-Violent Coercion* (1923); *The Power of Nonviolence* (1966) by Richard Gregg; Leroy Pelton's *The Psychology of Nonviolence* (1974); *Nonviolent Power* (1972) by Judith Stiehm; George Lakey's *Strategy for a Living Revolution* (1968); and Gene Sharp's three-part masterpiece *The Politics of Nonviolent Action* (1973).

It soon became clear that I was not a traditional pacifist. The notion most folks carry around of a pacifist is one who meekly submits to bullying and violence and relies upon moral suasion and suffering to achieve victory. While the idea of moral suasion can be important in a nonviolence campaign, it is generally only a small part of the mix.

Gene Sharp provides the best analysis of the mechanisms of nonviolent direct action. Because of my lifelong belief in the efficacy of nonviolence, it is useful to provide a lengthy passage from his *The Politics of Nonviolent Action* (1973).

> It is, however, possible to distinguish three broad processes, or mechanisms, by which the complicated forces utilized and produced by nonviolent action influence the opponent and his capacity for action and thereby perhaps bring success to the cause of the grievance group. These are *conversion, accommodation,* and *nonviolent coercion* ...
>
> In *conversion* the opponent has been inwardly changed so that he wants to make the changes desired by the nonviolent actionists. In *accommodation* the opponent does not agree with the changes (he has not been converted), and he could continue the struggle (he has not been nonviolently coerced), but nevertheless he has concluded that it is best to grant some or all of the demands. He may see the issues as not so important

59

after all, the actionists as not as bad as he had thought, or he may expect to lose more by continuing the struggle than by conceding gracefully. In *nonviolent coercion* the opponent has not changed his mind on the issues and wants to *continue* the struggle, but is *unable* to do so; the sources of his power and means of control have been taken away from him without the use of violence. This may have been done by the nonviolent group or by opposition and noncooperation among his own group (as, mutiny of his troops), or some combination of these (Pages 705-706).

According to Sharp, I did not have to see myself as someone who relied on converting my opponent, I could use nonviolent coercion—real power—to obtain goals. Nonviolent direct action was not for weak sissies, it required strength and could be a true test of power sans violence.

One of the groups I came across in my study of nonviolence was the War Resisters League (WRL). Officially formed in 1923, it has proselytized and practiced nonviolent direct action against war and the roots of war for decades—always in the forefront of the antiwar and social justice movements. It is the oldest secular antiwar organization in the US ("War Resisters League" 2013A and 2013B). At the time it was the nation-wide organization I needed. They provided tons of great information and support and an entree for meeting the heavies of the national antiwar movement. I formally joined in 1972 and remained an active member until the mid-1990s.

War Resisters League symbol

In 1973 Lori and I decided to up the ante slightly and wrote a protest letter to the Internal Revenue Service (IRS) that we sent along with our (1972) federal tax return. The letter noted that we were law-abiding citizens and would pay our full federal tax, but did not want our money to fund military spending. This was the first of 11 consecutive years of including a protest letter and refusing to pay a portion of the federal taxes due for the 1981 to 1983 tax years. While I still believe it was an important gesture—given my beliefs during this period—our efforts did not exactly stop the military-industrial complex in its tracks.

My senior thesis (spring 1974) at Cal State was a 50 page examination of violence and nonviolence as methods to resolve conflict. More specifically, how does each method affect the underlying values, the social requisites, upon which our country is based? The values, borrowed from Charles Hyneman's *Popular Government in America* (1968) include (1) commitment to and provision for individual and group autonomy, (2) commitment to equality, and (3) commonalty—a common mind on the objectives and methods of government (page 28). This was a logical think piece and, not surprisingly, I found that nonviolent direct action, regardless of the opponent's methods, tended to strengthen the social requisites for democracy. Dr. McCall was generous in his critique and wrote about my effort, "It is, I believe, the best paper I've read since I came here." (He arrived in 1970.)

In August 1977, while working on my PhD in political science at UC Santa Barbara, we took a vacation to the 10th Annual WRL Conference at Grinwood Conference Center, Washington, approximately two miles from Lacey. For those of you unfamiliar with Lacey (just about everyone), it is located two hours south of Seattle.

This was exciting, our second trip to the great northwest and our first meeting of some of the big names in the WRL and the antiwar movement in general. The conference center is located at Hicks Lake—a beautiful wooded retreat.

After registering and orienting ourselves, we joined an affinity group, the socialists. Affinity groups, which occasionally met during the four day Conference, were organized around some shared characteristic—socialism, sexual orientation, anarchism, and so forth. The purpose is to provide a bonding opportunity for groups of strangers.

For a group committed to nonviolence and social justice, the attendance by minorities was disappointing—about a dozen brown or black faces out of 175 or so attendees. But I can't fault the WRL, as an organization and individually they make everyone feel welcome.

Meetings to discuss various topics dominated the overall agenda. One on "Socialism" was led by Dave McReynolds, a WRL and Socialist Party USA heavyweight for years. Dave is a thoughtful and nice guy I got to know a bit over the years. A consensus emerged from the 14 people at this discussion that while the major means of production should be socially owned, small businesses and industries need not be.

Later Lori and I joined a "Disarming Ourselves" workshop. Its purpose was to examine our own lives regarding sexism, elitism, racism, and other "isms." At one point the large group broke up into two subgroups, men and women. This bothered me then as it does now. A paragraph from my journal of this trip is still appropriate.

> There was some discussion of breaking up into groups by sex and sexual preference. Some (myself included) thought it somewhat strange that a Conference of people trying to overcome these types of divisions keeps splitting into groups according to these divisions. Discussions and criticisms of this procedure continued for the whole Conference (Garrison 1977A).

Another feature of the Conference typified much of the progressive/antiwar/antinuclear power movement. This is the practice of "equalizing" who speaks at a meeting. Again one of my journal entries about an incident at the "Emerging Tactics in the Disarmament Movement" workshop (about 80 people attending) spells it out fairly well.

> One co-facilitator fucked up by making a huge deal of not letting men speak until some women had spoken. Finally a woman got on him for pressuring all the women. I think they are taking it too far. Traditionally men have dominated discussions, but I've noticed that the women here are not the mousy, "let your man speak" type (Garrison 1977B).

I saw this sort of artificial "quota" mechanism deployed in leftist/progressive meetings for the next 20 years. Every time it reared its head I objected; I usually lost the ensuing discussion and vote. I imagine it still exists. Anyone can feel a bit nervous about public speaking. However, forcing member of one subgroup to speak when maybe they are more comfortable listening for a while is pretty coercive—not such a good thing at a Conference of mostly serious pacifists.

 More individual discussions, meetings and workshops over the next two days. Yet another point of contention arose between me and many of the other attendees. It seemed as if most people were eager to discuss almost anything, but seldom questioned their assumptions. A good example was nuclear disarmament. The year before the Conference (1976) I earned my Master's Degree in political science at UC Davis. One of my areas of emphasis was international relations, where the grad students read almost everything of importance on disarmament. International relations was also an area of concentration at UC Santa Barbara where I was working on my doctorate. So I was pretty well read and had many analytical discussions on the subject of nuclear disarmament.

However, almost everyone at the Conference blithely believed that unilateral nuclear disarmament by the US was a good thing. What? While people made fun of mutually assured destruction (MAD), the fact is it worked. If the US pursued unilateral nuclear disarmament what would prevent the other then-superpower, the Soviet Union, from coercing and threatening our government with nuclear blackmail to obtain their goals? The goodness of Soviet leaders? Protests by the Soviet people? I doubt it. I'm all for mutual disarmament with guaranteed strong verification—every nation eliminating, or at least reducing the number of nukes simultaneously. Needless to say my position was not well received. This was one of those eureka moments when I realized that these folks had great intentions that, for them, trumped reality. No serious student of international relations could advocate unilateral nuclear disarmament.

This mindset of ignoring, or even never realizing, the implications (anticipated or unanticipated) of what they proposed was troubling. As I write this the Conference was more than 35 years in the past and I was an antiwar and socialist activist for about 20 of those years. But I would like to think that my activism was reality-based, what could work given the existing socio-political system. While we preached nonviolent revolution, change was almost always in an incremental manner. I know many of my comrades over the years lacked grounding in reality on many issues. Too often, certainly not always, there was an abundance of emotion and a dearth of rigorous analysis.

On the other hand, almost everyone at the conference was seriously concerned about important issues. They were decent people grappling with a world with thousands of nuclear weapons, seemingly endless wars, social inequality, and other ills. I was, and still am with them on most issues.

References

Case, Clarence. 1923. *Non-Violent Coercion*. New York: The Century Company.

Garrison, Tom. 1977A. Journal entry. August 12.

Garrison, Tom. 1977B. Journal entry. August 12.

Gregg, Richard. 1966. *The Power of Nonviolence*. First edition published in 1934. New York: Schocken Books.

Hyneman, Charles. 1968. *Popular Government in America*. New York: Atherton Press.

Lakey, George. 1968. *Strategy for a Living Revolution*. San Francisco: W. H. Freeman and Company.

Pelton, Leroy. 1974 *The Psychology of Nonviolence*. New York: Pergamon Press, Inc.

Sharp, Gene. 1973. *The Politics of Nonviolent Action*. Boston: Porter Sargent Publishers.

Stiehm, Judith. 1972. *Nonviolent Power*. New York: D. C. Heath and Company.

"War Resisters League." 2013A. Website. Last modification unknown. http://www.warresisters.org/.

"War Resisters League." 2013B. Wikipedia. Last modified October 20, 2013. http://en.wikipedia.org/wiki/War_Resisters_League.

Sly and the Family Stone Smoking Head Concert

Lori and I both smoked cigarettes. Yeah, yeah, I know a bad habit. Early on in my smoking career I learned to utilize this bad habit so as to amaze friends.

Along with smoking I enjoyed blowing bubbles. You know, those plastic bottles with soapy water and the magic wand with the circular plastic end that you blow on to form the bubbles. Regular bubbles are great; kids, the kid in all of us, cats, and dogs love them. Look close and swirling colors of the rainbow cover the bubble.

As special as they are, regular bubbles are pedestrian compared to smoke bubbles. Smoke bubbles? Here's what you do: take a drag on your cigarette, hold the magic wand to your mouth, blow out the smoke into the wand and a smoke-filled bubble forms. When it pops a small wisp of smoke gently floats away. Do this indoors in a room without swirling air currents and let the bubble burst on the floor. As it bursts a small mushroom cloud of smoke rises upward. Very cool, your own miniature re-creation of an atomic bomb explosion. Do this in a room full of people smoking those funny cigarettes and the crowd goes crazy.

By the spring of 1973 I had perfected the smoke bubble. Around this time Lori and I went to an outdoor concert in Bakersfield featuring Sly and the Family Stone. Mostly forgotten now, Sly's group was groundbreaking, the first major American rock band to be racially integrated and have women playing instruments and not just singing backup vocals or dancing around as eye candy. The group had a great stage presence and politics with a few hit songs. ("Sly and the Family Stone" 2013)

The concert was at the county fairgrounds stadium with bench seating. The crowd, as to be expected, was racially mixed with lots of black guys and gals sporting afros as was the fashion at the time. Lori and I were toward the top of the seating. No way was I going to attend a concert without my bubbles. As Sly and the group finally began playing (they were notorious for being late or some band members not even showing up due to excessive drug use) the crowd got into the music. I began blowing smoke bubbles. The air currents were such that the bubbles drifted down the seating and people in our section began to notice. What the hell was this? A floating opaque bubble that literally smoked when popped. As people realized what was going on their attention split between the group on stage and the magic bubbles.

Sensing a rare opportunity, I blew a monstrous smoke bubble that drifted down the stands, seemingly dodging hands reaching out to pop it. The smoke bubble collided with a black guy's afro and burst apart, smoke curled through his hair and around his head. Smiles and cheers erupted. Yes!

References

"Sly and the Family Stone." 2013. Wikipedia. Last modified August 13, 2013. http://en.wikipedia.org/wiki/Sly_and_the_Family_Stone.

The Chair of Power

In the fall of 1973, the beginning of my senior year, I took a class on the Sociology of Power from my sociology professor/mentor and friend Bill Hanson. Dr. Bill guided us on a journey through the various bases of power. You know the list: money, affection, fear, social standing, knowledge, logic, coercion, manipulation, and so on. A simple definition of power is the ability of A (an individual or organization) to influence the behavior and/or the thinking of B (again, an individual or organization) in accordance with A's objectives.

Bill Hanson, not in a chair of power, examining
a Christmas present, 1975.

While many nuances of lively classroom discussions and readings were interesting and useful in analyzing power, one stood out for me—defining situations and roles as a form of power. What does that mean? We all know how important government buildings are structured—high vaulted ceilings, marble floors, lots of brass fittings, maybe murals and columns. This physical structure defines the situation and your role in it. It projects feelings of governmental strength and power, which an individual does not have.

Additionally, it is not a coincidence in serious negotiations, say between an employer and a labor union or between unfriendly nations, that the shape of tables and seating arrangements are the focus of pre-negotiation negotiations. These pre-negotiations can establish one aspect of the parameters of power.

It seemed to me a relatively egalitarian new state college (California State College, Bakersfield which opened in 1970 and I was in the first entering freshman class) with eager students and mostly young faculty ought to minimize disparities in power between students and faculty. Obviously, this excepts knowledge as a power source since we students were there to increase our knowledge and cognitive powers from those who possessed them.

Similar to all public state college campuses in the 1970s, the faculty did not have luxurious offices, but decent enough. The 18 to 22 year-old student walks in and sits in a hard-back straight chair with hands nervously flopping around. The professor, on the other hand, has a padded swivel chair, resides behind a nice desk, surrounded with their diplomas and awards. Forget any power disparity due to knowledge. Who sits in the chair of power solely due to the structural setting? It ain't the student.

After gleaning this tidbit of knowledge about defining structures and roles, I went on a one student crusade to rectify the situation. Every time I visited a professor I requested to sit in the chair of power behind the desk while they took the pitiful student chair. All my professors patiently listened to my reasoning. Remarkably enough each one acceded to my "demand." They were all decent people, willing to experiment. It didn't hurt that Cal State Bakersfield was, at that time, a small school and I was personal friends with most of my teachers.

This partial role reversal lasted a few months until I graduated in June. I'm not sure it made a great deal of difference to me. I was already eager to follow the 1960s mantra of "Question Authority" and my teachers knew it. But I'd like to think that this slight alteration in situational power reminded my professors their knowledge and logic (and maybe a bit of experience) was the basis of their power, not a big chair.

Road Trip

It's two years into your marriage. You are 22 and your spouse 20. Let's see, what would force you together for weeks, no respite from each other? I know, a cross country car trip for five weeks. Yeah, that makes sense.

I just earned a Bachelor of Arts degree in Political Science graduate (1974). I did well in school (graduate magna cum laude with a 3.64 GPA) and thought highly of myself. After considerable discussion, we decided to embark upon that once in a lifetime trip—drive across the country.

We duly prepared: traded cars with a good friend, he took our 1964 Chevy Nova wagon and we got his Chevy van; packed plenty of camping equipment and food; had $958 in cash; bought a new blank book for daily journal entries (which, amazingly, we did); and brought Tolkien's *Lord of the Rings* trilogy for entertainment. Although young we were savvy enough to bring peace offerings for the natives we met along our trip. No, not glass beads and other shiny things; instead a stash of decent pot.

We left Bakersfield on July 1, 1974. It was nice to drive slowly (the van was hardly a speed machine anyway) and not be in a hurry to get anywhere. One of the first stops was Davis, California, home of UC Davis where I was accepted in the Master's Degree program in political science for the fall. We spent July 4th in Davis and reveled in the town's antics: a two minute parade downtown, adults racing kid's tricycles, a public bar-b-que, fireworks, and much beer drinking. The townies were friendly, much like the people with whom I grew up in Shafter. Maybe all small towns have friendly folks, or perhaps the unfriendly ones get fed up with the positive vibes and immigrate to the cities.

The lushness of northern California contrasted sharply with our home in the southern Central Valley. Forest covered mountains, instead of tumble weed covered fields, soothed the eye. We stopped for the night at a State Park in Crescent City, California. Here we met our first truly foreign people—Rosie and Mitchell from New York City. Amazingly enough, these barely comprehensible foreigners were making the same trip as us, only backwards. We shared food and some reefer. We parted the next day, but not before they provided a name and address of a safe harbor in New York City where we could stay.

A few days later in eastern Washington we spent time at Expo '74, the World's Fair in Spokane. During its six month run, the Expo had more than five million visitors—roughly 28 times the city's population ("Expo '74" 2013). The exhibits were interesting at the first environmentally themed world's fair. The Soviet Union's exhibit was a bit pushy, emphasizing the communal ownership of their natural resources. Of course, this communal ownership did not prevent their government from creating vast wastelands in the motherland.

We pushed on over the Rockies and into the rolling plains of South Dakota. On the same day (July 13) we saw Mt. Rushmore and experienced the mother of all thunder storms. The former was amazing, four 60-foot tall presidential heads carved in a granite mountain. An impressive feat. The latter scared the shit out of us. For more than an hour intermittent heavy rain was illuminated by dozens of lightning flashes. One struck less than 100 yards away, the electricity was palpable and the thunder rocked the van. Simultaneously beautiful and terrifying. I do love nature and agree with Aristotle who noted, "In all things of nature there is something of the marvelous" (Aristotle 2013).

Speaking of nature, a couple of days later near Rockford, Illinois we encountered mythical creatures—fire flies. Being a California native who had never ventured out of the southwest, I put fire flies in the same category as unicorns—cute beings that inhabit children's literature. Lo and behold, they do exist.

The next couple of days were spent in Springfield, Ohio. One of my political science professors at California State College, Bakersfield, Gene Clark, hailed from Springfield and was home for a visit. We stayed at his mom's house and were regaled with "when Gene was young stories." Quite amusing for me, his student only months before, quite embarrassing, as only moms can do, for him.

The seat of federal power beckoned and we took the bait. We spent three days exploring our nation's capital. I once again used my Cal State Bakersfield connection and we stayed with Bill Hanson's (my sociology professor and mentor) mom's house outside of Washington, DC.

Bill's mom and brother warmly greeted us as old friends (we had never met). They fed us and gave guided tours of the city—the imposing monuments and buildings, the tony areas, and the black neighborhoods. We were duly impressed with The Mall, the Smithsonian, and observing the House of Representatives from the gallery.

After a quick detour to Philadelphia and Independence Hall we rolled into The Big Apple. New York City was a time of firsts for us: the first time in the city, our first subway ride, and our first ride on the Staten Island ferry. Remember back in Crescent City, California and the New Yorkers we met, Rosie and Mitchell? We called the number provided and the people on the other end, on Staten Island, said of course we could stay with them—a home base.

So each day we commuted from Staten Island to Manhattan Island to explore. We utilized the modern day equivalent of streams and rivers for transportation, the subway. It was just like in the movies—noisy, covered with graffiti, and packed with humans. On the streets we marveled at the kamikaze taxis creating yellow metal streams while pedestrians darted in and out like some crazy fish species. Add in people of all races and ethnicities fashionably dressed or slouching around in virtual rags, a background of buildings as tall as small mountains, and you realize you ain't in Kansas (or Bakersfield) anymore.

I grew up watching Mickey Mantle, Roger Maris, Whitey Ford, Yogi Berra and the boys on the "Saturday Game of the Week." Yes, I'm a lifelong Yankees fan. No way were we leaving New York without seeing a game. Our last night we went to Shea Stadium (Yankee Stadium, the house that Ruth built, was being refurbished) for a game. The fans were, well they were New York Yankee fans—loud and rowdy. Of course the Yanks won 5 to 1.

We traveled through more impossibly green states to Boston. Boston was … yawn. Other than people speaking in some foreign language that vaguely resembled English, it was just another large eastern city.

We started home on July 29. We did make a detour to Saginaw, Michigan to visit my older brother Jim. Bad move. My relationship with him has been strained since … forever. He was a hard drinker with few positive vibes. At that point in my life I drank very little, if any. The same for Lori. We spent a day watching softball games and later bar hopping, him drinking and growing more sullen. My brother and his buddies did little to dispel the stereotype of the blue collar industrial worker (almost all were union members working at auto plants)—much drinking and/or ingesting drugs, sports as a major aspect of their lives, cars as something more than a machine to get from point A to point B, and material things being very important. Don't get me wrong, even at that point in life I enjoyed watching and playing sports (but not as a quasi-religious experience) and I certainly appreciated nice material goodies. I just had a feeling that those things were more than a part of life; they pretty much defined their lives.

The next day brought some much needed positive feelings. For the final time this journey I used my Cal State Bakersfield connection and we stayed at Rocky Hanson's (the spouse of Bill Hanson, my sociology professor and mentor; Rocky was also a good friend) parent's house outside of Dubuque, Iowa. After plowing through endless corn fields, we arrived and received a warm greeting from Bill and Rocky and Rocky's parents.

On our second day there Lori and I, Bill and Rocky, and Rocky's sister smoked a little ganja. Being a very amateur magician, I showed the gang the pencil trick—nothing quiet as enjoyable as seeing a bunch of stoned adults concentrating on a simple bit of prestidigitation. It was funny as hell. Then Rocky brought down the house with her famous "Rocky the Squirrel" imitation—putting her hands like little paws on the sides of her scrunched-up face and making squirrel noises. Later on we all went bowling and generally did pretty lousy, figure that.

From Iowa we had a pretty straight shot to California mostly along Interstate 80. A couple of days later we rolled into our starting point, Bakersfield.

Our journey took us through 26 states in 39 days. Boston was out easternmost destination. Along the way we visited several friends and made some new ones. What a great country—friendly people everywhere and much natural beauty. Adventure in every state, the trip of a lifetime.

References

"Expo '74." 2013. Wikipedia. Last modified August 25, 2013. http://en.wikipedia.org/wiki/Expo_%2774.

"Aristotle." 2013. *Parts of Animals*. The Quotations Page website. Last modification unknown. http://www.quotationspage.com/quote/24228.html.

Chapter Three
Winter 1981—Fall 1989
Intense Leftist Political Activity

Introduction

The sun being swallowed by the ocean created multihued colors bathing the lush coastal plain fronting the Santa Ynez Mountains—beautiful. As nature cycled through its daily routine proletariat families finished their dinner and eagerly awaited the latest installment of *Dallas.* The more upscale bourgeois leisurely plan their late supper and discuss the recent *Miami Vice* and *Moonlighting* episodes. Unbeknownst to these good folks, a group of socialist— democratic socialists, but socialists nonetheless—are planning to elect one of their own to the local ruling body, the Santa Barbara City Council. The City Council was a moderate to liberal group of politicians that never seemed to tackle the tough issues such as affordable housing, tenant's rights, and equal rights for gays and lesbians. Meanwhile, more than 3,000 miles away the Nicaraguan Contras, backed by covert US support, battled the ruling Sandinistas, supplied by the Soviet Union, for control of the country throughout the decade.

For me the decade was devoted, virtually non-stop, to anti-war and, later, increasingly leftist political activity. It was also a decade of great personal upheaval—divorce. For about a year after the divorce I fell in love with just about every woman I knew or met. My second marriage in early 1982 blossomed into a great partnership.

This activity was fueled by a strong commitment to leftist political ideology, youthful passion, some drugs, and the Rolling Stones. Coming of age in the 1960s, the, by the 1980s, older rockers like the Stones and The Who were my baseline music fix. Later, as New Wave rock 'n rollers crashed into Santa Barbara, I began to appreciate The Clash, Devo, Pat Benatar, the B-52s, Little Feat, and many others. Quite often my warm-up prior to a political event or candidate forum included some air guitar with Mick and the boys belting out "Sympathy for the Devil" or "Street Fighting Man." But

73

never drugs before public appearances—after all I did represent democratic socialism for most people with whom I came in contact.

Republican Ronald Reagan, elected president in a landslide over Democrat Jimmy Carter in November 1980, maintained his residence in the Santa Barbara area. Our task was not only to proselytize for democratic socialism, but do it in the president's adopted home town—no mean feat. The world-wide Cold War was replicated in Santa Barbara and the result was much the same—the Left lost.

Divorce and the Great Santa
Barbara Man Shortage of 1981

Happy New Year! A time for new beginnings—an understatement for the year to come. January 2, 1981, the new year kicks in and Lori decided to kick me. She left and said she wanted a divorce. She was unhappy and clearly stated several times in the last year that she cared little for me or the relationship. Was she serious? Hell yes.

You know the feeling when you are in a heated discussion and the other person delivers a series of lines that feel scripted. It's like they had a team of writers prepare the words for them. You, on the other hand, stammer back with a gem of a retort "so are you" or something just as lame. Then your opponent (for now my wife was an opponent) slings a barb worthy of Shakespeare. Suddenly you simultaneously feel stunned, angry at them, and about this tall (thumb and forefinger about an inch apart). It is the type of confrontation that, for days later, keeps running through your head and you feel "I should have said ..." Obviously Lori had prepared for this confrontation, probably for months. I was ambushed.

The next few weeks, anger at her and my pity party dominated my thinking and feeling. I realized this breakup was coming, but was good at denial. For a couple of months I secretly hoped she would die of tertiary syphilis. However, it was difficult to maintain such anger and self-pity for long—takes too much energy. Lori and I were very different people and "You Can't Always Get What You Want" (2013) (or what you think you want) according to Mick Jagger and Keith Richards. Looking back, Lori's decision to leave was courageous and the best for both of us.

My anger subsided and we got along pretty well for the next few months, sort of became almost friends. Since there were no kids and pitiful few possessions, the divorce process went smoothly. The divorce was final on October 29, 1981. I thought we should throw an "untying the knot party" to celebrate, well, our untying the knot. The party was held October 24, a few days prior to the Final Divorce Decree. We invited old and new friends and the 25 or so who attended had a good time. I only saw Lori a few more times after that, the last being about 30 years ago.

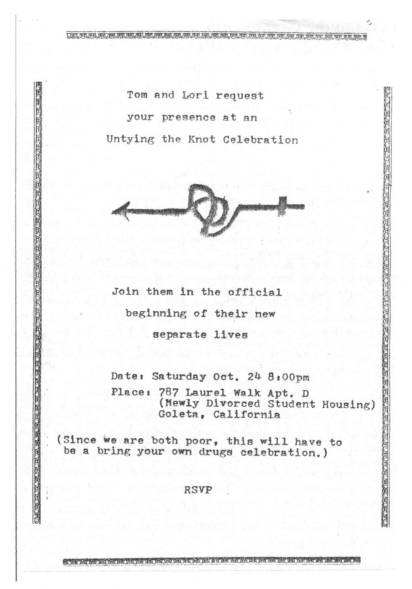

Tom and Lori request

your presence at an

Untying the Knot Celebration

Join them in the official

beginning of their new

separate lives

Date: Saturday Oct. 24 8:00pm
Place: 787 Laurel Walk Apt. D
(Newly Divorced Student Housing)
Goleta, California

(Since we are both poor, this will have to
be a bring your own drugs celebration.)

RSVP

Invitation to the "Untying the Knot" party, October 24, 1981.

There was no reason to dawdle and within a month or two of Lori leaving I was back in the dating game. During the remainder of 1981 I looked up a couple of old female friends and met two new ones. Unlike Lori, they actually seemed to enjoy my company. I wondered how could this be? All these beautiful, smart women dating me and sometimes more than dating? There was only one logical explanation.

For some reason, men between the ages of 25 and 35 or so in Santa Barbara in 1981 must have left the community in droves, perhaps abducted by aliens. (It is strange the media never commented on this major event. Most likely it was yet another conspiracy of silence.) The result was the Great Santa Barbara Man Shortage of 1981. Which makes sense, it's basic economics. If a commodity becomes scarce— such as available men in Santa Barbara—the value of such commodity, tends to rise. The unanticipated benefit of the shortage was my near atrophied intimacy skills blossomed.

Thanks to the man shortage I had good times. I dated, and in some cases loved, four decent women in a year. The parting of the ways was amicable in every case and I remained friends with each.

References

"You Can't Always Get What You Want." 2013. Wikipedia. Last modified October 20, 2013. http://en.wikipedia.org/wiki/You_Can%27t_Always_Get_What_You_Want

Defeat the Devil: Diablo Canyon Nuclear Power Plant

In December 1980 I took a leave of absence from the UC Santa Barbara Political Science Department and from writing my PhD dissertation. I knew I would get back to it once things settled down. (That was a bad case of wishful thinking.)

The year began with a fairly large change in my life—Lori left and we got divorced. (See the "Divorce and the Great Santa Barbara Man Shortage of 1981" story in this chapter for details of my divorce and subsequent dating exploits.)

My immediate need was a job. Let's see, what could I do? During the 1970s and '80s Santa Barbara had a thriving antiwar/peace community. There was even a storefront peace resource center called The Gathering Place (TGP). It was funded and run by a group of mostly wealthy, older, politically liberal women. Amazingly enough there was a job opening for a fulltime paid "Peace Action Coordinator." Hmmm, I was a war tax resister, had studied nonviolence for a decade, was a member of the War Resisters League, and was writing a dissertation on nonviolence and democracy—maybe I should apply for the job. I did and was hired in mid-February, 1981. Yahoo! A job actually doing what I had been studying for a decade.

Peace Resource Center
THE GATHERING PLACE
331 North Milpas Street
Santa Barbara, CA 93103
(805) 966-4404

The creative juices were unleashed. For the next seven months I lived the peace activist life. The job description was loose; I pretty much made it up as I went along. I had certain set responsibilities: staff the office; answer and return phone calls and correspondence; organize and promote TGP and its monthly peace educational events; find and contact speakers; develop literature; help write and produce the quarterly newsletter; organize fundraising events; staff a TGP table at events organized by other groups; and attend staff meetings. Beyond that it was my call. The direction I dragged TGP ultimately led to my demise. They favored moving slowly with gentle, generally small peacenik type events and people; I leaned strongly toward large rallies, confronting the powers that be, political action, rowdy peace people, and civil disobedience.

I got busy and established an account at the Isla Vista (the UC Santa Barbara student community) Recycling Center and began recycling our recyclables. (Why hadn't this been done before?) I ordered business cards, letterhead, and envelopes for TGP—we needed to look professional. I developed contacts with just about anyone and every organization in the Santa Barbara area that had any interest in broadly defined peace issues. For a community with about 80,000 population the list of active organizations that had peace/anti-war as at least part of their agenda was impressive—Committee in Solidarity with the People of El Salvador; Legal Defense Center; Network; Santa Barbara Coalition Against War and the Draft; Santa Barbara Draft Counseling Service; Santa Barbara Friends Meeting (Quakers); Santa Barbara Gray Panthers; Santa Barbara Indian Center; Santa Barbara People for a Nuclear Free Future; Santa Barbara Solidarity; Santa Barbara Tenant's Union; UC Santa Barbara Friends of The Gathering Place (which I stared); Southern California Clergy and Laity Concerned; United Nations Association; Women's International League for Peace and Freedom; and others.

MX MISSILES

- 200 missiles carrying 10 hydrogen bombs each
- Over $100 billion in tax dollars ($440 million annual operating costs)
- Drastic environmental changes in over 20,000 square miles of western land
- Decreased nuclear stability — increased chance of nuclear war
- Lower probability of nuclear arms control

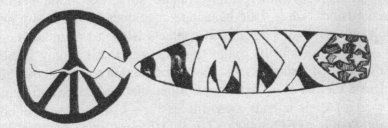

PARTIAL LIST OF ENDORSERS

Mary Grace Canfield
Dr. Jack Ceder, UCSB
Bob Creolian, ASB President SBCC
*Greg Cross, S.B. Coalition Against War and the Draft
*Corey Dubin, Citizens to Protect Pt. Concepcion
Dr. Ellis Englesberg, UCSB
*Richard Frishman, Legal Defense Center
*Jack Hagerty, Recycling Operations Coordinator, SUNRAE
*Mary Kornhauser, WILPF
*Glen Lazof, S.B. Solidarity
*Nancy Lynch, S.B. Draft Counseling
Tony Mitchell, Activist Network
*Genevieve Nowlin, U.N. Association
S.B. Coalition against War and the Draft
S.B. County Collective Opposed to the MX
S.B. Indian Center
S.B. Solidarity
S.B. Tenants Union
United Nations Association
UCSB Coalition to Stop the Draft
UCSC Friends of the Gathering Place
*Elliot Waidman, UCSB Hunger Action Group
*Roberta Weissglass, U.N. Association

*Organizations listed for identification only

JOIN US:

In learning about the MX Missiles and the potential impact on arms control, the environment, and your pocket book.

SPEAKERS:

Vice Admiral John M. Lee (retired)

Joe Griggs, Chairperson of the Great Basin MX Alliance of Nevada and Utah

Marlene Graham, Western Shoshone Sacred Lands Association of Nevada

Bring your lunch, learn about the MX Boondoggle, and enjoy music by JEFF LEVY and FRIENDS.

SUNDAY, MAY 3
12:30-3:30
ALAMEDA PARK

SPONSORED BY SOUTHERN CALIFORNIA CLERGY AND LAITY CONCERNED AND THE GATHERING PLACE
FOR MORE INFORMATION: 966-4404

The flyer for one of the events I helped organize and The Gathering Place co-sponsored, May 3, 1981.

The Gathering Place had monthly public meetings concerning various peace issues. This was an ongoing activity which I promoted by writing press releases, gathering sponsors, notifying other community groups, putting up flyers, and giving radio interviews. During the summer I led a series of four forums on Gandhi and nonviolence.

I was attending meetings of other like-minded groups two or three times a week, often working into the night. I was young and loved it. With the reluctant blessings of TGP Steering Committee I began working closely with other groups with similar interests. The first large rally I organized was an Anti-MX Missile rally at a local park. Of course it was a roaring success with several good speakers and scores of people attending.

In the spring I spent considerable time working with people affiliated with the Abalone Alliance. The Abalone Alliance was a coalition of autonomous anti-nuclear power, anti-nuclear weapons, and pro-safe energy groups and individuals in California ("Abalone Alliance" 2013; "Abalone Alliance" Undated). The local group was the Santa Barbara People for a Nuclear Free Future. Their main focus, along with the Abalone Alliance at that time, was to halt construction of the Diablo Canyon Nuclear Power Plant located in San Luis Obispo County—the adjacent county north of Santa Barbara County ("Diablo Canyon Power Plant" 2013). The general plan was to halt construction through education, outreach, political pressure, and, if necessary, a human blockade. I joined an affinity group, a support group, of which several members—including me—planned to participate in civil disobedience and blockade Diablo Canyon when the time came ("Affinity Groups" 1979). Our group's name was "Infinity," pretty clever. Due to my background in studying nonviolence and willingness to put in the time, I became one of several nonviolence trainers in the area. We held workshops on the reasons for the upcoming blockade and how to maintain nonviolent discipline—how not to lose your cool when being hauled off to jail. I helped train about 50 to 60 people for the blockade.

This hectic schedule of TGP work, helping organize some large rallies and open community meetings, and working with the anti-Diablo Canyon movement lasted till late September.

81

Me being arrested while blockading Diablo Canyon Nuclear
Power Plant, September 20, 1981.

On September 10, 1981 the blockade of Diablo Canyon
Nuclear Power Plant began. At the conclusion of the ten day action,
1,960 people, me included, were arrested for trying to blockade the
entrance to the plant. This was the largest arrest total in the history of
the US anti-nuclear power movement.

I was arrested on September 20 and spent three days in "jail" in
the gym at Cuesta College near San Luis Obispo. I assume hard jail
time changes a person. This was hardly hard time, and I emerged
unchanged. I met a bunch of interesting guys (the male and female
"prisoners" were housed in separate facilities), including an AIM
(American Indian Movement) activist checking out the almost totally
white middle class anti-nuke movement. One ongoing discussion stuck
with me—how friendly should we be with the guards? Were they "our
friends in green" and we should try to win them over, or were they the
coercive arm of the state and should be treated accordingly? No clear
group consensus on that one. I felt we were political prisoners.

As the torture of incarceration got to me I wrote a song memorializing the experience.

This Gym

I wrote this song on September 21, 1981 while in jail for blockading and unlawful assembly at Diablo Canyon Nuclear Power Plant. It is sung to the tune of "This Land is Your Land" by Woody Guthrie.

This gym is your gym.

This gym is our gym.

All the way from that end.

Right down to this end.

From the barbed wire fences.

To the Harvey's Honey Huts.

This gym was made for you and me.

If you get bored here.

There's lots of meetings.

And time to catch up on extra sleeping.

It's so exciting.

You'll hate leaving

This gym was made for you and me.

Just like a nuke plant.

There's lots of guards here.

Just like a nuke plant.

It's very safe here.

And all that barbed wire.

Just makes it so clear.

This gym was made for you and me (Garrison 1981A).

On September 22, 1981 I had my day in the San Luis Obispo Municipal Court. I read the statement below, pled "no contest" to

83

blockading and unlawful assembly at the Diablo Canyon Nuclear Power Plant, paid a $20 fine, and left.

> For me civil disobedience is not an act of futility or frustration. It is, instead, a positive affirming action which at some point must be taken if sanity and love are to have any place in our society. I and thousands of my brothers and sisters have worked, some for years, to stop the madness at Diablo Canyon Nuclear Power Plant. The struggle to stop this plant has been taken through the courts and the federal regulatory system. At each step the generic facts about nuclear power plants and specific facts about Diablo Canyon have been ignored. This issue is now being decided by the people through their nonviolent action.

> Like other people I voluntarily obey the laws of this country. However, given the structure of the current political and economic system and its direction particularly with regards to nuclear power, I had to withdraw my consent to obey the laws and, therefore, practice civil disobedience.

> This was done for both personal and political reasons. Personally I could not sit aside and let this nuclear power plant spew its poison into the environment. Politically if even one person is influenced by the actions of myself and my brothers and sisters, then this action has been successful. In addition, the nonviolent action centered around Diablo Canyon is helping to build a strong community which will continue to struggle for a nuclear free future until the technological Frankenstein of nuclear power has been eliminated from our home—the earth.

> In our struggle it is imperative that we remember the words of Martin Luther King, Jr. when he said, "We must learn to live together as brothers and sisters, or we will perish together as fools" (Garrison 1981B).

Despite our efforts, Diablo Canyon Nuclear Power Plant unit one went online May 7, 1985; unit two the next year ("Diablo Canyon Power Plant" 2013). Was it worth it? I worked at organizing for months; some people had been at it for years. Did I ever think "the people" would stop the plant? No. I do believe the educational component of the campaign—educating the general population about nuclear power and educating the activists about the power of nonviolent direct action—was worth the effort.

What about the anti-nuclear movement itself? I had, and still have, some serious criticisms. First was the way the meetings were run. Meeting facilitators tried to be extremely egalitarian and let everyone speak their piece ad nauseam. It was a noble goal but usually ended up producing very long meetings. This led to a related problem: how many working class people, after an eight-hour work day, would stick around for a multitude of endless meetings? Not many is the answer. As a result, the Abalone Alliance and its affiliates were almost entirely composed of the retired, students, and professional middle class people—and almost all white.

In addition, few of the participants were well grounded in political analysis. Was the scourge of nuclear power an aberration or the logical consequence of our political-economic system? Could participants be mobilized for actions around other issues? The vast majority of supporters and activists never approached these and other questions. I felt the leadership, wanting the broadest participation possible, tended to avoid the hard political discussions.

In any case, I had a job to return to. Or did I? The Gathering Place Steering Committee did not think it appropriate for a Peace Action Coordinator to practice civil disobedience at Diablo Canyon Nuclear Power Plant. What? Isn't that <u>exactly</u> what a peace activist should do? They took a moralistic view of nonviolence based on moral suasion, there was little room for the role and uses of power in nonviolent direct action. I had a much broader view and saw opposing power with power, albeit nonviolently, as the essence of nonviolent action. Their next step was obvious and I quit before they fired me.

(For a more detailed discussion of the mechanisms of nonviolent action, see "Antiwar Work and Nonviolence" in Chapter Two.)

References

"Abalone Alliance: Structure and Process." Undated. Twelve page information document produced by the Abalone Alliance.

"Abalone Alliance." 2013. Wikipedia. Last modified August 31, 2013. http://en.wikipedia.org/wiki/Abalone_Alliance.

"Affinity Groups." 1979. Four page information document produced by the Abalone Alliance. March 9.

"Diablo Canyon Power Plant." 2013. Wikipedia. Last modified August 24, 2013. http://en.wikipedia.org/wiki/Diablo_Canyon_Power_Plant.

Garrison, Tom. 1981A. "This Gym." I wrote this song on September 21 while in jail for blockading and unlawful assembly at Diablo Canyon Nuclear Power Plant. It is sung to the tune of "This Land is Your Land" by Woody Guthrie.

Garrison, Tom. 1981B. My statement read in the San Luis Obispo Municipal Court before pleading "no contest" to blockading and unlawful assembly at the Diablo Canyon Nuclear Power Plant. September 22.

New Job, New Love, New Life

After quitting my position as Peace Action Coordinator at The Gathering Place in late September 1981, I was unemployed, would soon be asked to leave married student housing at UC Santa Barbara (I was no longer married and was on a leave from my political science graduate studies), and between sweeties. Sounds like a maelstrom of chaos, but don't shed any tears. Within the next six months I established patterns that would structure my life for the next 15 years.

I was only unemployed for about two weeks when I landed the job I kept for the next 18+ years, managing editor (later editorial director) of *Current World Leaders*. It was a political science journal—generally focusing on international relations and comparative politics—published by the nonprofit International Academy at Santa Barbara. I enjoyed my new job, getting paid a decent salary to produce and edit a political science journal—heaven for a political junkie. At the time of my hire, the publication covered rather boring non-controversial topics and only reprinted previously published articles. Change was needed and I was the willing agent.

The journal needed interesting topics: over the years I covered immigration, women and politics, nationalism and ethnic politics, affirmative action and quotas, international terrorism, multiculturalism and linguistic politics, and many others. I also started using original essays, which clearly enhanced the publication's credibility. To further promote the journal, and continue my education, I worked hard to obtain papers on all sides of an issue. For example, the immigration issue featured essays favoring and opposed to illegal immigration in the US and discussions of immigration policies in other countries. While I had strong opinions on most topics I covered, I went to great lengths to include articles supporting each side of an issue. Let the readers decide which is the stronger argument. Even though I was removed from academe, this job kept me somewhat connected for almost two decades.

The International Academy was a non-profit company. Its founder, Eric Boehm, was also the founder of ABC-Clio, a respected academic publisher. Both companies were housed in the same facility in the lush low foothills of the Santa Ynez Mountains above Santa Barbara.

Deb, Spring 1982.

When I had worked only a few weeks at the International Academy, I literally ran into an ABC-Clio employee—Deborah (Deb) Looker, the manager of Clio's data processing service. We got to talking as people do after a collision, and discovered several life similarities. Like me she had fairly recently been divorced; had been in other relationships since the divorce; was interested in, well, just about everything; possessed real positive self-esteem derived from doing well in her job (not the self-esteem we see in the last couple of decades where everyone regardless of effort and achievement is treated as "excellent"); and was cute—what a combination.

Within a few weeks of colliding with her we began having lunch together on an expansive lawn overlooking the city, a great setting to get to know each other rather quickly. We laughed a lot, always a good sign. Deb noted that our budding relationship felt equal—it's was about time for me to hear that. In past years I had been labeled as too weak or too domineering by a few women.

On January 18, 1982, my birthday, we went our first formal date and saw *The Misfits* (2013). A great movie, the last one for Marilyn Monroe and Clark Gable and directed by John Huston. It was the beginning of the end for Marilyn and Clark and the end of the beginning for Deb and me. After that we were inseparable—not crazy in love, but growing to love each other. This is not to say everything was perfect, but we were both pretty much adults (me 30 and Deb 32) and knew how to handle adversity. This was different from my ex-wife in that with her there were things I didn't much like even during good periods.

Some basic things not given much mention in "How to find your true love" articles are important for relationships. For example, energy levels. My ex, Lori, had a very different energy level (low to my hyper) and this contributed to other problems. "So why don't you help more around the house?" "I'm tired." Thus, the great difference in energy levels contributed to a different level of acceptance of household messiness. Deb and I have similar energy levels, not a trivial matter.

Wedding ceremony, March 8, 1982

No reason to put off matters and on March 8, 1982 (International Women's Day) we were married in a civil ceremony at Alice Keck Park in Santa Barbara. It must have been a good decision for we are still together, like and love each other, share many interests, and have weathered the bad times. Once married Deb and I also became a DINK couple—double income, no kids that continues today.

First married kiss, March 8, 1982.

Like most couples, early on we experienced the wilds of passion and rites of ecstasy. However, unlike my first marriage, Deb and I find comfort in each other—not a small matter. I suspect many couples share the passion, but somehow miss out on the comfort. Comfort is a quiet victory, essential but often overlooked.

The wedding party—Janine (Deb's sister), Deb, me,
and our friend Scott.

References

Current World Leaders. Santa Barbara, California:
International Academy at Santa Barbara.

The Misfits. 2013. Wikipedia. Last modified October 15, 2013.
http://en.wikipedia.org/wiki/The_Misfits_(film).

War Resisters League and War Tax Resistance

Time to ramp up the activism. In July 1982, Deb, me, Scott, and other like-minded people in the Santa Barbara area formed a local chapter of the War Resisters League (WRL). Officially formed in 1923, the WRL has proselytized and practiced nonviolent direct action against war and the roots of war for decades—always in the forefront of the antiwar and social justice movements. It is the oldest secular antiwar organization in the US.

Some Santa Barbara WRL members at a rally, 1983.

I had been a member since 1972, Deb recently joined, and Scott was a long-time member who served for a time on the WRL National Committee. We began meeting monthly and soon had a core membership of eight to ten. For the next few years we agitated for peace. Our group co-sponsored public events, participated in events organized by other groups, produced several high quality pieces of literature, gave radio interviews, and sponsored several speakers. Basically, we tried to disrupt the military-industrial complex by verbal intimidation and nonviolent action. (The complex generally ignored our efforts.)

By far our most visible activity was our focus on war tax resistance. To facilitate this we established the Santa Barbara Peace Fund Escrow Account (SBPFEA) in October 1982. The Account was established as a repository for individuals to deposit phone tax and income tax money not being paid to the federal government—a form of war tax resistance. We educated ourselves and gave seminars on the reasons for war tax resistance, how to do it, and what to expect from the Internal Revenue Service (IRS) (Headman 1981A and 1981B).

War tax resistance ad that ran in the *Santa Barbara News-Press* (April 13, 1983) and the *Santa Barbara News & Review* (April 7, 1983)

Our first big action was a tax day (April 15) press conference and demonstration in 1983 in which about 20 people attended. Surprisingly for moderate-to-liberal Santa Barbara, we received considerable print media and radio attention that focused on the issues. We placed ads in local newspapers; a general statement about the WRL and war tax resistance was read; and eight people, including me, read individual statements on why they were participating in this form of civil disobedience. This event, and subsequent tax day events, was successful.

At its height, the Santa Barbara Peace Fund Escrow Account had more than 20 depositors and in excess of $4,000 in deposits.

I began attaching war tax protest letters with my (our for most years since I was married) federal income tax statement in 1973 for the 1972 tax year. The letters noted that my wife and I were law-abiding citizens and would pay our full federal tax, but did not want our money to fund military spending. By the early 1980s I began refusing to pay a portion of the federal taxes due along with a protest letter. (I did the latter, refused to pay all of the income tax due, for the 1981 to 1983 tax years). While I still believe it was an important gesture—given my beliefs during this period—our efforts did not exactly stop the military-industrial complex in its tracks.

By 1985 Deb and I, while still members of the WRL, slowly removed ourselves from its activities. We were getting burnt out and began focusing on other political work. In late 1984 we closed our SBPFEA account and paid the IRS back taxes plus interest. Within a year, the local WRL Chapter was seldom active. In 1992, after years of inactivity, I helped close the SBPFEA and disperse the funds.

While our involvement in the Santa Barbara WRL was relatively short, about three years, the activity level was intense. Without exception the local members were committed peace people— good folks. I did have criticisms of the local antiwar movement and local leftists that I voiced in an April 30, 1983 letter to good friend and former Cal State Bakersfield professor Bill Hanson and his wife Rocky. Portions of that letter are below.

> Toward the end of this effort [the April 15 press conference and demonstration] I got pretty burned out and irritable. Glad it was over. My major bitch was that

too few people did all the work, and I did most of it. For example, the woman who volunteered to organize the press conference copped out and I did it. That meant writing press releases, radio spots, get permits, etc. But as I reflect back, a lot of people did get more involved than they ever have. I purposely didn't do any IRS tabling and it went well. Deb did media liaison at the press conference and did a good job. People slowly are learning the skills needed to be effective organizers.

A related train of thought: Scott and I (Scott is a member of the National WRL Council) have been discussing/bitching about how so few organizers and peace centers (we have one in SB) do not think in a strategic long-term manner. They simply plan for one disconnected event after another. No thinking of how these will mobilize people for the long-haul, how to plug them into an organization which can effectively use their energy. And worst of all is the narrow focus. Like the belief that the fucking [nuclear] freeze will be a panacea. What about the underlying causes of violence we all face daily—sexism, racism, monopoly capitalism, hierarchical organization at the work place. These so-called "peace people," being nice moralistic middle-class folks, have a hell of a hard time moving beyond that to a realistic political analysis.

Now the above sounds harsh and it is. I do realize that moralism is the basis for most nonviolent action—as it should be, we are discussing moral issues. But we are not going to end nuclear power/weapons/sexism by being nice and pleading with the elites to give us a break. As we learned from all social justice struggles, we need to confront their power with an equally strong nonviolent power which forces them to meet our demands. As Gene Sharp would say "cut off or threaten to cut off their sources of power" (e.g., obedience, money, etc.). It would be nice if we could convert Ronnie and his gang through nonviolent action. It is frustrating working with "granola-heads" who believe that power is dirty, and by being "nice" and singing enough Jackson Browne songs, the opponents will come around.

On the other side are those who do practical thinking, but have lost their gentleness—our Marxist-Leninist friends. I've had a lot of contact with the Revolutionary Communist Party people (Maoists) in this area. I agree with much of their analysis (excepting two big points: democratic centralism/Leninism and the need for violence), but they have so much hatred. I would not like to see them controlling things. They forgot, if they ever knew, that basic lesson that we do not do all this political work for revenge, but to bring about meaningful, humane social change.

So it is difficult to find non-granola heads, non-Leninists to work with. Oh well, again I'm sounding more harsh than the facts. I do work with the mushy types. And the ones like that in our WRL local are becoming more political.

As long as I'm griping, here's another one. No humor. Boy, both the extremes have no humor. Never laugh at themselves—it's all too serious. Scott and I would like to start a magazine called "Lose" (after *WIN*). But I doubt if we would get many subscribers. Also theater. When the Queen of England came to Santa Barbara there was a small demonstration. I thought it would have been great to mock all the shit the city organized for her. Have a whole bunch of lefties dress up as queens and ride down the street in an open caddie convertible throwing dollar bills and have people with literature working the crowds. Do something to show how ridiculous the whole idea of royalty is. Well, anyway it was a thought.

Back to the war tax resistance (WTR) campaign. One reason why it is important to do WTR is that it is probably the first act of civil disobedience most people do (like starting with a zero risk action such as refusing to pay the phone tax). I'm sure it took a lot of courage for the other seven people at our press conference who did so, to stand up in public and challenge the government. Getting beyond or even reducing the fear of what the government will do to you is a huge step toward changing the beast. It was a very Gandhian action. One of the really neat things is that with one exception, all the people who spoke on the 15th are not granola-heads. Two are older women (over 55), one is a librarian, another guy works in a hospital, I'm an editor, Scott is a typographer. So we did not look like aging hippies, but more like serious dedicated common folk.

Deb and I began focusing on more overtly political activity—organizing a local Socialist Party Chapter, getting heavily involved in the Santa Barbara Tenant's Union and the local Gay and Lesbian Resource Center, becoming relatively big fish in the small pond of California Peace and Freedom Party politics, and running for Santa Barbara City Council.

References

Garrison, Tom. 1983. Letter from me to Bill and Rocky Hanson. April 30.

Hedemann, Ed. Editor. 1981A. *War Resisters League Organizer's Manual*. New York: War Resisters League.

Hedemann, Ed. Editor. 1981B. *War Resisters League Guide to War Tax Resistance*. New York: War Resisters League.

War Tax Resistance advertisement. 1983. *Santa Barbara News-Press* (April 13, 1983) and the *Santa Barbara News & Review* (April 7, 1983).

Justice Prevails!

On March 16, 1984, Deb and I officially joined the revolutionary bourgeoisie—we bought a house. Or more correctly, a duplex. It was a Spanish style, red tile roof charmer with hardwood floors, internal arches, and built-in cabinets. At that point we had been married a little more than two years and needed to invest in our future, have a garden, more space, and escape our last evil, yes evil, landlord. Along with political work, we now had the "opportunity" to spend the next 25 years fixing and maintaining our house that was built in the 1920s.

Prior to our marriage in March 1982, I was living in a collective. In November 1981 I joined three other adults (and two kids) who were collectively buying a house in Goleta (a suburb of Santa Barbara). I knew one member, Scott, and met the other two adults— Jim and Vonna. We all got along and I was invited to join the group. We decided to name our house TRACT ("Toward Revolution and Collective Truggle") HOUSE and our motto "Making the Ordinary Revolutionary."

It was great to be a homeowner. Physically TRACT HOUSE was an ordinary Goleta tract house—four bedrooms and green shag carpet. Scott and I discussed the revolutionary aspects of home ownership. No more rent to a parasitic landlord. We all feel a strong commitment to each other and the house. Both of these commitments were amazing to me. Going from a long marriage to alone for ten months and then a collective household is strange. However, it was a group of responsible and politically lefty adults—just what I needed.

We were going to make the ordinary revolutionary. Owning a home is ordinary, but a home-owning political collective is revolutionary. Our long range plan is to use TRACT HOUSE as a nonviolent revolutionary base camp in Goleta. We were like a guerilla group in the countryside. Getting to know the territory and people and building a solid base from which to spread the revolution. More specifically we were all committed to getting involved in Goleta politics. We viewed this as a long-term struggle. I thought I would be there for years.

I believed that long-term grassroots organizing is the key for the Movement and to do that effectively a stable base, support from a collective, and intimate knowledge of the community is necessary. All will happen.

As fate will have it, all did not happen. In January 1982, Deb and I started dating and spending much of our time at TRACT HOUSE. Everyone got along. But by the time we got hitched, March 8, 1982, it was clear we would not reside at the collective household. Seven people, including two kids and a dog, in a four bedroom house was a bit crowded. We wanted to save money for a down payment for our own place by living at Deb's apartment.

For the next two years, the first year or so with a roommate, we began to realize that our landlord, "Icky", was evil and out to get us (we were not paranoid). Odd, because we were perfect tenants— always paid the rent on time, kept our place clean, and even took care of the communal grounds.

In April 1983 the evil one requested that we sign a rental agreement addendum that made us, the tenants, liable for pest control. The whole complex had roaches and rats and controlling this problem was clearly, and legally, the responsibility of the landlord. We refused and a few days later we received a rent increase—the first example of illegal retaliation by "Icky."

On November 9, 1983, we received a "Rules and Regulations" addendum to our rental agreement. It was full of absurd and vague rules such as "Garbage … should be placed in the outside containers on a daily basis." and "All doors must be locked during absence of the resident." We did not need a landlord to tell us how often to take out the trash or to lock the door when we leave. Since this was a legal

99

document, we would not sign it and notified "Icky" to that effect. He responded by becoming angry and verbally abusive. Four days later we received a rent increase—a second blatant case of illegal retaliation. That it was retaliation for not signing the addendum was obvious since our last rent increase was only seven months earlier. We received three rent increases in 15 months to that point and that was excessive even for the tight Santa Barbara rental market.

We had had enough of the "Ickster" and intensified our search for a house to purchase. Good thing too, since on February 14, 1984 we received yet another rent increase—a $55 a month increase. Thus, we were subjected to three rent increases in less than one year. The next day we gave our 30-day notice along with a request to return our cleaning deposit. The real battle now began.

Me and Deb and Louise the cat at our first house, Spring 1985.

We moved into our new place on March 16 and life was good. Only one problem, the evil one refused to return ANY of our cleaning deposit. We spent hours and enlisted friends to help spackling and cleaning. Not only did "Icky" refuse to return any of our cleaning deposit, he said we owed him an additional $4.09.

On April 4, 1984 Deb and I filed a Small Claims Court suit against "Icky" in Santa Barbara Municipal Court. After a couple of delays on his part (he said he was vacationing in Europe, sure on our money) we had our court date on June 22. Attorneys are not allowed in Small Claims Court. No problem, I led the judge through the events, presented evidence, and questioned witnesses. "Icky" floundered and got angry. At one point, while glancing around the courtroom with furtive eyes, he blatantly lied while under oath (along with several smaller lies); said we repaired our bicycles in the living room which resulted in greasy carpet (not true). I know under oath lying happens, but it was still shocking. I could understand lying while under oath in a case involving tens of thousands of dollars or your freedom, but lying for a few hundred bucks?

We asked for $626.19 in damages, including $200 due to the defendant acting in bad faith, and were awarded a judgment of $593.54 plus $9 in court costs. Yippee! Justice prevailed.

Most pugnacious slime like "Icky" would slither away and pay the judgment. Not our boy. He filed an appeal to Superior Court and the battle renewed. Superior Court allows attorneys and "Icky" had one. Feeling rather Clarence Darrowish from our earlier victory, and not having the inclination or bucks to hire an attorney, I took on "Icky's" dream team attorney. (His lawyer was well known around town as the landlords "gunslinger.") We squared off on November 2, 1984.

Besides our own testimony, Deb and I had three other witnesses and several documents. "Icky" was his normal charming self—not. On November 8 we received the judgment—$365.27 for damages, $10 for bad faith by the defendant ("Icky"), and $9 court costs. Victory!

In the normal course of events, this story is over. But, you don't know "Icky" like we do. He took his last shot and refused to pay the judgment. We filed an "Enforcement of Judgment" on November 28. A few days later we received the payment.

This was an exciting victory in several ways. "Icky" was one of the landlords known in Santa Barbara for keeping cleaning deposits. Few tenants ever challenged him in court—too much trouble. Very few tenants ever won these sort of cases, the Santa Barbara courts at that time were known as landlord friendly. It took us almost eight months, and a lot of work, from the initial filing to succeed. But justice prevailed in the end and I did get to play attorney.

We realize most landlords are decent people providing housing at reasonable rents. But the evil one and his ilk deserve a special place in Dante's *Inferno*—permanent residence in at least the fourth circle, greed, or more likely the eight circle, fraud.

Santa Barbara Tenants Union

Being tenants in a high rent community, Santa Barbara, was difficult. Due to the lack of buildable space within the city, few apartments were built since the 1970s. Being a desirable place to live, market forces dictate an upward pressure on rents. The supply is basically static while demand, the pool of potential renters, increases slowly decade after decade. During the 1980s approximately 60% of the households rented.

That was the background in which Deb and I found ourselves, a tough rental market. Being good socialists of some sort (not yet members of the Socialist Party, USA) we joined the Santa Barbara Tenants Union (SBTU) in early 1982, and remained members until the late 1980s when its activity level dropped sharply. The SBTU grew out of a rent control campaign in 1978. That campaign, the first of four within a decade, lost 37% to 63% at the polls. The rent control campaign in 1980 did worse, losing 32% (yes) to 68% (Wilkins 1986).

At least some of the SBTU's leadership (they often held office in the SBTU) were affiliated with the League of Revolutionary Struggle (LRS), a nationwide communist organization formed in 1978. The LRS considered itself anti-revisionist and took inspiration from the Communist Party of China and its leader Mao Zedong. It was heavily invested in racial and ethnic identity politics ("League of Revolutionary Struggle" 2013).

How could we tell they were commies? The LRS published a newspaper called *Unity*. Even for a lefty paper it was pretty bad—full of slogans and stories of struggle against capitalism by just about anybody as long as they were non-white. By this time I was fairly well connected with the local reds, some LRS people and a few Revolutionary Communist Party (RCP) types. The only people who sold *Unity* were members of the SBTU's leadership. When Deb and I asked if they were LRS members the reply was always, "I am a supporter of the *Unity* newspaper." Come on. Nobody except a dues-paying LRS member would try to sell that rag.

Deb and I had no problem with commies. Well, maybe a little problem with the fact that they were Marxists-Leninists and believed in the dictatorship of the proletariat. I had some concern that, if they were honest, they would most likely initiate violence (as opposed to self-defense) to achieve their ends. Ohhhh, and we had maybe a tinsy problem with the most likely outcome if their kind gained power—that people like Deb and I would be some of the first to be lined up against a wall and shot. Other than those small caveats, we were fine with the local commies.

However, we did have a problem with political people hiding a primary affiliation. I can just envision that after the revolution in Santa Barbara some of the SBTU leaders, in leadership positions in the post-revolutionary government, telling the people, "Oh, did we forget to mention that we are commies?"

So this transparent lying about their political affiliation means that when the "revolution" comes it will be led in Santa Barbara by political activists who are, if not skilled at lying, at least comfortable with it. A great start for a new humanistic order.

Of course, lying about one's principal political affiliation has a long tradition on the Left. There may have been justification for underground political work (including lying about leftist political affiliations) in Czarist Russia or 1980s El Salvador. But in 1980s America?

I twice ran for Santa Barbara City Council (1985 and 1987) openly as a socialist. In several years (early 1980s to mid-1990s) of very intense political activity—all of it done openly as a member of the California Peace and Freedom Party and the Socialist Party, USA—I never had a major problem with the public due to being a socialist and promoting socialism. Neither did any of the score or so core members of our local socialist group. In both campaigns the SBTU, somewhat reluctantly in 1987, endorsed me.

Putting the lying aside, the SBTU did help hundreds of tenants. They represented individual tenants in disputes with landlords and were a thorn in the side of the established powers in Santa Barbara. The SBTU testified before the Santa Barbara City Council and various city committees numerous times concerning tenant issues.

For several years I was on the Steering Committee and co-chaired the Office and Tenants Rights Information Committee. I spread the gospel of rent control in the 1986 and 1988 electoral campaigns (both lost handily) by speaking to other community groups hoping to gather their support (Hulse and Burns 1988). Deb and I also walked precincts and distributed literature.

Like most communist groups, the LRS was active in the Democrat Party (although not always openly as LRS members). Nationally they played an important role in the Rainbow Coalition and the 1984 and 1988 campaigns to elect Jesse Jackson as president.

Locally, the LRS folks and their supporters also exhibited an incredible ability to politically support almost anyone—excepting, of course, the most blatant conservative—as long as that person had black or brown skin and was a Democrat.

They demonstrated this behavior when Democrat Tom Bradley, a black moderate (at best), ran for governor of California in 1986. Other than being black, Bradley had no progressive/leftist credentials. The SBTU had fairly radical by-laws and, as noted above, some members of the leadership were LRS members. Deb and I, being serious and open leftists, argued strenuously at a general membership meeting that the SBTU should endorse the Peace and Freedom Party (the only avowedly socialist party with ballot status in California of which Deb and I were members) candidate—a Hispanic woman, Maria Elizabeth Munoz—instead of the milquetoast Bradley for governor. While we managed to convince several Tenants Union members who were not LRS "supporters" to endorse the true leftist candidate, the majority voted to endorse Bradley (the vote was 13 to seven for Bradley).

Understand the underlying political context. An endorsement by the SBTU for any candidate for statewide office would only influence at most a couple of hundred voters in Santa Barbara—almost certainly not enough to make a difference for any candidate. But, by openly backing a socialist (the PFP candidate) the organization would help build a base outside the Democrat Party for progressives and leftists. On the other hand, backing a tired old moderate Democrat would mean almost nothing and build little except allegiance to what almost everyone in the leadership agreed was a corrupt Democrat Party. It didn't matter that Bradley would offer at best lukewarm support for the goals of the Tenants Union, while the PFP candidate would whole heartedly support those goals. Bradley was a black Democrat—that was enough.

References

Hulse, Jane and Melinda Burns. 1988. "Rent issue suffers fourth loss." *Santa Barbara News-Press*. November 9.

"League of Revolutionary Struggle." 2013. Wikipedia. Last modified October 18, 2013. http://en.wikipedia.org/wiki/League_of_Revolutionary_Struggle

Wilkins, John. 1986. "Rent control measure defeated for third time." *Santa Barbara News-Press*. November 5.

Go Reds, Smash State

In the fall of 1983 Deb and I were two of the founding members of the Santa Barbara Chapter of the Socialist Party, USA. It became our political home base for well over a decade and provided historical and moral support—a "user friendly" organization for radicals who were not anti-democratic Leninists or muddle headed former hippies.

The Socialist Party (SP), USA was organized in 1901. It was somewhat influential in the first two decades of the 20th century, but  eventually dwindled to a few thousand members. It is a multi-tendency organization open to a wide spectrum of opinions and disagreement. The SP rejects dogma and promotes internal debate. It is oriented around principles, and solidarity within the party comes from the ability of those with divergent views on some issues to engage in a collective struggle toward social revolution. Most socialist and communist parties adopted some form of "democratic centralism," which stifled internal debate once a majority had spoken (members holding minority viewpoints were expelled or forced into silence) and inevitably led to vicious internal fighting. Simply examine the history of leftist parties in the US that adopted "democratic centralism" to understand the wave after wave of internal fights and party splits. The SP never embraced that tradition and was open to debate on all issues ("What's the Difference?" undated; *Socialist Party Membership Handbook* 1985).

The Socialist Party structure and tradition fit our local SP Chapter like a hand in a glove. Our members came from a variety of backgrounds and political organizations including Solidarity: A Socialist-Feminist Network, the New American Movement, the Socialist Labor Party, and the War Resisters League.

In keeping with the Socialist Party tradition of non-sectarianism, some members of our local group joined a new nationwide socialist organization, Solidarity (S), in the mid-1980s (*Solidarity: Founding Statement* 1986). In 1987 five members of our local group attended the founding convention of Solidarity in Chicago. Since that time several members of the Santa Barbara Chapter of the

Socialist Party belonged to both groups. Technically, we called ourselves the Socialist Party/Solidarity (SP/S).

Our dual chapter was fairly controversial in socialist circles. In the beginning, both Solidarity and the Socialist Party were wary of members who belonged to other socialist organizations. We had to obtain clearance from the respective National Committees to join another socialist organization. However, our local group made it very clear we strongly believed in Left groups working together for common purpose and in dual membership. If either National Committee didn't care for that, then it was not an organization to which we should belong. Needless to say, our local was in the forefront nationally in promoting the dual membership concept.

There were three major reasons why dual membership was not a problem. First, both the SP and Solidarity support independent electoral political work and so did our local group. Over the years, we supported candidates for Santa Barbara City Council (me), the Isla Vista Recreation and Park District Board of Directors (the only local government in Isla Vista where UC Santa Barbara is located), and other local government boards. Our candidates were successful in some races. We always ran openly as socialists and did not support Democrats. Thus the position of the SP and Solidarity on not supporting Democrats coincided with our own.

Second, both the SP (as noted above) and Solidarity were multi-tendency. The SP had a long tradition of non-sectarianism. Solidarity less so, especially in its first couple of years, but developed in that direction without losing its fighting spirit.

Finally, both national organizations were internally democratic. Our local socialist group was not fond of democratic centralism in any form.

While we had plenty of lively debates over what policy or program to support or oppose, our shared belief in the need for a socialist transformation of society bound us together. We also separated ourselves from the many local liberals, and most other socialists and communists, because we worked openly as socialists. We did have many contacts with and worked with liberal organizations on specific issues. But working in the Democrat Party, as many socialists did (and still do), and supporting the lesser of two evils or the most liberal candidate, only served to draw socialist elements away from more productive political activity.

The founding and rapid growth in members and activity of our local SP/S Chapter coincided with the apogee of New Wave music. Even a zombie shuffles his feet (or tries to) and plays a sloppy air guitar when the B-52s "Planet Claire" is cranked up. And who can resist the haunting lyrics and signature sound of "Sweet Dreams (are made of this)" by the Eurythmics ("New Wave music" 2013).

As New Wave music utilized complexity and diversity in the music and lyrics, our local group represented the New Left—a Left that was complex, diverse, and interested in more than union labor/class issues of the Old Left ("New Left" 2013). Among other topics our anti-hierarchical group was in the forefront of tenant's issues, equal rights for gays and lesbians, and legalizing personal drug use—we truly believe in people power as the goal. We were poised, we thought, to be a New Wave in politics sweeping tsunami-like across the Santa Barbara political landscape.

Our entire group identified, to one degree or another, with the political New Left. A prime tenant was participatory democracy, or working to empower individuals so they can fully control their own lives. One of the group's most energetic members, Glenn, put it well in one of the many information sheets ("What is Revolutionary Sewer Socialism?") our local group produced.

> I think there can be an approach called Revolutionary Sewer Socialism which uses local governments to build peoples' institutions and peoples' power outside the state and thereby set the stage for an eventual socialist revolution. While Stalinists and some Social Democrats theoretically view the capitalist state as an instrument of bourgeois rule, in practice they often end up treating the state as if it were neutral. This is a byproduct of their elitist perspective which ultimately does not trust the direct empowerment of working people. *They seek to do things for the working people rather than develop a*

working class that does things for itself. [emphasis added] Incidentally, the North American working class understands this a great deal better than does the Revolutionary Left. This explains part of the reason workers have been so slow to give the Left their confidence. They are not all that anxious to trade capitalism bosses for Stalinist bosses, nor should they be (Lazof 1990).

In essence, the members of our group did favor and worked toward the original Marxist notion that after a transitional period society would be reorganized with the state withering away in favor of communes of freely associated producers. Quite different from the hierarchical nanny state favored by most leftists and liberals today (or back in the 1980s).

One thing that kept our group together was our progressive (and lucrative) suggested dues structure. The dues were based on the national organizations to which the individual belonged and that persons' income. Annual national dues for the SP were low (a minimum of $10.); for Solidarity $240. If a member belonged only to the SP, their local dues were 1% of their net income per month divided by the number of people they support. If they belonged to Solidarity, it was 2%; and the monthly dues were 3% if they belonged to both groups. (I belonged to many national, state, and local political organizations and none had a dues structure like our local group.)

We took in $150 to $200 per month—a lot for a local organization (especially back in the 1980s and early '90s). But we had many expenses. As noted above, the local group paid the annual dues to the SP and Solidarity for all members who made an attempt to attend meetings and pay at least something each month. (Keep in mind that our dues structure was only a suggestion for members—some paid more and some paid less than what is suggested. But most members adhered to them in a disciplined manner.) We also paid the dues for members, if they so desired, who joined local, state, and national organizations that directly related to our local interests and work. For example, I belonged to the Left Green Network and the local group paid my annual dues.

In addition, we strongly believed that our group—after all we were in the forefront of the revolution—should be represented at national meetings which our members wanted to attend regardless of the cost. Thus, we paid airfare and registration fees for some lower income members to attend national meetings in other parts of the country. They connected with like-minded folks and reported on the state of the revolution in different parts of the country.

Our local group also regularly donated money to other groups and candidates for office. For example, we contributed $40 to Bernie Sanders for Congress (Vermont) in 1988 when Bernie was still a real socialist and not just a toady for the Democrat Party. We gave to local campaigns and the SP presidential campaigns.

Finally, although it was close to self-sustaining in the early 1990s, we subsidized our local bi-monthly newsletter, *LEFT OUT*.

As a group we focused on three major areas—internal discussions and education, gaining exposure for socialism by organizing and participating in local events, and publishing (since 1987) our own bimonthly local newsletter, *LEFT OUT*.

Tim and Deb carry the Socialist Party banner in the 1984 Evict Reagan March/Rally. Probably the first time a socialist contingent had openly marched in anything in Santa Barbara history.

We had discussions around important issues at the monthly meetings. Internal education was taken seriously; we sponsored

111

numerous public lectures, often led by experts in the field, to educate ourselves and the community about important topics. These included "Animal Liberation," "US Politics in the Wake of Contragate," "The Palestine-Israeli Conflict," "Feminism and Ecojustice," "The Cold War and the Arms Race," "Why Should Christians and Marxists Dialogue?" "Why the Democrats Aren't," and several others. Over the years, our members spoke at dozens of meetings and events.

Our local group was akin to a whirling dervish when it came to activities designed, at least in part if not totally, to promote socialism. We locally produced eight flyers and two 8 ½ X 11 booklets and reprinted numerous information sheets from the national SP and other organizations. We marched and carried our blood red banner in annual Santa Barbara Peacewalks; marched in the Evict Reagan March/Rally (1984); twice (1985 and 1987) ran a candidate (me) for Santa Barbara City Council; participated in the Santa Barbara Renters Conference (1986); ran a successful candidate for the Isla Vista Recreation and Parks District Board of Directors (1990); organized and hosted May Day picnics for several years; and participated in Earth Day events. We had information tables at these and many other events.

Socialist Party member Jack speaking at the Socialist Party-sponsored May Day picnic, early 1990s.

Perhaps our greatest impact locally came as a result of participation by our local members in other political activity and in the workplace. They brought a socialist perspective to these areas. We had

112

members on the Board of Directors of the Peace Resource Center; on the Board of Trustees of the Santa Barbara Peace Fund Escrow Account; on the Board of Directors of the Gay and Lesbian Resource Center; on the Board of Directors of the South Coast Information Project; on the Santa Barbara City Council-appointed Rental Housing Mediation Task Force; on the Isla Vista Community Council; on the American Civil Liberties Union Board of Directors; on the Santa Barbara County Central Committee of the Peace and Freedom Party; and on the Isla Vista Recreation and Parks District Board of Directors ("A Brief History of the Socialist Party/Solidarity, Santa Barbara Chapter" 1991). All these organizations undoubtedly benefitted from the influence of our local SP/S members.

The groups' longest running project was *LEFT OUT*, our bimonthly newsletter. (The official full title was *News the Other Media LEFT OUT*.) We intended the newsletter to be a compilation of analyses, opinions, and a calendar of events that were compatible with a democratic socialist, non-sectarian viewpoint. While focused on local issues, we often published articles of a wider interest.

Most locally produced political newsletters, especially in the dark ages prior to the widespread use of desktop publishing and the Internet quite simply sucked. Not ours. After the first year or so, it was six pages, printed on good paper stock, with professional layout and graphics. Not to be too full of ourselves, but a big reason for its success was that Deb and I served on the editorial board and/or production staff every issue for the entire six year run of the newsletter. We brought certain skills to the project. My day job was editing a political science journal at a small non-profit publishing company. Because it was small, I also did the production of the journal. Deb was a supervisor at a different local publishing company who assisted in production and was a fine editor. We had the skills and experience to ensure *LEFT OUT* looked professional on a shoe string budget.

Although we did reprint the occasional article, most were original. Just about every member of our group wrote at least a couple of articles over the years. Local progressives also submitted and we printed their stories. We accepted advertising, letters to the editor, and had paid subscriptions.

Under the pseudonym of The Cat I wrote a column "Scratching in the Dirt" which appeared in almost every issue. What fun—I skewered the actions of local politicians and pontificated about whatever issue grabbed my attention. I also wrote approximately 25% of the articles over the lifetime of *LEFT OUT*. At its height we had almost 200 subscribers, about a third actually paid for the privilege of reading our newsletter. After six years of continuous publication, *LEFT OUT* died of natural causes with the May/June 1993 issue.

A lot of activity over the years. But it was not all political work. We figured the socialist revolution could be furthered through having fun, and anyway enjoying life was important to us. For example see the "Socialists as Party Animals" story later in this chapter for details of the annual (beginning in 1986) "Socialist Sports Festival and Bar-B-Que."

Socialist Party members: Deb (far left); me (second from left); Scott (fifth from left); and Laura (second from right) and non-SP member friends at the annual California Socialist Party campout at Big Sur, California, July 1985.

A few months prior to becoming charter members of the Santa Barbara Chapter of the SP in the fall of 1983, Deb and I attended the annual California Socialist Party campout at beautiful Big Sur,

California. This was a three-day event held each year on the July 4th weekend to gather, exchange ideas, meet new comrades, and do some great hiking. We attended each year through 1992 and often led discussion groups. One year we performed our magic act, the comrades were mystified by our prestidigitation. We also encouraged many local lefties and friends, family members, and assorted fellow travelers to attend—and many did.

The Santa Barbara contingent was often the largest at the campout, even though the population base was tiny compared to the Los Angeles or San Francisco Bay area. Our local crowd may have not been the "Sultans of Swing" (Dire Straits), but our laughter, drugs, good food, commitment to democratic socialism, and irreverent style most certainly livened up the party.

Being a local dominated by Baby Boomers, the Santa Barbara Chapter was a bit more into luxuries and drugs than the typical California SP member. We would prepare full-on meals of shrimp scampi while our comrades from around the state were dining on hot dogs and pork and beans. We offered to share, but did not have enough for the entire group. We did, however, have enough pot to share with those who were so inclined.

The annual July 4th campouts were better than even SP or other political organizations' national meetings to connect with like-minded comrades. Where else can your discuss the differences between Stalinism and Trotskyism with an older comrade who personally knew Trotsky? Several electoral and other political campaigns had their genesis at these campouts.

For me and Deb our home in the Socialist Party was cozy and useful for about a decade. As noted in several stories in this chapter, I always had reservations concerning some leftist positions—equality of outcome vs. equality of opportunity; the closeness, or at least absence of wariness, some reds felt toward the government; the ease in which many lefties bought into political correctness; the leftist support of victim mentality, coupled with derision of the idea of personal responsibility; and, seriously, the lack of humor or ability to laugh at our own foibles on much of the Left (excepting most comrades in our Santa Barbara group). Even given my doubts, it was political home. I still have good feelings toward (and contact with) some of the local comrades. But by the early 1990s my concerns could not be overlooked. In the mid-1990s I was adrift politically and no longer considered myself a socialist. My "Why I Left the Left" story in Chapter Four explains why I left the Left.

References

"A Brief History of the Socialist Party/Solidarity, Santa Barbara Chapter." 1991. Information sheet produced by the Santa Barbara Chapter of the Socialist Party/Solidarity. April.

Lazof, Glenn. 1990. "What is Revolutionary Sewer Socialism?" Information sheet produced by the Santa Barbara Chapter of the Socialist Party/Solidarity. June.

LEFT OUT. 1987 to 1993. Bimonthly newsletter published and distributed by the Santa Barbara Chapter of the Socialist Party/Solidarity.

"New Left." 2013. Wikipedia. Last modified October 11, 2013. http://en.wikipedia.org/wiki/New_Left.

"New Wave music." 2013. Wikipedia. Last modified October 17, 2013. http://en.wikipedia.org/wiki/New_Wave_music.

Socialist Party Membership Handbook. 1985. Pamphlet (38 pages) published and distributed by the Socialist Party, USA. June.

Solidarity: Founding Statement. 1986. Pamphlet (44 pages) published and distributed by Solidarity. March.

"What's the Difference?" undated. Information sheet produced and distributed by the Socialist Party, USA.

Storming the Gates of Santa Barbara City Hall

As said the Bishop in *Ladyhawke* (1985) "Great storms announce themselves with a simple breeze, and a single spark can ignite the fires of rebellion." My two campaigns for Santa Barbara City Council were designed to be that spark of rebellion, unfortunately the good people of Santa Barbara disagreed.

Being intensely interested in politics, it comes as no surprise I had political ambitions. At least as early as December 1983 I was mentioning the possibility of running for Santa Barbara City Council in a letter to an old friend.

I did not just appear on the political scene and throw my hat into the electoral politics ring. Years of preparatory work preceded the decision. But, I should have had my head examined—Deb and I were in for years of almost non-stop political work, along with full-time day jobs. It was truly a team effort, and not just me and Deb.

The idea is to embed oneself in the community, get involved, and learn the issues. To have an impact and build the movement—not just run as a novelty socialist—required making contacts with other community groups and politically active individuals, basically develop allies.

From my previous job in 1981 as the Peace Action Coordinator at The Gathering Place I had considerable contacts in the local peace community (See "Defeat the Devil: Diablo Canyon Nuclear Power Plant" story in Chapter Three). Along with Scott and Deb, I founded the local chapter of the War Resisters League in 1982 (See "War Resisters League and War Tax Resistance" story in Chapter Three) which increased the peace community contacts and involvement. Deb and I were also active in the Santa Barbara Tenants Union since early 1982 (See "Santa Barbara Tenants Union" story in Chapter Three), knew the issues and the major players. And we were founding members of the Santa Barbara Chapter of the Socialist Party (SP) in the fall of 1983 (See "Go Reds, Smash State" story in Chapter Three).

Building up to the City Council run, I became a member of the Board of Directors of the South Coast Information Project and was appointed by the Santa Barbara City Council to serve on the Rental Housing Mediation Task Force (I was later elected Secretary and then Vice Chairperson of the Task Force by fellow Task Force members) in

1984. This organization gathered information about landlords and tenants and mediated disputes between them (but only for landlords and tenants who voluntarily used the service). Around this time I also joined Network, a local political/environmental organization, and the local chapter of the Gray Panthers.

Given that the Socialist Party was my primary affiliation, the one that represented the foundation of my political beliefs, I began discussing a potential city council run with the local group in the fall of 1984. I and the local Socialist Party Chapter—which gave it all for my campaigns—wanted an electoral campaign that grew out of community activism. I certainly met that criteria. Because of my earlier political/community work, my city council campaign did emerge organically and was not an artificial attempt at power grabbing. It was an attempt to use electoral politics as one aspect of an overall strategy of movement building. Even though local elections were formally non-partisan, everyone knew who was a Democrat or Republican. We wanted to make sure the electorate knew who the socialist was.

A campaign committee (about eight hard core members for each campaign) was formed, mostly SP members, and we sent out the first of many fundraising letters on January 17, 1985 (for the November election). This was the beginning of almost three years of non-stop political work. I ran for the November 1985 election; for a City Council-appointed seat on the Council to fill a vacancy in December 1986 (along with 28 other applicants); and for the November 1987 election. It was not uncommon to attend three to four evening meetings per week with a full weekend schedule. This pace lasted till the end of my second city council campaign in November 1987. (Deb and I also had full-time jobs.) Think of the most hectic week of your life in the last year and imagine doing that for about three years. Unless you have tons of money and can hire "people" to do all the necessary footwork and recordkeeping, this is not a sport for the faint of heart. I was fortunate to have a dedicated and professional core group who worked relentlessly during the campaigns.

The official pin for both campaigns.

On May 16, 1985 I formally announced my candidacy on the steps of City Hall. Some of the major points of the campaign were: protect tenants by passing an ordinance preventing unjust evictions; tenants should receive a fair interest on all deposits; passing an ordinance barring job and housing discrimination against gays and lesbians; divest public employee retirement money from corporations that do business with South Africa; and reign in out-of-control offshore oil drilling. The cornerstone of our issue platform was a scheme to help people control their own housing, a perennial problem in high rent Santa Barbara. We developed the idea that a substantial transfer fee should be levied on large rental housing complexes sold to speculators who do not live in the complex. Money gathered from this fee would be used to help fund affordable housing projects. Fair rent control would be incorporated into the program.

In 1985 six candidates vied for three four-year term council seats (each voter had three votes), including all three incumbents. Politically two were liberal, two moderates, one conservative, and one socialist (me). Interestingly, the winners included one liberal, one moderate, and the lone conservative.

TOM GARRISON
CITY COUNCIL

Front cover of my 1985 campaign literature.

119

During the 1985 campaign I attended 8-10 public candidate forums, appeared on TV and radio, and met with hundreds of people individually and in groups/organizations. While tiring, campaigning was fun. I did the traditional shaking babies and kissing hundreds of hands. No, that's wrong, kissing babies and shaking hands. I'm eternally grateful to Deb for help in the latter. I'm pretty good at making small talk, but woefully lacking in remembering names unless I've met the person more than a couple of times. Deb is great at remembering names and tidbits of family information. Countless times while at one event or another, I'd whisper to Deb for information about the person we were approaching or was approaching us. She filled my short term memory and in seconds I greeted the potential voter, "Hey Bob, how are you? So is Jane still working that part-time job? The kids doing well in school?" I'm sure this personal touch, very important in local politics, gained us respect and most likely scores or hundreds of votes.

Other than teaching, and being an honest politician is akin to teaching, where else can you discuss serious ideas with thousands of concerned citizens? The fact that I was running openly as a socialist only added to the fun. People would search me out to see what a red was like. The semi-anonymous rage so often displayed in the Internet age was absent. Almost all media people and regular citizens were respectful and polite. I got along well with the other candidates and developed a liking for the conservative, Sid Smith. He, like me, did not try to tailor his message for each particular audience. As a candidate, attending many events with the other candidates, you are able to quickly see who panders to each audience and who honestly promotes their program. Over the next three years of nonstop campaigning I found that many liberal candidates and their supporters, although certainly not all, were the most willing to obfuscate their message in order to gain votes.

A few prominent liberals wanted me to lie and say I was simply another "progressive" Democrat—a stupid idea for several reasons. "Progressive"/liberal Democrats are a dime a dozen in Santa Barbara. At least one runs for every office in the county. I was not a Democrat and was not about to lie concerning my basic political affiliations, even though I surely would have received more votes if I had. But it would have been a betrayal of the public trust and my own values.

During both campaigns our campaign literature noted my membership in the Socialist Party and the Peace and Freedom Party—I ran openly as a socialist. What is the use of being a socialist and not openly pushing it? A socialist running as a "progressive" or liberal Democrat is simply one more liberal Democrat and does not advance the democratic socialist revolution in any meaningful manner. If nothing else, my running openly as a socialist showed people who met me during the campaign that a red could also be a thoughtful believer in democracy (and that I did not have horns).

An example of liberal pandering, and some courage, was the candidates forum and dinner hosted by the Apartment Association in October 1985. This was the lion's den for rent control advocates. One liberal candidate, incumbent Gerry DeWitt (a personable guy I liked), skirted the issue and said the voters had decided—rent control had lost elections in 1978 and 1980 (Rankin 1985A). This was extremely odd since DeWitt was a darling of the local progressive community (virtually all of who supported rent control) and was endorsed by the Santa Barbara Tenants Union, which was the principal organization backing rent control since its inception in 1978.

On the other hand, the other liberal in the race, Shelly Rouillard who was a Tenants Union activist like me, had the guts to admit she supported rent control. As noted (Rankin 1985A) in the *Santa Barbara News-Press*:

> The two willing to stand up before about 70 people at the Apartment Association dinner at the Santa Barbara Inn Thursday night and endorse rent control were Tom Garrison and Shelly Rouillard.

> ... Garrison—who candidly noted he's the only socialist among the six candidates...

> Garrison, a soft-spoken young man clearly the most liberal candidate, bluntly told the audience "when I'm on the council it [rent control] will come up" as he presses for it, even though he himself is a landlord, living in one half of a duplex and renting out the other half.

Garrison explained that he sees rent control as one means of achieving his key goal—giving people the maximum amount of control over their lives.

Lest you think I'm being a bit harsh on the liberals, here is what the *Santa Barbara News-Press* ("Editorial" 1985) wrote in their endorsements for the election:

DeWitt waffles alarmingly on rent control; we hope he eventually sees there is no difference between rent control in mobile home parks (which he fought for) and rent control in the general housing market (which he claims to oppose).

This was just one example of many in my two campaigns in which liberals/progressives altered their message to suit the audience, a real show of adhering to one's principals—not. This real world experience, endlessly repeated over the decades since, goes a long to explain my general antipathy to liberalism. Many liberals, especially the leadership, show no shame in lying to the public. I found open socialists and conservatives (and libertarians since I became one in the late 1990s) much more consistent in their private and public political discussions.

Mainstream media covered our campaign in a serious manner, giving as much space as they would any first time (in 1985) and avowed socialist (both campaigns) candidate. Given a major purpose of my campaigns, to spread the gospel of socialism and show that socialists are human too, they played into our hand by renaming me in print as "socialist Tom Garrison" in many articles.

In contrast to many campaigns by third parties and non-traditional candidates, ours was serious. I became a clothes horse, attending in proper suit and tie every public event to which I was invited. We produced several pieces of campaign literature, heavy on the issues, along with professional buttons, bumper stickers, and yard signs. A local radio personality helped produce a professional 30-second radio spot which aired the two weeks prior to the election. We walked, dropped campaign literature, and talked with potential voters in almost every precinct. The campaign committee issued several press releases and worked the media. Through various fundraising events and letters (pre-email days) we raised nearly $4,500 in the 1985 campaign—a decent sum for a first-time candidate.

Endorsement ad for my 1985 campaign,
Santa Barbara News-Press, November 3, 1985.

Many voters (I know I do) check endorsements as election day draws near. If people I know and respect, or don't respect, endorse a certain candidate you gain a bit of information about that candidate. This is especially true in local elections in a medium-size city (about

123

80,000 population) where everybody seems to know each other (especially the political class). Like a squirrel gathering nuts for the winter, we gathered endorsements. By the closing days of each campaign, it was an impressive list: several UC Santa Barbara professors; the executive director of the Santa Barbara Gay and Lesbian Resource Center; the news director of a local radio station; attorneys; a marriage, family and child counselor; the Santa Barbara Tenants Union; the Santa Barbara Chapter of the Service Employees International Union; a couple of doctors; organizations to which I was an active member (Socialist Party, War Resisters League, Peace and Freedom Party) and scores of "regular" people.

My two campaigns were run by committees of decent hard working leftists and fellow travelers. I still have nothing but admiration for almost all who were at the center of the campaigns and the many foot soldier volunteers. Among many interesting discussions that emerged during both campaigns, one demonstrated the illogical pandering to the god of multicultural "diversity" and identity politics even among our Santa Barbara comrades.

To become a US citizen, one must demonstrate competence in the English language. My campaign committees had serious discussions about whether to print some of our campaign literature in Spanish. Many felt that doing so would help us gain the Latino vote. (More than one-third of the population in Santa Barbara is of Hispanic ancestry.)

Deb and I consistently argued that since only citizens could register to vote, and since naturalized Hispanic citizens must have competence in the English language (or they could not become citizens), there was no need for Spanish language campaign material. Those not competent in English could not become citizens and, thus, could not vote. Further, since virtually all Hispanic-ancestry citizens born in the US would speak English by the time they could register to vote, there was absolutely no need for Spanish language campaign material.

Our logic won the day, but it is interesting that the folks working in my campaigns would even broach this subject in a serious manner. Their arguments demonstrated the power of multiculturalism and the need of the Left to pander to identity politics.

"Rose's Authentic Gypsy Astrology" ad for the 1987 campaign. *The Independent*, October 29, 1987.

Given our politics and Baby Boomer status of most people in my campaigns, we were fairly creative in our advertising. Wine tours, local rock bands at fundraisers, catchy radio ads, and print ads in the daily and weekly newspapers. The apogee of our advertising efforts was the "Rose's Authentic Gypsy Astrology" ad from the 1987 campaign. It was ½ page with authentic astrology signs and realistic horoscopes—the catch being that each horoscope ended with a pitch to vote for me on November 3. Very clever.

Eventually November 5 came and the votes were counted. It was a low turnout, 42%, and I finished sixth out of six candidates receiving 3,736 votes (I certainly don't have that many friends). 17.7% of the voters chose me as one of their three choices (three open seats)—almost one in five. Not bad for a first time openly socialist candidate at the height of the Reagan Presidency and in his adopted home town.

A year later a sitting Santa Barbara City Council member won election to the county Board of Supervisors. This open seat was filled by a vote of the Council. I, and 28 other applicants, vied for the job. We completed questionnaires and were briefly interviewed. Needless to say, the City Council was not too excited about appointing a socialist to the open seat.

As 1987 approached it was time to crank up the political machine and my campaign committee had its first organizational meeting on December 9, 1986. The first fundraising letter was sent out in February 1987. This campaign was a replay of 1985 with one important difference, 12 candidates (two incumbents) running for three seats. This meant each candidate fought for time at candidate forums and space in newspaper reporting.

An interesting aspect of this election was the Santa Barbara Tenants Union running a slate of two candidates, Annette Cordero and Sheila Price (See "Santa Barbara Tenants Union" story in Chapter Three). Odd because while I was a Tenants Union member since 1982, had served several terms on the Executive Committee, and fully supported rent control I was not asked to join the slate. I would not, and my campaign committee would agree with me, join a slate with non-socialists (at least they did not say they were socialists), but given my history I should have been asked.

126

Like 1985, this campaign was filled with candidate forums, TV and radio shows, and dozens of meetings with organizations and individuals. And like 1985, all the other candidates, including the liberal Annette Cordero and Sheila Price, declined to support an ordinance preventing housing and job discrimination against gays and lesbians.

The October 22, 1987 issue of *The Independent* (the local liberal weekly newspaper) noted:

> Garrison is the only candidate among the 12 who calls for greater city protection for gays and lesbians from housing and job discrimination. Not gay himself … (Welsh 1987).

Decades later it still pisses me off that in two election cycles not one candidate out of 16 besides me would openly support non-discrimination in jobs and housing for gays and lesbians. So much for liberals supporting legal equality for all.

The campaign mercifully ended November 3. I was burnt out and Deb and I were both tired of being constantly "on" and in the public eye for the last three years. On the other hand, we asked for it and gave our all for democratic socialism. This time around I finished eighth out of 12 candidates and received 1,887 votes—10.2% of the voters chose me as one of their three choices. My campaign raised $5,525.

Were we successful? By traditional measures, no. I was not elected. But judged by our own goals, the campaigns were very successful. We exposed the good citizens of Santa Barbara to a democratic variant of socialism. They could hardly miss that I was a socialist given our campaign literature and an assist by the media—yet thousands voted for me. Dozens of volunteers, many in their first political activity, got involved in the campaigns and exposed close-up to real socialists. Several community groups—tenants (just cause eviction and rent control), gays and lesbians (a local anti-discrimination ordinance), and working class families (affordable child care)—benefitted due to our promoting issues that would give them more control over their lives. And by the end of the each campaign other candidates were at least occasionally grilled about issues my campaigns emphasized.

Besides the above, two points stand out. First, my core belief has not changed from these campaigns more than 25 years ago. No, not that capitalists are pigs. In their Sunday edition (November 3, 1985) prior to the election the *Santa Barbara News-Press* wrote about me:

> He emphasized that his views on policies stem from his basic belief in maximizing people's control over their lives (Rankin 1985B).

That theme, and specific policies derived from it, was in most news articles during both campaigns. It should be, I said it enough times. While some specifics have changed, my basic belief in empowering people has not. Interesting that it fits New Left socialism and libertarianism.

Secondly, my distrust of most liberals was strengthened (and exists today) from my campaign experiences. In a letter (a portion is below) to my old friends Bill and Rocky Hanson dated December 14, 1985 I recounted my intense feelings concerning liberals.

> Big lessons from the campaign.

> I hate liberals. They bent over backwards to not support us. I've talked to a couple of non-supporters in their "community" and the excuses they gave are just that— excuses. They had no real reasons—one of them quoted gossip about me (wouldn't give a name or the specific problem) as a reason. It seems as if someone said I wasn't a feminist. How does one explain or defend themselves against unsubstantiated vague gossip? Well, that is the level of political discourse for most liberal activists in S.B.

> I could also tell you some great stories about how they play the "ends justify the means" game. They only have principles when it serves them. Virtually all the liberals I know are opportunists and spineless. I have to work with them, but I will never trust them again. *They aren't into bringing about a new age where real people have more control over their daily lives. They are into "do-gooderism"—"let's help the poor common folk."* [emphasis added]

And they have no problem with ignoring ideas like democracy and openness when they find it expedient.

As I said, I do have to work with them (there are a lot of them around), but it is not a pleasant thought. ...

Our strongest supporters were other radicals/socialists/communists or "common" folk. The few Reds in town were great, so were the regular folks. I now fully realize that the vast majority of liberals are not "almost" socialists—they are a different breed.

I still feel proud of our campaign's efforts. Good people donated money and much time to promote democratic socialism. We were high on politics and believed the impossible might just be possible.

References

"Editorial." 1985. "City Council." *Santa Barbara News-Press*. November 3.

"Endorsement advertisement." 1985. *Santa Barbara News-Press*. November 3.

Ladyhawke. 1985. Directed and produced by Richard Donner. Distributed in the United States by Warner Brothers. Released in 1985.

Garrison, Tom. 1983. Letter from me to Bill and Rocky Hanson. December 21.

Garrison, Tom. 1985. Letter from me to Bill and Rocky Hanson. December 14.

Rankin, Jerry. 1985A. "2 candidates back rent control." *Santa Barbara News-Press*. October 4.

Rankin, Jerry. 1985B. "Intriguing alternatives on the ballot." *Santa Barbara News-Press*. November 3.

"Rose's Authentic Gypsy Astrology" advertisement. 1987. *The Independent*. October 29.

Welsh, Nick. 1987. "Who's Left?" *The Independent*. October 22.

Gays and Lesbians

In January 1985 Deb began serving on the Gay and Lesbian Resource Center (GLRC) Board of Directors. Quite a coup since she was the first heterosexual (or "breeder" as our gay friends liked to say) and first socialist to serve on the GLRC Board. Over the next few years we worked politically with Santa Barbara's gay and lesbian community, partied with them, and got to know several individuals pretty well.

My campaigns, in 1985 and 1987, for Santa Barbara City Council were strongly supported by leaders in the gay and lesbian community, even though many were not leftists or even liberals. They did understand that my campaign strongly supported issues close to them. For example, in both campaigns I was the only candidate to openly, and repeatedly, call for a local ordinance to protect equal rights in jobs and housing regardless of age, sex, race, religion, or *sexual orientation*. Even the liberal candidates shied away from this "controversial" issue. It was the right thing to do, so we did it.

But it was not all politics. Deb and I attended the annual Unity Week Prom for several years. The first couple of years we were the only "breeder" couple attending. We presented awards at one prom and received "special thanks" for our contributions at others.

At one event in 1986 the caterers cancelled at the last minute. Deb and I and a couple of gay folks, Geni (executive director of the GLRC) and Vern, pulled it together, cooked like crazy and delivered the goods to the event. No one knew the difference. One GLRC Board member sent us a nice note afterward (Houlihan 1986).

September 29, 1986
Dear Debby & Tom:

Thank both of you for hard, hard work this past weekend to salvage our anniversary banquet. Without your help it would have been a disaster and real embarrassment to the Center.

My guess is that most of our guests didn't even realize that we had pulled everything together in 48 hours. That's the true mark of professionalism: when the job seems so easy that you think anyone can do it when you watch it happen.

Again my heartfelt thanks for a job done so well in such a short period of time.

In the spring of 1986 Deb and I joined a mostly gay and lesbian (at least in Santa Barbara) campaign, the Central Coast Citizens

Against LaRouche (No on Proposition 64). This statewide proposition would have restored AIDS to the list of communicable diseases. There was no reputable evidence that the HIV virus spread by means other than shared needles and unprotected sex. This was designed to attack AIDS patients by allowing health officials to quarantine them.

We attended meetings, contributed money, and, more importantly, spoke at meetings of the many other groups to which we belonged. Proposition 64 was defeated by a margin of 71% to 29% in the November 4 election ("California Proposition 64" 2013).

References

"California Proposition 64." 2013. Wikipedia. Last modified July 8, 2013.
http://en.wikipedia.org/wiki/California_Proposition_64_(1986)

Houlihan, Thomas C. 1986. "Thank You Note from Thomas Houlihan to Me and Deb." September 29.

Peace and Freedom Party

At some point a democratic socialist must cleanly break with the corrupt two party system. Since many socialists work within the Democrat Party, let's use that as an example. For decades leftists have argued for or against working within the Democrat Party. Those pursuing an "inside" strategy work within the party and attempt to gain control or at the least influence the leaders and policies. The problem is this strategy, more often than not, co-opts the people using it. In order to gain influence they compromise a little here on an important principal, give a little there, and are soon indistinguishable from the Democrats they were out to change.

An "outside" strategy recognizes the problem above and attempts to create independent power bases separate from the two major parties. These may be electoral, such as the California Peace and Freedom Party, or non-electoral like community organizations.

On July 15, 1985, I registered to vote with the socialist-feminist Peace and Freedom Party (PFP)—the only socialist party with ballot status in California. This was about a month after I formally announced my candidacy for Santa Barbara City Council on the steps of City Hall. (See "Storming the Gates of Santa Barbara City Hall" in this chapter for details of my two Santa Barbara City Council campaigns.) Prior to this I was registered as an Independent. It was time to affiliate with a ballot status socialist party—time to become a small fish in the larger pond of statewide leftist politics. I was a dues-paying member of the Socialist Party (SP), (since early 1983) but it was very small and did not have ballot status anywhere. The electoral portion of the revolution would have to be fought through the PFP.

The PFP was founded in 1967 by people wanting to vote for something they could support, not another round of voting for the lesser of two evils. It is avowedly socialist in working toward an  economy where industries, financial institutions, and natural resources are owned and democratically managed by the people as a whole. It has run hundreds of candidates and been in the forefront of many leftist movements in California over the decades (*About the Peace and Freedom Party of California* 1987).

One reason I put off joining the PFP was that it historically suffered serious sectarian infighting. This was to be expected since the PFP had the coveted ballot status. If you were a leftist running for a partisan office in California, you gravitated toward the PFP (excepting those misguided souls who pursued an "inside" strategy within the Democrat Party). Thus, it seemed as if every leftist group of any size in California at one time or another made a run at taking control of the PFP. While not averse to some sectarian nonsense, I did not want to devote too much energy to infighting. Little did I know that in the coming years I would become a serious player in fighting off nefarious attempts by cults and tiny socialist groups to take over the PFP.

After joining, Deb and I became active in the Santa Barbara County PFP. At this time it was only limping along with few activities. Very little, if any, community outreach. The county PFP Central Committee endorsed both my Santa Barbara City Council campaigns (1985 and 1987) and occasionally ran candidates for the State Assembly or Congress. Over the years a few PFP registrants won office in the non-partisan Isla Vista Recreation and Parks District Board of Directors. Isla Vista is the student dominated community adjacent to UC Santa Barbara.

That was it—not a state of affairs much furthering the revolution. We knew some long-time PFP members—of the non-sectarian committed to democracy type (the democratic socialist faction to which Deb and I and all Santa Barbara SP members were affiliated)—scattered around the state who strongly encouraged Deb and I to reenergize the Santa Barbara County PFP by running for the Central Committee. They wanted more democratic minded, non-sectarian socialists in the party for future battles against the crazies. We were committed socialists and certainly needed more political work, why not?

We sort of guilt-tripped ("come on, a real socialist would help out and run for the PFP Central Committee") some of our Santa Barbara Socialist Party Chapter members to join us in running for the PFP County Central Committee in the June 7, 1988 election. Not surprisingly, since no one ran against us, we all won. Central Committee elections for all ballot status parties in California are held every two years. Deb and I and Jack, a stalwart in our local SP Chapter, ran and won the 1990 and 1992 elections and formed the nucleus of the Central Committee for six years. The other four slots were filled by various members of the local SP Chapter. Since no one else wanted the job, I was elected Chairperson and served in that capacity until 1994.

Peace and Freedom Party
Organizing Meeting

Ready for a change? If yes, then consider attending the kick-off meeting of the Santa Barbara Peace and Freedom Party (PFP)!

This is it, the public meeting you have been waiting for. Hear Dr. Gerald Horne (state chairperson of the Peace and Freedom Party) discuss his recent campaign for the U.S. Senate. Be there when Tom Garrison (chairperson of the S.B. County Peace and Freedom Party) unveils the history of the Peace and Freedom Party. Come and just listen, or help build the Party by joining a committee. Refreshments will be available. If you care, be there.

Thursday February 18 – 7:00 to 9:00 pm

Center for Black Studies, 4603 South Hall

U.C. Santa Barbara

Sponsored by the S.B. County Peace and Freedom Party. Call 968-0856 or 965-4817 for more information.

One example of my efforts to increase the visibility of the Peace and Freedom Party, February 18, 1993.

We quickly began to spread the PFP gospel in Santa Barbara. Our first communication/fundraising letter to party registrants went out on July 20, 1988. The numerous events organized by the local SP

Chapter were now usually co-sponsored by the PFP. Unfortunately, we were quickly sucked into the endemic in-fighting.

Between 1988 and 1992 the nemesis of democratic socialism came in two guises—the Internationalist Workers Party (IWP) and the New Alliance Party (NAP).

The former was a Trotskyite group with few members. But the members they did have were totally committed to their brand of revolution, and to "sharing" that vision with the PFP. In a 1988 letter, Herb Lewin, a major leader of the IWP, wrote to one of the democratic socialist mainstays, Charles Curtiss in Los Angeles (Lewin 1988):

> But when it comes to the class struggle, we are not pacifists. We are prepared to fight the capitalist class with *whatever it takes* [emphasis added].

In the same year in an open letter to PFP registrants, Curtiss wrote (Curtiss 1988):

> A major lesson … is that freedom of speech, press and assemblage, and the right to express one's thoughts are essential to socialism and its achievement. The transition to socialism needs the thoughts of all, given freely and without fear.

More than a slight difference in attitude toward democracy.

The New Alliance Party was essentially a cult founded in 1979 and controlled by psychologist Fred Newman of New York. It called itself "pro-socialist" and at various times allied itself with groups such as the Nation of Islam, led by Minister Louis Farrakhan ("New Alliance Party" 2013) Nationwide most leftists who encountered NAP supporters felt they could not be trusted, were opportunistic and unprincipled, and the leadership was heavily involved in a New York City psychotherapy cult. Perhaps the harshest criticism came from Dennis Serrette, a black union leader who was NAP's 1984 presidential candidate. He notes in *The Guardian* (an independent Left newspaper):

> "The New Alliance Party is basically a therapy cult centered around the person of Dr. Fred Newman," charges Serrette, who left the group in 1985. "Newman and his household maintain total control over member's lives, where they live and work, their wealth and also

their relationships." Serrette denies that the party is black-led, despite the presence of African-Americans in many of its more visible posts. Newman, who is white and who has long been one of the Alliance's principle theorists, actually makes all the important decisions, while brooking no dissent, Serrette adds (Kelley 1987).

The 1988 and 1990 biannual PFP State Conventions, which I attended, were fractured among the three groups. The 1988 convention in Oakland featured NAP bussing in people who were elected in districts in which they did not live or were registered to vote with the Democrat Party. After a credentials fight, NAPsters left the convention en mass, gathered at a pre-arranged location, and declared themselves the "true" PFP. They nominated their long-time candidate Lenora Fulani as the PFP candidate for president. The other two factions continued meeting and nominated Herb Lewin for president. It was so confusing that California's Secretary of State refused to recognize either convention as representing the majority of delegates and no PFP presidential candidate appeared on the ballot (Eu 1988).

The 1990 State Convention in Sacramento was volatile, but did manage to conduct business and elected state party officials and candidates for the November statewide election.

In August 1992 I attended my last State Convention (Deb also attended) in San Diego, a presidential election year. By now I was thoroughly fed up with battling the New Alliance Party and their continual attempts to gain control of the PFP. The IWP was dead, so our (the democratic socialist majority in the PFP) focus was laser-like in beating back the NAP. My main contribution in this battle, beside attending many state Central Committee meetings and voting for the good guys, was publishing *The New Alliance Party: A Media Analysis* in July 1992. This 47 page, 8 ½ X 11 pamphlet reprinted 17 articles, all of which dealt, at least in part, with the NAP. The majority were newspaper stories from *The Guardian* and *In These Times*— independent Left newspapers with nationwide distribution. Readers of my pamphlet could quickly note that different writers from several different publications raised serious questions about NAP over a period of years. I distributed the pamphlet at the convention and sold copies for years.

Eventually the democratic socialist majority prevailed and nominated Ron Daniels, co-chair of the National Black Independent Political Party for president over NAP's Leonora Fulani. We also won most other statewide offices. By the mid-1990s NAP disbanded and the PFP could focus on real issues instead of fighting off opportunistic cults.

The Santa Barbara PFP continued to agitate for socialist candidates and increase party registration. On June 7, 1988 (the day I was first elected to the County Central Committee) the Santa Barbara County PFP had 663 registrants; on June 2, 1992 (the day I was last elected to the County Central Committee) we had 997 people registered to vote with PFP.

The entire period I was involved in the PFP was mostly devoted to the survival of a democratic Left in California. Not much fun.

References

About the Peace and Freedom Party of California. 1987. Pamphlet produced and distributed by the Peace and Freedom Party. May 16.

Curtiss, Charlie. 1988. "Democracy—The Issue Before the Peace and Freedom Party." Open letter to Peace and Freedom Party members. March 20.

Eu, March Fong 1988. "Peace & Freedom Presidential Nominee, State Officials in Question." News release from California Secretary of State March Fong Eu. August 24.

Garrison, Tom. 1992. *The New Alliance Party: A Media Analysis.* Compiled by Tom Garrison. Published by the Santa Barbara County Peace and Freedom Party Central Committee. July.

Kelley, Kevin J. 1987. "New Alliance: Therapy cult or political party?" *The Guardian.* December 23.

Lewin, Herb. 1988. "An Open Letter to Charles Curtis." Open letter to Charles Curtiss and Peace and Freedom Party members.

"New Alliance Party." 2013. Wikipedia. Last modified April 28, 2013. http://en.wikipedia.org/wiki/New_Alliance_Party.

Socialists as Party Animals

Everyone knows the image of the typical American socialist— a guy, usually with a beard, shouting slogans, angry faced, and waving the red flag of revolution. Well, not in Santa Barbara. Here the typical socialist was smoking a joint, probably doing a few lines of Bolivian marching powder at parties, and calmly discussing the societal prerequisites for democratic socialism.

Deb and I and several local socialists we knew formed the Santa Barbara Chapter of the Socialist Party (SP), USA in the fall of 1983. We became dues paying SP members that January. Over the dozen years the group was active Deb and I often organized social events for fellow comrades and to entice the curious. We enjoyed the company of our fellow reds.

Early in 1986 we hatched a plan to organize and host, and have the local SP chapter sponsor, an annual socialist sports festival and bar-b-que. We both loved sports, participating and viewing, and thought it would be a fun event. The sports festival, held at our house, was clearly the highlight of the spring season for Santa Barbara area socialists. The festival featured six events (table tennis, checkers, darts, basketball, cube building, and water balloon toss) and the top three finishers each won a prize. As a nod to political correctness, all participants received a certificate of participation suitable for framing.

Deb and I had great fun observing the underlying competitive nature of many local socialists when the games began. We were not being mean, just amused when some generally self-identified as non-competitive and so much into cooperation individuals transformed into Michael Jordan when you put a table tennis paddle in their hands. I observed similar behavior at other socialist conferences and events. Humans evolved as both competitive and cooperative animals—it's in our DNA. It is sad, however, to see the competitive side squashed by the evil magic of political correctness.

This annual event, which drew between 20 and 30 people each year, lasted five years. The local socialists and fellow travelers enjoyed themselves.

Dear

You have been chosen from a list of thousands of worthy people to receive this special invitation to the

Second Annual Santa Barbara Socialist Sports Festival and Bar-B-Q

Events:

Table Tennis (Begins at 2:30 pm)
Checkers (Begins at 2:30 pm)
Darts (Begins at 3:00 pm)
Basketball (Begins at 3:00 pm)
Cube Building (Begins at 3:30 pm)
Water Balloon Toss (Begins at 4:30 pm)

You meet the best people at a socialist gathering

I sure am glad I'm a Socialist

Place: 1013 Niel Park Street
Date: Saturday May 16
Time: 2:30 pm till?

There is a $3.00 entry fee (to help cover the cost of the prizes for the awards ceremony—the first three finishers in each event will win a prize) which entitles you to enter up to three events. Also, remember to bring something to Bar-B-Q and, if possible, some chips, a side dish, desert, etc. to share. Drinks will be available at a no-host bar.

Please RSVP by May 12 by calling 965-4817.

Sponsored by the Socialist Party/Solidarity, Santa Barbara Chapter
P.O. Box 60208, Santa Barbara, CA 93160

Invitation to the Second Annual Santa Barbara Socialist Sports Festival and Bar-B-Que, May 16, 1987.

Fair competition is okay. Deb and I played co-ed softball off and on (mostly on) for more than 15 years. For three years or so in the early 1990s we played a few matches in southern California on the United States Table Tennis circuit and were ranked nationally. My top ranking was 885 and Deb's 1209. Hardly Olympic quality but hundreds of players were ranked below us and we had fun.

I never understood the animosity some reds feel toward participating in competitive sports. Perhaps it stems from the fact that there will be winners and losers. So what? Choose any endeavor and some people are better than others—naturally endowed with quick reflexes, work their butts off in practice, have better vision, or whatever. It is physical activity and fun. Not everyone will be a winner, because no matter how much we deny it or try to legislate it away we cannot make people equal in all abilities. As Milton and Rose Friedman (Milton won the 1976 Nobel Prize in Economics) noted:

> A society that puts equality—in the sense of equality of outcome—ahead of freedom will end up with neither equality nor freedom. The use of force to achieve equality will destroy freedom, and the force, introduced for good purposes, will end up in the hands of people who use it to promote their own interests (Friedman 1980).

Even in my "reddest" days I agreed with Friedman, not just in sports but in all endeavors. I was never a fan of equality of outcome, but always a strong supporter of equality of opportunity. I was never with the leftist program on this issue.

References

Friedman, Milton and Rose. 1980. *Free to Choose: A Personal Statement.* New York: Harcourt.

Self-defense and the Left

I grew up in a rural community, Shafter, in California's southern Central Valley. Like many kids in such an environment, I was not a stranger to guns. Around ten or so I got a BB gun for Christmas. Some neighborhood buddies and I would jump on our bikes and go on the occasional safari in the fields surrounding the town. Stealthily we tracked the always dangerous sparrows and sometimes crows. I can't recall ever killing a bird, but do remember some crows mocking our meager hunting skills.

My dad would go on annual deer hunting trips, sometimes as far away as Utah. He always brought back venison. I assume he was a pretty good hunter since generally deer do not walk up to you waiting to be shot. A few times he took some of the kids target shooting. I can't say I was overly familiar with guns, but did know the basics and was not afraid of them.

Since the early 1980s, Deb and I were active leftists in a liberal to moderate community. We became public and open socialists once I began running for Santa Barbara City Council in 1985. Because we were so active politically I sometimes gave a little consideration to self-defense and took a stick fighting class in the mid-1980s. A lot of fun and useful for learning techniques of self-defense only using a stick (of course, a baseball bat was the best "stick"). Unlike the movies, going for your opponents head is often a poor tactic.

I did not want to be either of us to be defenseless, or rely on cops showing up 30 minutes later, if bad guys—either agents of the state, right wing crazies, or common criminals—came a knocking at our door.

Deb and I discussed having guns in our house for a few years. She was not excited about the idea. But I was persistent and not above playing the "what if we get attacked because of our politics" card. Finally in May 1987 we bought the perfect self-defense weapon, a Winchester pump action 12 gauge short barrel shotgun. A couple of years later we added a Ruger 10/22 semi-automatic rifle.

We diligently went to the range to familiarize ourselves with the weapons. While not sharpshooters, we can hold our own if need be.

Nowadays liberals and many on the Left are all for gun control. That seemed odd then for lefties and even more so now. In the 1980s the serious Left (at least in Santa Barbara) was not enamored with the state. While we would try to harness its power, we saw that it could easily be used against us. We were not paranoid; we simply realized that the government could round us up, especially if we were unarmed. Many of the leftist crowd with which we associated in Santa Barbara owned guns. At least some of us had no desire to go gentle into that good night.

Chapter Four
Winter 1990—Winter 2000
The Questioning Years

Introduction

This decade began with Deb and me continuing our political activity at a reduced level. I was still heavily involved in Peace and Freedom Party and Socialist Party politics. However, by the middle of the decade our local socialist party group had ceased to exist and the *LEFT OUT* newsletter died in June 1993.

Most of this decade I was in my 40s—a good time to reflect. I had lived long enough experience intensity and adversity in several areas: a divorce and second marriage, years studying politics as an undergraduate and graduate student, a high level of political activity, and holding down the same job for many years. At the same time I needed new challenges, ways to keep the intensity up. My path was well worn; perhaps it was time for questioning and changes.

Challenging fears was a good start. We all have certain fears: being abandoned, speaking in public, spiders, dying—the list is long. I long ago conquered my fear of public speaking. For my birthday in 1990 I initiated a series of birthday events to challenge my few remaining fears. That year it was the fear of having my skin punctured. So, of course, I got my left ear pierced. Hurt like hell but I only cried a bit.

Two years later it was time to challenge my most intense fear—heights where there is little or no protection and if I fell death was a real possibility. Around my birthday in 1992 I jumped out of a hot air balloon with only a bungee cord tethering me to the balloon. That cleared out the cobwebs.

By 1990 I had been a solid very active open leftist for almost a decade. I figured the Federal Bureau of Investigation (FBI) ought to at least keep an open file on people like me. On June 8, 1990 under the provisions of the Freedom of Information Act, I requested copies of any and all files maintained by the Federal Bureau of Investigation relating to me. A few weeks later I received a reply. Evidently I was

not a small fish in California leftist politics; I was a nonexistent fish. I didn't need to see my face on a FBI wanted poster in the post office, but hell, I expected them to have at least a thin file. I clearly had a bad case of overblown self-importantitis. How embarrassing.

Having been a socialist of some sort my entire adult life, it was time to test some basic tenants of that doctrine. How about trying a little entrepreneurship? Deb and I were tired of being those special members of the bourgeois—great job titles and professional standing but raking in relatively low salaries. What to do? We both had worked in the publishing industry for more than a decade, how about starting a publishing company. And that, in March 1993, was the genesis of Pacifica Communications and *Guide to Political Videos*.

By the mid-1990s and needing a change, Deb and I began to explore the desert areas in southern California. While we loved the lush coastal lands, our explorations there were wearing thin—too easy, too green, too safe. The desert, on the other hand, was wild and did not suffer fools gladly. Foolish people died in the desert. Thus began our love affair with Native American petroglyph sites, old mines and ghost towns, slot canyons, azure blue skies, and magnificent multihued rock formations. The southwest became our destination of choice.

You know that exposed third rail in an electrical railroad that carries high voltage to power the train? The one that if you touch it, you suddenly become dead? During the mid-1990s I had one essay and two letters to the editor published in local newspapers criticizing illegal immigration—to the consternation of many of my erstwhile political "comrades". It soon became clear that regardless of how detailed and rational an argument you spin criticizing open door illegal immigration, touching that issue on the "wrong" side is like touching the third rail—ostracism by many "comrades" and friends, a sort of leftist political death.

By the latter part of the decade I was seriously questioning some basic assumptions, tactics and strategy, and the efficacy of democratic socialism. I began seriously researching and reading libertarian literature. I wrote and had published (in *Liberty*—a libertarian magazine) in January 2000 an essay titled "Why I Left the Left." A revised and updated version of that essay concludes this chapter.

Many readers may recall two widely repeated axioms arising from the 1960s: "Question Authority" and "Challenge Authority." For me, these truisms were guidelines for the 1990s. I challenged the authority of some fears; questioned the authority that always criticized entrepreneurship; challenged my own beliefs about desert adventures; took on the local liberal/leftist establishment concerning illegal immigration; and finished the decade by leaving my political home of about 15 years.

Scared? I Ain't Scared of Nuthin!
(Well, Maybe a Few Things)

I think I'm about as brave as any American male, braver. Many studies show vast numbers of Americans, at least 75 percent by most estimates ("Fear of Speaking in Public" 2013), experience some degree of anxiety when speaking in public (known as glossophobia). For many people, it is ranked as their greatest fear—greater than accidents, diseases, or even snakes.

I felt glossophobia. In high school and my undergraduate years I seldom spoke in class. Not because I didn't know answers or have decent questions, but because I was afraid. However, breaking out of my shell in graduate school classes and teaching undergraduates allowed me to later give scores of speeches as a peace organizer, Santa Barbara City Council candidate, and general socialist rabble rouser. I appeared on many TV and radio shows and managed to overcome my anxiety. Not just overcome, but I became a more than decent pubic speaker.

I always felt a perverse desire to confront the fears gnawing at my confidence. As the big four-o approached, I began a series of birthday events to challenge my remaining fears. (And maybe a bit to prove to myself I wasn't some "has-been" fearful of accepting physical challenges.) You know, like the dread of having your skin punctured. Come on, who doesn't panic when imagining a bullet digging into your flesh with that icky splat sound, like a hand spanking a baby's butt? Or the terror generated when a knife thrust pierces your belly and bright red arterial blood begins to seep around the edges.

Bullets and knives were a bit much so I decided to start small and on my 38th birthday (January 18) in 1990 I had my left ear pierced. I know, I know, it's something nearly every female and more and more males do in their lifetime, but give me a break. I was 38 years old and voluntarily piercing my flesh. A guy has to start somewhere. After confronting the flesh piercing fear, I moved on to other concerns.

Next year around my birthday in 1991, I tackled my largest anxiety causing situation—fear of heights. By fear of heights, I don't mean climbing a tree to rescue a cat or repair a roof. I mean heights where there is little or no protection and if I fell death was a real possibility.

As with skin puncturing I started small, a glider flight in the Santa Ynez Valley about 30 miles north of Santa Barbara. I'd flown in powered airplanes many times without any problem—high altitude but you are encased in a steel hot dog with wings and engines. But what about a steel hot dog without engines? Actually it was a very pleasant experience, silently gliding along riding the updrafts. However, it was not a true challenge—I didn't have to worry about engines failing.

Me ready for lift off, January 1991.

Enough of this sissy stuff. The next year (1992) I turned 40 and went for some serious anxiety producing heights. Deb and I decided jumping out of a hot air balloon with only a bungee cord tethering me to the balloon was more of a challenge. You bet.

On Saturday January 25, after a night of hard partying we drove to the foothills above Santa Barbara to the hot air balloon launching site. I was surprised, but happy, to note that there was not a "one-size-fits-all" row of coffins near the launch area. Even in winter, the brush around the site was velvet green with a spectacular view of the sparkling Pacific Ocean. It was a good day to die. Since I had a slight (maybe more than slight) hangover, becoming a red spot on the ground was not such a bad option.

147

I signed in, paid my money, and watched other idiots, I mean "brave" souls, rise to the heavens in a wonderfully colorful balloon. The routine was quickly established: put on a harness, attach the bungee cord to the harness and an anchor in the balloon then rise up in the balloon (at least 500 feet) attached to the ground by very long ropes; stand on a two by three foot shelf on the OUTSIDE of the balloon; then jump to your death.

Bungee balloon for the jump of death, January 25, 1992.

My name was called, here we go. Deb dragged me over to the balloon and I squirmed into the harness and made damn sure the bungee cord (what is a bungee cord other than a really thick rubber band) was connected at both ends. We ascended into the heavens, perhaps my final destination in a few minutes. I stepped, well trembled, out onto the shelf and looked down. No way. Then the manhood test commences. The crowd below begins a countdown, "five, four, three, two, one, jump!" I jumped. The wind whipped my face and through my hair. But strangely, I didn't feel I was falling. Instead the ground was making one hell of an effort to reach up and smash my frail bag of liquid and bones body. Before that happened I began slowing down, the bungee cord reducing my velocity. "Ha, ha, you don't get me this time," I yelled at the earth. After bouncing up and down a few times the balloon descended. Back on the ground I stumbled over to Deb and we embraced. Wow!

That was an experience. You might think any fear of heights would dissipate. Nope. I'm still uneasy around heights with little protection from falling, like hiking on a narrow trail up against a near vertical cliff, while using a chain pounded into the rock as a handhold. Deb and I have done several such hikes over the years.

Or the challenge a few years later when we visited the Stratosphere Casino and Tower in Las Vegas. The Tower, jutting 1,149 feet into the Vegas skyline, is the tallest freestanding observation tower in the United States. At the top are several rides. One, Big Shot, has 16 seats arranged around a smaller square tower. Each volunteer straps into a seat against the small tower atop the large tower more than 1,000 feet above the ground. In seconds 16 people are catapulted 160 feet into the air at 45 miles per hour ("Stratosphere. Las Vegas Thrill Rides" 2013). Yeah, that's for me. Of course we tried it. I thought my shaking would loosen the flimsy looking bolts holding this Rube Goldberg contraption together. We survived.

For me, some fears, such as public speaking have little impact. I suspect because ultimately I control my performance—if I prepare and thoroughly know the subject, speak slowly and clearly, make eye contact, and keep my gesticulating under control (I would be mute if my hands were tied) I will do well. No problem. However, if I am traversing the last half mile of the Angels Landing Trail in Zion National Park all bets are off. As the official Zion National Park website notes:

> The last half mile is across a narrow sandstone ridge. Anchored support chains are attached along some sections of the sheer fin. Sheer cliffs at high elevations

while hiking on a narrow fin. Not suggested for children or those with a *fear of heights* [emphasis added]. Avoid standing near the edge at all times! Do not hike the trail when it is wet, storming, or when high winds are present ("Angels Landing" 2013).

The last section of Angels Landing Trail, Zion National Park. Notice the very narrow trail with an elevation gain and vertical cliffs on either side, September 2006.

What they don't mention is that over the years several people have plunged to their death hiking the Angels Landing Trail. Of course someone with a fear of heights would avoid this trail. Nope, Deb and I conquered this trail in 2006 while in our 50s.

I'm at the age where there is no doubt that my fear of heights is permanent. There are two major differences between this fear and a more mundane fear such as that of public speaking. First, with the former I have no control over several crucial variables—a fellow hiker jostling me and I lose my footing, a violent gust of wind knocking me off a cliff face, and so on. Secondly, while I may be embarrassed due to poor public speaking, a mistake on a narrow elevated hiking trail can easily lead to major injury or death. Some fears are relatively easy to conquer with experience, while others, no matter how often they are challenged, linger on like an annoying cold sore that never goes away.

References

"Angels Landing." 2013. ZionNationalPark.com website. Last modification unknown. http://www.zionnational-park.com/zion-angels-landing-trail.htm.

"Fear of Speaking in Public." 2013. Website. Last modification unknown. http://fearspeakingpublic.org/.

"Glossophobia (Fear of public speaking)." 2013. Wikipedia. Last modified October 16, 2013. http://en.wikipedia.org/wiki/Glossophobia.

"Rube Goldberg." 2013. Wikipedia. Last modified October 22, 2013. http://en.wikipedia.org/wiki/Rube_Goldberg.

"Stratosphere. Big Shot." 2013. Last modification unknown. http://www.stratospherehotel.com/Tower/Rides/Big-Shot.

"Stratosphere. Las Vegas Thrill Rides." 2013. Last modification unknown. http://www.stratospherehotel.com/Tower/Rides.

Great Expectations

Being an open and very public socialist in 1980s America comes with certain expectations. Regarding electoral politics the expectation is that you will not win. Over the years of intense political activity by the Santa Barbara Chapter of the Socialist Party members or fellow travelers won minor nonpartisan local offices (Isla Vista Recreation and Parks District Board of Directors). Unfortunately while I and my supporters worked our butts off, I did not win in my two highly publicized and professional campaigns for Santa Barbara City Council. (See "Go Reds, Smash State," "Storming the Gates of Santa Barbara City Hall," and "Peace and Freedom Party" stories in Chapter Three for details.) We hoped and worked to win, thought it was possible albeit unlikely, yet met the expectation by losing.

Another expectation is that socialists acting openly and enthusiastically in a moderate-to-liberal tourist town in coastal California would be treated rather harshly by the media. While my campaign did not garner the level of the print and electronic media attention we had hoped for, the coverage we did receive was surprisingly fair. Sure, the local media renamed me "socialist Tom Garrison," but that played into our game plan. We wanted the citizens to know what a real socialist was about and were not shy about using the "S" word in our literature. I began every speech, of dozens, by making it clear I was a socialist. Overall the media surpassed our expectation and was generally fair.

Having worked with liberal Democrats for years, I did not expect much from them. I hoped they would see the obvious—that on almost all issues in a local city council campaign my position and theirs were at least similar, if not exactly the same. Yet that hardly seemed to matter to them. Some local liberal leaders encouraged me to suppress or hide my socialist affiliation. Sure, begin my electoral campaign career by lying to the public. They were often in the forefront of my critics. (See "Why I Left the Left" later in this chapter for details on my relationship with local Santa Barbara liberals.) Neither I nor our local Socialist Party group expected much from the local liberal elite—we were not disappointed.

By the end of the 1980s I had almost a decade of high visibility, openly socialist political work behind me. Each year since 1973 I sent a protest letter with my federal taxes and had withheld paying a portion of my federal tax bill for several years in the early 1980s. In 1981 I worked as a paid Peace Action Coordinator, helped organized several very public anti-war demonstrations, and had been arrested for blockading and unlawful assembly at Diablo Canyon Nuclear Power Plant. I was a founding member of the Santa Barbara Chapter of the War Resisters League and had led seminars on war tax resistance. Deb and I were also founding members, in the fall of 1983, of the Santa Barbara Chapter of the Socialist Party—the most active leftist group in Santa Barbara for more than a decade. Twice (1985 and 1987) I ran openly as a socialist for the Santa Barbara City Council. In 1988 I was elected to the Peace and Freedom Party County Central Committee (the only socialist party with ballot status in California) and served as its chair for six years. These are the highlights and do not included dozens of public presentations. So what?

After all that leftist political for years, I expected the federal government to have paid some attention. I realize I was a medium-sized fish in the relatively small pond of California leftist politics, but hell what good is the Federal Bureau of Investigation (FBI) if they don't keep track of people like me?

On June 8, 1990 under the provisions of the Freedom of Information Act ("Freedom of Information Act [United States]" 2013), I requested copies of any and all files maintained by the Federal Bureau of Investigation relating to me. On July 24, 1990 Emil P. Moschella of the FBI replied to my June 8, 1990 Freedom of Information Act request by saying that, "A search at FBI Headquarters of our electronic surveillance indices, as well as the indices to our central records system files, revealed no record responsive to your Freedom of Information-Privacy Acts (FOIPA) request other than your previous request and our response to you dated September 2, 1976" (Moschella 1990). (I filed a previous Freedom of Information Act request in 1976 when I was a nascent unaffiliated socialist. I did not expect much from that request and my expectation was met.)

What does a guy have to do to get noticed by the FBI? A solid decade of radical political work and I'm not even on federal government's radar. How embarrassing.

References

"Freedom of Information Act [United States]." 2013. Wikipedia. Last modified October 18, 2013. http://en.wikipedia.org/wiki/Freedom_of_Information_Act_(U nited_States).

Garrison, Tom. 1990. Freedom of Information Act request for information on Tom Garrison filed by Tom Garrison. June 8.

Moschella, Emil P. 1990. Chief Freedom of Information-Privacy Acts Section, Information Management Division. Federal Bureau of Investigation. US Department of Justice. July 24.

I am Somebody

We all crave recognition for our accomplishments. We, rightfully so, get excited about doing well. The type of achievement matters little—baking an excellent cake or becoming a rocket scientist. (Obviously excepting becoming the world's best serial killer or similar negative/evil "achievements.") My nomination for the most excited person generated by a rather mundane achievement has to be Navin R. Johnson, played by Steve Martin, in the 1979 comedy *The Jerk*. Navin acquires a job and a place to sleep in a gas station. The gas station became his home and he is subsequently listed in the phone book.

> Navin: The new phone book's here! The new phone book's here!
>
> Harry [the gas station owner]: Boy, I wish I could get that excited about nothing.
>
> Navin: Nothing? Are you kidding? Page 73—Johnson, Navin R.! I'm somebody now! Millions of people look at this book every day. This is the kind of spontaneous publicity—your name in print—that makes people. I'm in print. Things are going to start happening to me now (*The Jerk* Quotes 2013).

I understood Navin's feeling, perhaps not quite as intensely, of "I am somebody" when I saw my name and biography listed in the 4th edition of *Who's Who in Writers, Editors & Poets* in 1992. My biography was later listed in the 25th edition of *Who's Who in the West* (1995); the 1st edition of *Who's Who in the Media and Communications* (1997); and the 27th edition of *Who's Who in California* (1998).

Being the editor of *Current World Leaders* for more than a decade at that time, my name was printed in dozens of issues. And by then I had had a few articles published in progressive publications and newsletters, plus many essays in the Santa Barbara Socialist Party's *LEFT OUT*. Not to mention seeing my name in print scores of times during the two campaigns for Santa Barbara City Council in the 1980s. (See "New Job, New Love, New Life," "Go Reds, Smash State," and "Storming the Gates of Santa Barbara City Hall" stories in Chapter Three for details.)

I realized that being listed in these various Who's Who reference books was mostly a method by the publishers to generate some income. Once "nominated" to be included in their listings, a deluge of "offers" immediately jammed your mailbox. Offers to sell you—a distinguished person of achievement—a gold embossed personalized copy of the publication for a nominal fee (actually not so nominal) if you acted immediately. Okay, it was an appeal to vanity as much as a real reference book.

Given all the above, it was still a slight ego boost to be included in some Who's Who listing—"I am somebody."

References

The Jerk Quotes. 2013. Imbd.com website. Last modification unknown. http://www.imdb.com/title/tt0079367/quotes.

The Jerk. 1979. Wikipedia. Directed by Carl Reiner. Released 1979. Last modified June 24, 2013. http://en.wikipedia.org/wiki/The_Jerk.

Who's Who in California. 1998. 27th edition. Arson City, NV: Who's Who Historical Society.

Who's Who in the Media and Communications. 1997. 1st edition. New Providence, NJ: Marquis Who's Who.

Who's Who in the West. 1995. 25th edition. New Providence, NJ: Marquis Who's Who.

Who's Who in Writers, Editors & Poets: United States & Canada. 1992-1993. 1992. 4th edition. Highland Park, IL: December Press.

Lucy the Vibes Monitoring Cat

Being heavily involved in progressive/leftist/environmental politics since the early 1980s, I attended hundreds of meetings—large meetings, small ones, mellow meetings, and contentious meetings. Some of them were well run and efficient, others not so much. In order to increase efficiency, intra-group decision-making, and ensure everyone's opinion was heard, various progressive organizations published guides to help people organize and facilitate meetings (Cover et. al. 1978; Hedemann 1981; "Rules of Procedure" 2005). One role many guides included was that of a "vibes watcher/monitor."

Lucy relaxing on the lawn, 1990

The vibes watcher's task was to monitor the "climate" or overall tone/mood of the meeting. If tensions increase, anger flares, or a speaker is interrupted in a disrespectful manner, the vibes watcher intervenes, reminding the group of its common goals and commitment to cooperation. A short break may be called, or a moment of silence to keep people focused and relaxed. In short, a vibes watcher's job is to minimize "bad vibes."

While not all organizations adopted a vibes monitor role for meetings, many did and it was generally useful. Meetings can get contentious and a calmer atmosphere is usually conducive to real accomplishments.

Being core members of several political groups and party animals (See "Defeat the Devil: Diablo Canyon Nuclear Power Plant," "War Resisters League and War Tax Resistance," "Santa Barbara Tenants Union," "Go Reds, Smash State," "Storming the Gates of Santa Barbara City Hall," "Gays and Lesbians," "Peace and Freedom Party," and "Socialists as Party Animals" in Chapter Three) Deb and I hosted many meetings and parties at our house. Our family for much of the 1980s and all the '90s included Lucy and Sonya, our cats.

We adopted Lucy in 1986 as a young tortoiseshell domestic shorthair—a beautiful cat. Since our place was a hotbed of radical activity with many visitors, Lucy grew up being comfortable in large groups of people.

Everyone thinks their children or pets are the best. That's understandable. Well, it was literally true for Lucy. She had a sweet personality and was an excellent hunter. Birds and the occasional mouse were staples in her hunting repertoire. I wonder how many domestic cats catch bats on the fly? Lucy would bring us small furry rodent-looking animals and only when she presented her "present" did it open its wings. "That ain't no mouse, it's a bat," I said.

Lucy's hunting instinct led to her ability to fetch. Throw a crumbled-up cigarette pack (the only object she would return) and off she was in attack mode, returning the pack to us for another round. I know cats can be taught to fetch, but she was the first I had personally witnessed.

For most cats that would be plenty. However, being raised around many different people, often interacting in a group, Lucy took it upon herself to be the unofficial vibes watcher at meetings and parties. Her tactics were a bit different than those delineated in meeting guides, but hell, she was a cat! Typically, she would patrol the floor, acquiescing in typical cat manner to friendly pets or rubs. If someone began talking loudly or in an agitated manner, Lucy approached them and gently nipped at their hands or arms—clearly communicating they should take a breath and calm down. When in full blown vibes watcher mode, she would sit or lie on the back of a couch and watch. Anyone becoming too loud received a gentle nip at their hair or ears reminding them to mind their vibes. It surprised those who were unaware of her job, but it almost always worked. Nearly everyone would calm down when Lucy gently munched on their arm.

Lucy the vibes watcher springing into action, 1992.

Almost there.

Mission accomplished.

I do love my animal companions. They usually do cat or dog activities and I'm fine with that. Lucy was special, the best vibes monitor I've encountered.

References

Coover, Virginia, Ellen Deacon, Charles Esser, and Christopher Moore. 1978. *Resource Manual for a Living Revolution.* 2nd edition. Philadelphia: New Society Press.

Hedemann, Ed. Editor. 1981. *War Resisters League Organizer's Manual.* New York: War Resisters League.

"Rules of Procedure for the Green Assembly of San Benito County." 2005. Adopted November 2005. Last modification unknown. http://www.greencalifornia.org/gpsbc/rulesproc.html

Guide to Political Videos

Let's see, virtually all of our friends were making good salaries with great benefits by working for government or government funded institutions. Deb and I were tired of being those special members of the bourgeois, impressive job titles and professional standing but raking in relatively low salaries. What to do? We both had worked in the publishing industry for more than a decade, how about starting a publishing company. And that was the genesis of Pacifica Communications.

Pacifica Communications logo

In March of 1993 Deb and I founded Pacifica Communications—our own company to publish *Guide to Political Videos*. It didn't much matter that we both had fulltime day jobs and remained fairly active politically, we were still young and full of energy—and wanted to make a bunch of money. The premier issue came out in the fall of 1993.

The *Guide*, published bi-annually, included descriptions/reviews of broadly defined political videos including politics of the environment, campaigns and elections, foreign policy, gay and lesbian issues, health care, the peace movement, and women's issues just to name a few. We also included distributor/producer, title, price, and advertiser indexes, and full bibliographic and ordering information. The *Guide* was intended to provide a needed and easy-to-use resource for a variety of customers including college, high school, and public libraries; all types of political organizations including (among others) peace, environmental, and social justice groups; teachers at all levels; retail video outlets; bookstores; and individuals interested in politics. Each issue contained at approximately 350 new video listings from more than 50 distributors.

Deb and I did an amazing amount of direct mail advertising. In the 3 ½ years of its existence, we spent too many nights stuffing thousands of envelopes and putting them in zip code order as required by the Post Office for bulk mailing. Since it was a two person company, we did all the work—contacting video distributor/producers, data entry, editing, layout and graphics, marketing, and order fulfillment. Looking back, how we managed it all with fulltime jobs and some semblance of normal lives is almost incomprehensible. While we utilized our home computer, this was well before the Internet and online resources were widely available and user friendly.

While it existed, the *Guide* receive rave reviews from those all too few people who used it. In an article about Christmas gifts, Ron Sheldon of the *People's Weekly World* (the national newspaper of the Communist Party, USA) noted:

> For the teacher friends on your gift shopping list there's the *Guide to Political Videos*, a thoroughly researched list of videos with political themes for purchase or rent. The *Guide* is geared toward classrooms showings including short educational videos along with more celebrated feature films. The index is organized by subject matter so the book can provide quick reference for that perfect film to show the classroom, you know the one that exposes the real reasons behind our government's foreign policies... (Sheldon 1995).

In a February 16, 1994 letter to Pacifica Communications the editor of *Third World Resources*, Tom Fenton, wrote:

> ... we know what a valuable tool it [*Guide to Political Videos*] is going to be to activists and educators (Fenton 1994).

While those who actually saw and used the *Guide* thought it was a useful resource, as hard as we tried the exposure did not translate into thousands of sales. In our best year we made only a couple of thousand dollar profit—not much for literally hundreds of hours we worked each year.

The height of our success came on January 25, 1996 when Pacifica Communications won the *Business Digest* (Santa Barbara) magazine's Best of Business Award in the category of Communications. I won't say we stuffed the ballot box illegally, but we did encourage all our friends, acquaintances, and strangers on the street to fill out a ballot and make sure to include Pacifica Communications in the appropriate category.

Despite all our work, accolades from our pitiful few subscribers, and winning the Best of Business Award in Communications, in December 1996 Pacifica Communications died. Our last published issue was the fall of 1996. One night as we put our after-day-job work to bed well past midnight for the umpteenth time, Deb and I looked at each other and said enough is enough. Time to move on.

References

Business Digest. 1996. "Best of Business Award in Communications." January 25.

Fenton, Tom. 1994. Editor. *Third World Resources*. Letter from Tom Fenton to Pacifica Communications dated February 16.

Guide to Political Videos. 1993-1996. Santa Barbara, CA: Pacifica Communications. Published bi-annually (spring and fall) from the fall of 1993 to the fall of 1996.

Sheldon, Ron. 1995. "Holiday gift ideas for lovers of progressive film." *People's Weekly World*. Volume 10, Number 29. December 16.

Desert Rats

The lush Santa Ynez Mountains provide the backdrop for Santa Barbara squatting along the coastal plain. No doubt coastal California is beautiful. However, the coastal mountains of central California remind me of a slightly over the hill French whore with a heroin jones and too much makeup—they're easy and languid. Sure the hills and valleys are lush and green. But it generally takes little effort to explore. You also can't see very far in most places because of all the damned trees. In contrast, desert mountains and canyons, which Deb and I came to love, are like a skanky meth addled blonde. They are rough, energetic, and do not give in easy. Personally, I much prefer the challenge.

Since I was raised and spent my first 24 years in California's rather drab Central Valley, for a few years I was enamored with the coastal region—it is beautiful. Most vacations with my first wife, Lori, and with the keeper, wife number two Deb, were to coastal areas. We explored the cities and natural wonders around Big Sur, Monterey, Santa Cruz, and the redwoods above San Francisco, along with local hikes.

Roy Purcell murals near Chloride, Arizona, January 1996.

164

Deb and I had been through desert areas on gambling trips to Laughlin and Las Vegas, Nevada. In the mid-1990s we decided to explore the area around Chloride, Arizona, about 45 miles northeast of Laughlin. The Chloride murals are a must see—incredible brilliant huge contemporary rock paintings in a canyon near the metropolis of Chloride (population about 150). These murals, by the now-famous artist Roy Purcell, remind one of the mysticism of William Blake coupled with the mastery of Michelangelo.

Purcell completed the project, titled "The Journey: Images from an Inward Search for Self," in 1966. Some murals are four feet in diameter and others soar 30 feet tall. Purcell's images include a 25 foot tall woman with an all seeing eye above; a stylized rodent with romping antelope; Buddha-like figures; yin-yang symbols; twisting snakes; a rendition of Chloride; and more ("Roy Purcell's Murals in Chloride" 2013; "Purcell Galleries of Fine Art" 2013). We were hooked on desert vacations.

Around the same time Deb and I began exploring Death Valley National Park. It is not the drab, horrible desert of popular mythology. The canyons and surrounding mountains could be moonscapes. And after two or three Long Island Ice Teas at Stovepipe Wells Village in Death Valley you will think you're on the moon. Hike Artist's Palette with its blue-green to pale orange and pink rock formations to get a feel for the sharp reality of this desert wonderland (Digonnet 1997).

This emerging pattern intensified. We spent just about all vacation time exploring the great American Southwest. Among other places in Arizona we visited Tombstone and avoided a gun fight; saw the wild burros at Oatman; stayed in a Spartanette travel trailer in Bisbee; examined a Titan missile silo near Tucson and managed to avoid starting World War III; did not see aliens at Meteor Crater; and hiked around Sedona and the Grand Canyon. Anyone who has visited the latter two knows the multihued Navajo sandstone formations are magnificent.

Darwin Falls near Death Valley, 1997.

In California favorite adventures included various parts of the Mojave Desert—Death Valley National Park, Anza-Borrego Desert State Park, Joshua Tree National Park, and the Mojave Desert National Preserve. We hiked to petroglyph (rock art carved into stone by Native Americans) sites scattered throughout the area; old mines and processing mills; ghost towns; and, our favorite, canyons and desert waterfalls. On our travels we discovered several remote communities including Roy's Café in Amboy on Route 66 ("Roy's Motel and Café." 2013). It has an interesting history and an extinct volcano, Amboy Crater, a few miles away.

We began our desert rat explorations in the mid-1990s. The value added included physical challenges (more so as we aged); a better understanding of Native American peoples and culture; being very impressed by the will power to carve something out of the harsh wilderness by early settlers and miners; deeper appreciation of solitude since many of the places we searched out had no visitors other than us; and being awed by the beauty of nature. Aristotle put it well, "In all things of nature there is something of the marvelous" ("Aristotle" 2013).

Deb and her sister, Laurie, on a rock bridge, Sedona, Arizona, September 1999.

Our desert adventures only increased in frequency and distance from home in the 2000s.

References

"Aristotle." 2013. *Parts of Animals.* The Quotation Page website. Last modification unknown. http://www.quotationspage.com/quote/24228.html.

Digonnet, Michel. 1997. *Hiking Death Valley.* Palo Alto, CA: Michel Digonnet.

"Purcell Galleries of Fine Art." 2013. Last modification unknown. http://www.purcellgalleries.com/.

"Roy's Motel and Café." 2013. Wikipedia. Last modified October 17, 2013. http://en.wikipedia.org/wiki/Roy%27s_Motel_and_Cafe.

"Roy Purcell's Murals in Chloride." 2013. Roadtripamerica.com. Last modification unknown. http://www.roadtripamerica.com/places/chloride.htm.

Illegal Immigration: The Third Rail of Leftist Politics

One thing everyone on the Left learns quickly is that some points of view are intolerable. If you oppose affirmative action—giving extra consideration for jobs and college admission because of the applicant's skin color—you had better keep it to yourself if you want to remain a tribal member in good standing. Arguably the touchiest issue is illegal immigration. Publically state that you oppose open borders and government assistance for anyone sneaking over the border and you will be attacked by longtime comrades, friends, not to mention strangers. This is the third rail of leftist politics, speak out on this issue and you will suffer politically, and often personally.

I experienced ideological intimidation during the 1994 Proposition 187 campaign ("California Proposition 187" 2013) and its aftermath. The proposition was designed to deny state welfare benefits to illegal immigrants. (On November 8, 1994 it passed 59% to 41 %.) I wrote a couple of letters to the editor and an opinion essay that were published in local newspapers (Garrison 1995A; Garrison 1995B; Garrison 1996). Of course, some local liberals replied, and in print I was referred to as mean-spirited and probably racist. In addition, a couple of friends refused to take my arguments seriously, and publicly derided me for questioning the Left/liberal belief that America is an open house with complete benefits for anyone who can sneak over the border. However, 30-35 people, including a few "progressives," phoned or wrote me and supported my position. Unfortunately, they would not go public with their views. All this over some published letters and essays that were replete with logic and facts.

This questioning of the condition of my spirit and my supposed racism would seem very odd for anyone who knew my history—like the fact that in the preceding 15 years I had voted for, given money to, and publicly worked in electoral campaigns wherein 70 to 80% of the candidates were brown or black and most often women. Yes, I certainly have a history of racism.

But then facts are not the point, the point is to threaten people with vile labels if they overstep the bounds of politically correct thought; yet another clear example of intolerance for diversity in thinking. I could have been angry, but holding on to anger is like drinking poison and expecting the other person to die—probably won't work.

VOICE FROM SANTA BARBARA/TOM GARRISON   *Santa Barbara News-Press*

June 7, 1995

Rational discourse in discussing immigration

BARBARA CUMMINGS/LATS

L ike many (probably most) Americans, I am more than ready to have a national dialogue concerning immigration.

The issue is talked about, but usually not in a rational, fair manner. All too often, hyperbole and outright distortions replace honest analysis.

A case in point of the use of distortion is the recent "Latino Spectrum" column by Roberto Rodriguez and Patrisia Gonzales "Barricade along the U.S./Mexican border."

They argue that the borders of seven members of the European Union have come down regarding the free flow of labor. Why can't the United States and Mexico do the same, they ask.

On face value that sounds sensible.

However, they are distorting the real truth by comparing apples and oranges.

The European Union members that have removed border restrictions among themselves for the movement of labor are all highly developed, industrialized countries sharing similar cultural backgrounds.

The fact is that over the last 20 years, virtually all European Union members have greatly strengthened their borders regarding immigration from outside the Union.

Internal movement is facilitated, while movement into European Union countries is greatly reduced.

Many Europeans are at least as worried, and probably more, than are Americans about the flood of illegal immigrants into their countries.

Thus, if we follow the honest lesson from the European Union — and not the specious argument of Rodriguez and Gonzales — our government should certainly increase funding for the Immigration and Naturalization Service and even fund more border barriers.

The border between the United States and Mexico is very similar to that between the European Union members and non-union members, and not at all similar to the border among European Union members.

In a similar vein, Rodriguez and Gonzales distort the facts about the contributions of illegal immigrants once in the United States.

Regarding illegal immigrants they say that ". . . those who do come have been highly productive and wealth-generating members of the economy who give far more than they receive."

They obviously have not kept up with the research on the costs of illegal (and legal) immigration. In a recent article (Current World Leaders International Issues, April 1995) Professor of Economics Emeritus Donald L. Huddle of Rice University finds that illegal immigrants and their own citizen children (children born in the U.S. are automatically American citizens even if both their parents are here illegally) cost taxpayers an additional $12 billion to $16.4 billion annually for education, public services and incarceration after deducting all local, state and federal taxes paid in by them.

In addition, this study and several others have found that during the past 20 years immigrants (both legal and illegal, although this is especially pronounced for illegals) into the United States are increasingly poorly educated and have few job skills.

With population pressures straining the environment, this country does not need millions of new immigrants with few chances of landing any job outside of low-skilled manual work. The competition for those jobs is already intense and more immigrants only depress wages for working people who are citizens.

Rodriguez and Gonzales also play the guilt card.

I am tired of the guilt argument. Anyone who questions illegal immigration is called a racist.

This maneuver now seems to be mandatory for any pro-immigration article.

They sarcastically say that ". . . blaming immigrants for our problems makes us feel good."

I am tired of the guilt argument. Anyone who questions the usefulness of illegal immigration is guilt-tripped and/or called a racist. I feel neither "good" nor "bad" (and doubt if very few people do) when discussing this topic. I simply want a rational fact-based dialogue.

And while illegal immigration may not be the root cause of social, economic and environmental problems, there is little doubt that it exacerbates almost every problem we face, especially in California.

We should not let this demagoguery hide the facts — illegal immigration is not needed. America has a huge surplus of undereducated and low-skilled workers.

Illegal immigration costs taxpayers billions of dollars a year. It depresses wages for working Americans. It contributes to the strain on our resource base. And it is illegal — which often seems forgotten by illegal immigration advocates — and it can be drastically cut, albeit not eliminated, with enforcement of the laws and strict border enforcement.

Tom Garrison is the editor of Current World Leaders International Issues, a Santa Barbara-based international journal.

My June 7, 1995 immigration essay, *Santa Barbara News-Press.*

I don't understand open border advocates. Because someone breaks the law for a "good reason" we as a society should overlook the transgression? Title 8, Section 1325 of the US Code states:

> Any alien who (1) enters or attempts to enter the United States at any time or place other than as designated by immigration officers, or (2) eludes examination or inspection by immigration officers, or (3) attempts to enter or obtains entry to the United States by a willfully false or misleading representation or the willful concealment of a material fact, shall, for the first commission of any such offense, be fined under title 18 or imprisoned not more than 6 months, or both, and, for a subsequent commission of any such offense, be fined under title 18, or imprisoned not more than 2 years, or both.

Progressives would have us believe that as a society we should ignore the fact that if a person commits a crime to accomplish their goal, and—maybe—presents no future harm then the crime should be forgiven. I see, so the burglar who breaks into the progressives' house to watch TV and eat their food should be forgiven if they commit no future crime.

Would progressives look the other way if it was personal? If the illegal immigrants camped out on their lawn and used their resources for decades? I doubt it. But because the appearance of "fairness" is so crucial to their thinking they have no problem with illegals using societal resources. As libertarian icon Murray Rothbard (2013) notes, "It is easy to be conspicuously 'compassionate' if others are being forced to pay the cost."

A few months after my second letter to the editor appeared (April 13, 1996) I had a meaningful conversation about illegal immigration with Carmen, a long-time local progressive activist. I followed up the conversation with a lengthy letter top him. The entire letter is below. In it I mentioned some important issues in the illegal immigration debate, especially the rank emotionalism and lies of the open borders advocates.

July 30, 1996
Dear Carmen,

I appreciate your taking time to talk with me the other night at Ming's in a serious manner about your concerns with my position on immigration. Disagreeing with someone is no big deal, but I do dislike being treated as a stereotype. It is to your credit that you did not fall into that trap. By the way, you are the one of three or four people who criticized my position and did it in a rational, non-emotion laden manner. On the other hand, I have had about 30 to 35 people support my position, several of whom would be considered progressive types. And, what I think is amazing, only one person who talked to me about limiting immigration sounded like a racist. I feared my analysis—which has nothing to do with race/ethnicity—might attract some of the racist nuts.

I did not easily take a public position (a couple of letters to the editor and an essay in the past 14 months or so) on such a controversial issue without a hell of a lot of study and discussion.

Perhaps a bit of information about my situation may help. As you may know, for 15 years I have edited a political science journal published locally. (I have enclosed a promotional brochure and the most recent *Almanac* issue.) In one part of the journal (*International Issues*) we publish articles from differing points-of-view. While I have strong views about many of the topics we cover, I try very hard to get decent articles from each position. Our philosophy (and also my personal position) is that we present well written and thought out articles from all sides of a controversial issue and let the reader decide their own position. I strongly believe this is the fairest method of educating people concerning important issues in a true democracy.

In the past six years I have done two issues of my journal on immigration. In addition, I have closely studied the issue for the last 10 to 12 years. I have read scores of academic and journalistic articles dealing with all sides of this issue. For the most recent issue on immigration (April 1995, a copy of which is enclosed) my journal had only one article criticizing open door immigration and eight which either supported immigration or were academic wishy-washy (but clearly thought lots of immigration was fine). Not the kind of balance I want, but the article criticizing illegal immigration (by Donald Huddle) was excellent.

To me, the immigration issue is closely related to population growth questions, environmental problems, and labor economics. Even Marx would agree that we must acknowledge and take into account into any analysis such factors as technological change (which means we have a decreasing need for poorly educated and low skilled workers), population growth, and environmental degradation (all part of the objective situation).

I have enclosed copies of the original article (dated April 25, 1995) that caused me to write to the *S.B. News-Press* and my reply to Rodriguez and Gonzales' distorting the truth. (Something I will mention in more depth later.) They also use the "race/guilt card." Of course, racism exists but these two (along with a majority of articles supporting open door immigration) always assume that anyone who opposes massive immigration must be a racist—bullshit.

I'm also sending along a recent article from a local progressive, my reply, and the reply from Linda Thom (retired Santa Barbara County budget analyst, she held that position for many years). The progressive's article is very typical of pro-immigration arguments (especially in the mass media)—full of distortions and emotion. My reply (this is my full reply, the one printed by *The Independent* contained only about 1/5 of what I wrote and, thus, was not even close to providing the full meaning of my letter) sets out (in a broad manner) many of the problems I have with open door immigration.

While the two pieces of mine I'm sending are brief, they do give the flavor of my criticisms of current immigration policy. Anyway, this is probably enough written material to start.

About a week ago I attended a public debate about immigration (see the enclosed copy of the notice). Unfortunately only about 20 people attended. Overall, the debate was fairly good. However, a prominent local attorney (who, the moderator said, does immigration law and I know is a big advocate of open door immigration) just had to use the big lie technique. Over and over, even after he was corrected, he said legal immigration into the U.S. amounted to only about 270,000 per year. Well, that is a total lie. Legal immigration into the U.S. has run about 700,000 per year (usually somewhat higher) for many years. (I can produce many articles and quotes from INS officials that show the 700,000 figure to be true.) Now either the attorney is ignorant of the basic facts (in which case he should not be on a public debate panel), or he practices the "big lie" technique—say a lie often enough and people will start to believe it. And this particular fact is important (as I'm sure he knows) because if his figure was correct, that means that legal immigration is only about 1/3 of what most people think—hence no big problem, or at least much less of a problem.

Why this incident sticks out is because I have found that many pro-immigration advocates tend to distort the truth (e.g., the enclosed Rodriguez and Gonzales essay). That bothers me a great deal. Especially since many outspoken pro-immigration people are "progressive" types. As a progressive/democratic socialist most of my life (I'm not sure what I am now), I always made sure of my facts and analysis (as much as humanly possible, especially concerning basic facts) before speaking or writing in public. That honesty, to me, has always been a cornerstone of progressive politics. By god, we may not win many battles but we did not lie to the people. That puts us way beyond most regular political types.

Well, in my study of this issue over the years, I have found that there is a lot of distortion (to put it mildly) on the pro side. I have a real problem being associated with people who lie in public (via speaking or writing).

Carmen—seriously I do appreciate your wanting to have a real discussion (as opposed to a name-calling emotion-driven shouting match) about this issue. On the other hand, I realize that the prospects of my changing your position on this issue are as slim as you changing my position. Nevertheless, civilized honest dialog with opponents is important.

I'm totally open to meeting with you to further discuss this issue. (I sucked down some of your drink at Ming's so I owe you one.) In addition, I am willing to meet at any time with just about anyone (excepting people who are totally emotional about this issue, I doubt if they would listen to anything I said, and that does not make for a very interesting discussion) to discuss/debate this issue.

Take care,

Tom Garrison

Unfortunately I never received a reply from Carmen.

If nothing else, liberals and leftists should at least tone down the emotionalism and admit that illegal immigrants have broken the law and should not be given a free pass via amnesty. Illegal immigration is not at all similar to the civil rights struggle wherein thousands of decent people broke immoral laws. There is nothing immoral about a country having immigration laws. Basic civil rights, equal treatment for black and white citizens for example, bears no resemblance to millions of people illegally crossing a national border. And the civil rights activists willingly went to jail after breaking unjust laws. It is way past time for a reasoned debate on the issue.

References

"California Proposition 187." 2013. Wikipedia. Last modified October 12, 2013.
http://en.wikipedia.org/wiki/California_Proposition_187_(1994)

Garrison, Tom. 1995A. "Rational discourse in discussing immigration." *Santa Barbara News-Press*. Essay. June 7.

Garrison, Tom. 1995B. "No Victims Allowed." *The Santa Barbara Independent*. Letter to the editor. July 27-August 3.

Garrison, Tom. 1996. "Let's have reasoned debate on immigration issue." *Santa Barbara News-Press*. Letter to the editor. April 13.

Garrison, Tom. 1996. Letter from me to Carmen Lodise. July 30.

Rothbard, Murray. 2013. Libertarian Quotes website. Last modification unknown.
http://libertarianquotes.net/R/Murray-Rothbard.html.

US Code Title 8, Section 1325. 2013. U.S Government Printing Office. 2011 edition. Last modification unknown.
http://www.gpo.gov/fdsys/pkg/USCODE-2011-title8/html/USCODE-2011-title8-chap12-subchapII-partVIII-sec1325.htm.

Dad's Death—Do I Have Cirrhosis of the Soul?

I assume most people grieve when a parent dies. Certainly seems the human thing to do. My father died on October 23, 1995 at the age of 70.

My parents Final Judgment of Divorce was granted in 1968 when I was 16. Over the years since I moved out of my mom's place at 18, I had sporadic contact with my father—visiting him around Christmas and occasionally during the summer. He never visited wherever I was living. I sent Christmas and birthday cards and the occasional letter updating my life. Christmas and birthday cards from him, never regular, fairly soon became nonexistent.

My dad, "Tommy," at one of his favorite
activities, fishing, circa 1980s.

Okay, my dad was not a great communicator as I became an adult. Hell, he wasn't much of a communicator when I was a child. A lousy parent? Not really, just typical of fathers in the 1950s and '60s. As a group they were not terribly touchie-feelie. As much as I knew my paternal grandfather (he died when I was five, but I did spend a lot of time with him), dispensing warm fuzzies was not his style either. I guess the apple does not fall far from the tree.

Tommy, my dad, did do at least some of the "dad" stuff with his kids as we grew up—how to throw a baseball, play dominoes and table tennis, and the subtleties of fishing. He was an enthusiastic, and good, fisherman and sometimes hunter. Both parents encouraged us kids to save money and the lesson took with me. Dad was also a coin collector and I followed him in that hobby. Alas, I'm the only sibling who carried on the numismatic tradition. To this day I always search my pocket change for that elusive 1909 S-VBD penny.

I also remember mom accompanying me to more than one Shafter High football or track awards ceremony because dad was working, or at the Shafter Motel playing poker, or who knows where. As with most father-son relationships, it was a mixture of some good and some not so good.

Given all this, I did not feel neglected, or particularly close to my father. I was an active kid with school, sports, and just screwing around with friends. The absence of micromanagement by parental units was mostly a blessing. You either learn personal responsibility for your behavior and grow up damn quick or end up as a bum.

When he died after battling cancer, I felt indifferent. He was my father, but I didn't feel particularly close to him or upset about his passing. My lack of feeling bothers me. While I'm much more "in touch with my feelings" than my father ever demonstrated, maybe we are more alike than I choose to admit. Or perhaps I simply have a bad case of cirrhosis of the soul and am incapable of grieving. Naw, I've cried like a baby when a beloved cat dies.

Why I Left the Left*

"Point of racism."

Along with the ever popular "point of sexism," these additions to Roberts Rules of Order often echoed at statewide meetings of the California Peace and Freedom Party (PFP). You have to understand that one would be hard pressed to find a group less imbued with racist or sexist thoughts or behaviors than the leadership of the California Peace and Freedom Party—the only avowedly socialist party with ballot status in California. Yet, during debate members of some factions would often challenge any speaker who even mildly criticized or challenged the ideas of a person of color or woman by shouting "point of racism" and/or "point of sexism." Leftist democracy in action—try and intimidate your opponents by labeling them as racists and/or sexists. It is important to know that these folks were hypersensitive about race and sex and calling them racist or sexist was a powerful tool. It sounds ridiculous now and was silly then.

As a member of the PFP State Central Committee, I experienced these activities many times from the mid-1980s to the mid-1990s. These were only a minor, and somewhat amusing, sidelight to the major themes of why I left the Left.

Basically there are four characteristics of the Left that made it impossible to continue with my leftist affiliations. I'll mix personal observations with a wider analysis and empirical evidence. The four characteristics are: (1) a lack of respect for and understanding of the concept of personal responsibility for one's own actions; (2) unnecessary lying that undermined the democratic process; (3) a slavish adherence to "affirmative action" preferences, identity politics, and multicultural "diversity"; (4) and a strong intolerance for real diversity of ideas.

As time went on, I found myself more and more at the non-leftist part of the political continuum. While not the only issues that split me from the Left, there are representative of how the Left (and contemporary liberals in general) just don't get it.

Personal Responsibility

Our local Socialist Party chapter had a meeting soon after the April 1992 riots in Los Angeles that followed the original Simi Valley trial and acquittal of the Los Angeles police officers who were charged with attacking Rodney King. As you recall, during those riots, a white truck driver, Reginald Denny, was savagely attacked by several black men for no reason other than that Denny was a white man in the wrong place at the wrong time. Damian Williams, of the "71 Hustlers" a prime attacker of Denny, used a piece of concrete to fracture Denny's skull in 91 places. Williams also did the "revolutionary" act of pulling down the pants of another unconscious white victim and spray-painting his genitals black while a mob watched and laughed (Caldwell 1998). Even though Williams' actions were captured on videotape, he was later acquitted of the most serious charges (Will 1998, P. 80).

At our meeting one member proclaimed that we need to understand the black thugs (not their words) who attacked Denny and to see that their actions were not their fault but rather a function of societal oppression. Incredible! These thugs attack a totally innocent white man and we're supposed to tolerate it because the attackers are black. In our present culture feelings trump behavior.

Look at the facts. Damian Williams had a long history of gang-related violence. He could clearly make a choice between attacking a white man with whom he had no grudge and not attacking—the choice was his. But at least one member (and most likely several other sympathizers) of our local socialist group accepted and advanced the idea that poor Damian Williams was not to blame for his purposeful and vicious attack on a truly innocent victim who happened to be white. Society made him do it. Amazing.

Another very popular and obvious example of dismissing personal responsibility is the fairly recent idea of classifying alcoholism as a disease. Come on. If you believe that, then it is the only disease to have ever been eradicated by willpower. Quitting may be a difficult process, but an alcoholic can end his "disease" by simply *choosing* not to drink. That is, taking responsibility for his actions and not drinking.

If this were not the case, how else could we explain the millions of former alcoholics who simply choose not to drink and don't? Does their "disease" simply go away? In a sense yes, it does, once they decide to display some willpower and character.

It may be true that some folks have a genetic predisposition toward alcoholism. But that just means that once they know this, they should not drink. Abstaining may not be easy and requires willpower, but that certainly does not mean alcoholism is a disease.

However, the Left and liberals do seem to strongly latch on to any excuse for why an individual's crappy behavior is not his fault. Usually the mantra is that society is to blame. In this case, it is the mythical "disease" of alcoholism. Why is so difficult for leftists/liberals to simply say that someone does not have much character and/or willpower and this leads them to abuse alcohol. The answer is obvious—once the way is open to honestly discuss personal failing as a reason for destructive behavior, then other personal failings may also be attributed to an individual's own actions and not the fault of society. The whole underpinning of the Left and liberalism would be badly shaken. Leftism/liberalism relies on the proposition that, for the most part, people are not capable of controlling their own lives and need the government (for liberals) or the new socialist society (for leftists) to protect and watch out for them—the nanny state.

It is true society plays a role in molding people and that a black person in a racist society may face problems not of his own making. But contemporary America is not oppressively racist and there are plenty of chances for any hard working person who makes thoughtful choices to carve out a decent life. However, leftists/liberals are thoroughly immersed in the narcissism of minor differences. Noted civil rights activist Dr. James Meredith points out that:

> ... somewhere along the line, someone in power decided that the proud black race, a people who build cultures in Africa and built many of the physical structures of this nation, could not survive without a host of federal programs and giveaways.... A "dependency mentality" was created and fostered by black and white liberals looking to buy power. . . . I have come to realize that while white racism exists, our main roadblocks in the '90s are ones that have been created by our own so-called leadership (Meredith 1997, P. 18).

The situation today—approximately 40 percent of Americans receive federal government handouts of cash and valuable benefits (more than 45 million receive food stamps), financed by the 50 percent of citizens who actually pay taxes—further undermines personal responsibility. Assuming some percentage those receiving handouts are in a bad situation through no fault of their own, our nanny state system—fully supported by liberals and leftists—still enables tens of millions of Americans (and who knows exactly how many illegal aliens) to abrogate personal responsibility. The sad reality is that decades into the welfare/nanny state, virtually nothing has changed. According to political scientist and authority on public administration James Q. Wilson:

> ...there are three simple behavioral rules for avoiding poverty: finish high school, produce no children before marrying, and no child before age 20. Only 8 percent of families who conform to all three rules are poor; 79 percent of those who do not conform are poor (Will 1997, P. 88).

All three rules are dependent upon personal responsibility. Act responsibly and your chances of living in poverty plummet. Individual responsibility, not society, is the key. Ask your favorite leftist/liberal if they agree and you will get a litany of "reasons" why people are victims of society, corporations, the rich, or some other boogeyman—anything but personal responsibility. After all, a villain is needed to justify the security blanket of the nanny state.

Unnecessary Leftist/Liberal Lying

During the 1980s my wife, Deb, and I were very active in the local Santa Barbara Tenants Union (SBTU). Other than our local socialist group, the Tenants Union was the most active "progressive" organization in Santa Barbara at that time.

At least some of the SBTU's leadership (they often held office in the SBTU) were affiliated with the League of Revolutionary Struggle (LRS), a nationwide communist organization formed in 1978. The LRS considered itself anti-revisionist and took inspiration from the Communist Party of China and its leader Mao Zedong. It was heavily invested in racial and ethnic identity politics.

How could we tell they were commies? The LRS published a newspaper called *Unity*. Even for a lefty paper it was pretty bad—full of slogans and stories of struggle against capitalism by just about anybody as long as they were non-white. By this time I was fairly well connected with the local reds, some LRS people and a few Revolutionary Communist Party (RCP) types. The only people who sold *Unity* were members of the SBTU's leadership. When Deb and I asked if they were LRS members the reply was always, "I am a supporter of the *Unity* newspaper." Come on. Nobody except a dues-paying LRS member would try to sell that rag.

Deb and I had no problem with commies. Well, maybe a little problem with the fact that they were Marxists-Leninists and believed in the dictatorship of the proletariat. I had some concern that, if they were honest, they would most likely initiate violence (as opposed to self-defense) to achieve their ends. Ohhhh, and we had maybe a tinsy problem with the most likely outcome if their kind gained power—that people like Deb and I would be some of the first to be lined up against a wall and shot. Other than those small caveats, we were fine with the local commies.

But this transparent lying about their political affiliation means that when the "revolution" comes it will be led in Santa Barbara by political activists who are, if not skilled at lying, at least comfortable with it. A great start for a new humanistic order.

Of course, lying about one's principal political affiliation has a long tradition on the Left. There may have been justification for underground political work (including lying about leftist political affiliations) in Czarist Russia or 1980s El Salvador. But in 1980s America?

I twice ran for Santa Barbara City Council (1985 and 1987) openly as a socialist. In several years (early 1980s to mid-1990s) of very intense political activity—all of it done openly as a member of the California Peace and Freedom Party and the Socialist Party, USA—I never had a major hassle with the public due to being a socialist and promoting socialism. Neither did any of the score or so core members of our local socialist group.

Keep in mind that this was the apogee of the Reagan-Bush years and I was doing openly socialist political work in Ronald Reagan's adopted home town. As a matter of fact, I think my campaigns and other political work by myself and others in our local socialist group greatly benefited from our honesty and being a novelty.

I was treated fairly and with respect by moderates and conservatives and the local media. I had dozens of intense yet civil discussions with capitalists and other running dogs.

The only real problems came from liberals who wanted me to lie and say I was simply another "progressive" Democrat—a stupid idea for several reasons. "Progressive"/liberal Democrats are a dime a dozen in Santa Barbara. At least one runs for every office in the county. I was not a Democrat and was not about to lie concerning my basic political affiliations, even though I surly would have received more votes if I did. But it would have been a betrayal of the public trust and my own values. It still seems odd that Democratic Party activists encouraged me to lie.

During both campaigns my campaign literature noted my membership in the Socialist Party and the Peace and Freedom Party—I ran openly as a socialist. What is the use of being a socialist and not openly pushing it? A socialist running as a "progressive" or liberal Democrat is simply one more liberal Democrat and does not advance the democratic socialist "revolution" in any meaningful manner. If nothing else, my running openly as a socialist showed people who met me during the campaign that a "red" could also be a thoughtful believer in democracy (and they could see I did not have horns).

"Affirmative Action" Preferences,
Identity Politics, and Multicultural "Diversity"

My campaigns were run by committees of decent hard working leftists. I still have nothing but admiration for almost all who were at the center of the campaigns. Among many interesting discussions during my two campaigns for Santa Barbara City Council was one that emerged in both campaigns and demonstrates illogical pandering to the god of multicultural "diversity" and identity politics.

To become a US citizen, one must demonstrate competence in the English language. My campaign committees had serious discussions about whether or not to print some of our campaign literature in Spanish. Many felt that doing so would help us gain the Latino vote. (More than one-third of the population in Santa Barbara is of Hispanic ancestry.)

My wife and I consistently argued that since only citizens could register to vote, and since naturalized Hispanic citizens must have competence in the English language (or they could not become citizens), there was no need for Spanish language campaign material. Those not competent in English could not become citizens and, thus, could not vote. Further, since virtually all Hispanic-ancestry citizens born in the US would speak English by the time they could register to vote, there was absolutely no need for Spanish language campaign material.

Our logic won the day, but it interesting that the folks working in my campaigns would even broach this subject in a serious manner. Their arguments demonstrated the power of multiculturalism and the need of the Left to pander to identity politics.

Like most communist groups, the LRS was active in the Democrat Party (although not always openly as LRS members). Nationally they played an important role in the Rainbow Coalition and the 1984 and 1988 campaigns to elect Jesse Jackson as president.

The LRS folks and their supporters also exhibited an incredible ability to politically support almost anyone—excepting, of course, the most blatant conservative—as long as that person had black or brown skin and was a Democrat.

They demonstrated this behavior when Democrat Tom Bradley, a black moderate (at best), ran for governor of California in 1986. Other than being black, Bradley had no progressive/leftist credentials. The Tenants Union had a radical constitution and, as noted above, some members of the leadership were LRS members. My wife and I, being serious and open leftists, argued strenuously that the Tenants Union should endorse the PFP candidate (a Hispanic woman, Maria Elizabeth Munoz) instead of the milquetoast Bradley for governor. While we managed to convince several Tenants Union members who were not LRS "supporters" to endorse the true leftist candidate, the majority voted to endorse Bradley (the vote was 13 to seven for Bradley).

Understand the underlying political context. An endorsement by the Santa Barbara Tenants Union for any candidate for statewide office would only influence at most a couple of hundred voters in Santa Barbara—almost certainly not enough to make a difference for any candidate. But, by openly backing a socialist (the PFP candidate) the organization would help build a base outside the Democrat Party for progressives and leftists. On the other hand, backing a tired old moderate Democrat would mean almost nothing and build little except allegiance to what almost everyone in the leadership agreed was a corrupt Democrat Party. Moreover, it would show that the Tenants Union supported a black male candidate over a Hispanic woman. It didn't matter that Bradley would offer at best lukewarm support for the goals of the Tenants Union, while the PFP candidate would whole heartedly support those goals. Bradley was a black Democrat—that was enough. A clear example of identity politics wining over issue-based ideological politics.

One of the most impressive examples of identity politics and race pandering was the hoopla surrounding the June 29, 1995 US Supreme Court decision (a five to four vote) ordering the state of Georgia to redraw its 11th Congressional District in a manner that omits race as the "predominant" factor. Subsequent redistricting of five "racially gerrymandered" black-majority Congressional districts into white-majority districts in Florida, Georgia, and Texas spurred leftists, liberals, and so-called black leaders to predict (read their words) Armageddon for black folks in America.

The ruling was "the first step in the resegregation of American electoral democracy," according to Wade Henderson, legal director of the National Association for the Advancement of Colored People (NAACP). He added "If race can't be a factor, it's going to be almost impossible to preserve these black districts" (Muwakkil 1995, P. 20). Cynthia McKinney, the black female Democrat incumbent in Georgia's 11th district, lamented the ruling as "...a setback for democracy" and said that she believed that "The issue of fairness has been squarely left behind" (Muwakkil 1995, P. 20). That paragon of virtue President Clinton called the decision a "setback in the struggle to ensure that all Americas participate fully in the electoral process" (Barrett and Seib 1995, P. A16). And Rev. Jesse Jackson said this limit on racial gerrymandering would produce an "ethnic cleansing of Congress" (Will 1996).

Guess what? The sky did not fall and black people were not once again in slavery. All five black incumbents in the former black-majority and now white-majority Southern districts won their races in the November 1996 Congressional elections. Maybe Americans, even white Southerners, are not as racist as identity politics leaders would have us believe.

By early 1996 I had become fed up with affirmative action preferences in government, college admissions, etc. I took a small, entirely unscientific, survey to gather empirical evidence as to the extent of discrimination against women in college and the workplace. Over a couple of months, I asked co-workers and friends if they had ever been discriminated against in school or the workplace because of their sex. I polled nine women, from their early 20s to their late 40s, and asked if they felt they had suffered sexual discrimination at any point during the last ten years. (I used ten years because I figured that even the most retrograde men had at least heard of sexual discrimination by the mid-1980s and knew that it was unacceptable and could be illegal.) None, that's correct *none*, of the respondents reported *any* discrimination based on their sex.

Of course, the sample was small and my method unscientific. But if sexual discrimination was as rampant as leftists and feminists would have us believe, I figured at least half the women I talked to would report some sexual discrimination in the past decade. And if we are to believe feminists and the advocates of preferences and quotas, it is damn near impossible that not one of the nine women had been a victim of sexual discrimination.

I know sexual discrimination exists. But from my own observations, questioning, and much reading, I cannot believe that it is anywhere as pervasive as feminists and quota advocates would have us believe. Perhaps they need to keep "victimhood" alive to maintain their own jobs in Women's Studies programs and the cottage industry of sexual discrimination.

In a March 23, 1998 *Newsweek* essay Meg Greenfield clearly stated the major problem with identity politics (and by extension support of affirmative action preferences, quotas, and multiculturalism):

> To let yourself be transformed into the emblem of some cause, any cause, or demographic category, and to draw your identity and take your marching orders from it is to kick away your freedom, your independence and your individuality. It is to suspend all these and

basically to lose your influence over events that matter to you. You will find you have forgotten how to speak out with views that do not conform to those of the group or that you will have been led not to trust such views. You will see life through a very narrow lens and be very much in the control of those who do the defining of the group interest (Greenfield 1998, P. 76).

Intolerance for True Diversity of Ideas

Several years ago my wife and I got into a political discussion with another couple while on a trip to Las Vegas. While cruising around sin city in our rental car, I remember relating how I had two good friends who are conservative—two undergraduate teachers with whom I still maintain contact after graduating decades ago. The guy, let's call him Mr. N, replied that he had never met a conservative who he believed was not a fascist in disguise. No matter what I said, Mr. N would not accept the idea that a conservative could be principled and decent person—that there exists such an animal as a Burkian conservative who is not racist, not sexist, not anti-democratic, but simply has an ideology that challenges many tenants of modern liberalism.

I encountered the same or similar attitude dozens of times with leftists and liberals, albeit usually in not such an unvarnished manner. The truly unfortunate thing is that I doubt if Mr. N ever had a serious discussion with a principled conservative. It might lead to some doubt and the notion that a conservative could be seen as a real person and not simply a stereotype.

It was a bit of a shock to realize that Mr. N—while not a leftist but a strong liberal—could not accept as valid the idea that there exist people of good will who were not of his political persuasion. He was clearly being intolerant of other political views. I realized that the much touted diversity of the last 35 years or so does not seem to include the most meaningful type of diversity—a diversity of ideas.

Years ago I came across an interesting article in *The Wall Street Journal* that reported on a study at the University of Colorado and academic tolerance, or lack thereof (Carroll 1998). It is the premier public university in a state in which registered Republicans (at that time) outnumber Democrats by more than 100,000—a state in which the Republican Party controlled both houses of the state legislature from the mid-1970s to the mid-1990s. The article noted that in 13 social science and humanities departments at the University's main campus in Boulder, Democrats outnumbered Republicans by a ratio of 31 to one. Of the 190 professors affiliated with a political party 184 were Democrats. Not a single Republican turned up in major departments such as English (29 Democrats) and psychology (20 Democrats). There was a single Republican in anthropology (10 Democrats), education (21 Democrats), sociology (12 Democrats), and two Republicans in political science (14 Democrats) (Carroll 1998). Students could easily go through four years of "liberal" education without taking a social science or humanities class from a single Republican professor. Undergraduates find themselves in an environment in which liberal professors don't merely dominate the faculty, they essentially are the faculty.

A more recent study in 2005 and reported in the *Washington Post* by Howard Kurtz finds similar results from a survey of 1,643 fulltime college faculty across the country. By their own description, 72% of those teaching at American colleges and universities are liberal and 15% are conservative. At elite schools, the disparity is more pronounced—87% of the faculty is liberal and 13% conservative (Kurtz 2005). These are only two of several studies that reach the same conclusion.

This ideological hegemony is the obvious result of diversity that only takes race/ethnicity and gender into consideration. What happened to the idea an undergraduate education was intended to provide diverse ideological stimuli and produce graduates who are able to think critically about a range of subjects? Unfortunately, as other studies show, the University of Colorado at Boulder is not an anomaly in its slavish adherence to a very narrow notion of diversity. How is this ideological bias different in method and result from McCarthyism of the 1950s?

I personally experienced ideological intimidation during the 1994 Proposition 187 campaign and its aftermath. The proposition was designed to deny state welfare benefits to illegal immigrants. (On November 8, 1994 it passed 59% to 41 %.) I wrote a couple of letters to the editor and an opinion essay that were published in local newspapers (Garrison 1995A; Garrison 1995B; Garrison 1996). Of course, some local liberals replied and in print I was referred to as mean-spirited and probably racist. In addition, a couple of friends refused to take my arguments seriously, and publicly derided me for questioning the Left/liberal belief that America is an open house with complete benefits for anyone who can sneak over the border. All this over some published letters and essays that were replete with logic and facts.

This questioning of the condition of my spirit and my supposed racism would seem very odd for anyone who knows my history—like the fact that in the preceding 15 years I had voted for, given money to, and publicly worked in electoral campaigns wherein 70 to 80% of the candidates were brown or black and most often women. Yes, I certainly have a history of racism.

But then facts are not the point, the point is to threaten people with vile labels if they overstep the bounds of politically correct thought. Yet another clear example of intolerance for diversity in thinking.

Conclusion

Around this time, the mid- to late 1990s, I began to reconsider my commitment to socialism. I, and most of Santa Barbara socialist group, advocated New Left decentralized power. Marx's idea of the withering away of the state and voluntary cooperation among empowered citizens was our goal and guideline for action. For me, accepting free markets was simply applying my end state to current actions. And since I was always a Libertarian on social issues—such things as supporting gay rights, pro-choice, gun ownership via the 2nd Amendment, legalizing personal drug use—the evolution into a classical liberal/libertarian was not as drastic as one may think. As I began to read libertarian thinkers and magazines (*Reason* and *Liberty*) I came to see that the decentralized aspects of New Left ideology fit well with free markets and free minds. By the late 1990s I considered myself as a libertarian and joined the Libertarian Party.

I have not found the four characteristics discussed in this essay that typify leftism/liberalism in libertarianism. Libertarianism is founded on personal responsibility and limited government. While they probably exist, I have yet to encounter libertarians who practice political lying. Affirmative action and identity politics are not, for libertarians, worshiped at the altar of political correctness. Finally,

189

Libertarians are a diverse group who are tolerant of ideological diversity.

The Left betrayed me. As a young man I eagerly read about the Left, Marxism, socialism, and leftist heroes. My understanding was that the Left was striving to create a society wherein people could fully use their talents and together create a true democratic society. It seemed obvious that taking responsibility for one's actions was a necessary part of the equation, as was being a stand-up citizen/activist by not engaging in political lying. Equally obvious was the need to end racism and sexism, but not by creating new systems where some people are given extra consideration because of their skin tone or sex—a long-term recipe for polarization and divisiveness. I also expected the new society to display a real tolerance for a diversity of ideas—a crucial aspect in avoiding "thought police" I then assumed was necessary, and still strongly believe is a keystone for a better society.

"To hold the same views at 40 as we held at 20 is to have been stupefied for a score of years" ("Stevenson" 2013).

This is a revised and updated version of an essay originally published in the January 2000 issue of *Liberty* magazine. In this form, this essay also appears as one of 23 stories in my book *Why We Left the Left: Personal Stories by Leftists/Liberals Who Evolved to Embrace Libertarianism*. You can purchase the ebook or print version at any estore.

References

Barrett, Paul M. and Gerald Seib. 1995. "Supreme Court Redraws Political Battleground With Broad Attack on Race-Based House Districts." *The Wall Street Journal*. June 30.

Caldwell, Christopher. 1998. "Anatomy of a Riot." *The Wall Street Journal*. February 2

Carroll, Vincent. 1998. "Republican Professors? Sure, There's One." *The Wall Street Journal*. May 11.

Garrison, Tom. 1995A. "Rational discourse in discussing immigration." *Santa Barbara News-Press*. Essay. June 7.

Garrison, Tom. 1995B. "No Victims Allowed." *The Santa Barbara Independent*. Letter to the editor .July 27-August 3.

Garrison, Tom. 1996. "Let's have reasoned debate on immigration issue." *Santa Barbara News-Press*. Letter to the editor. April 13.

Greenfield, Meg. 1998. "Kicking Away Your Freedom." *Newsweek*. March 23.

Kurtz, Howard. 2005. "College Faculties A Most Liberal Lot, Study Finds." *Washington Post.com.* March 29. http://www.washingtonpost.com/wp-dyn/articles/A8427-2005Mar28.html.

Meredith, James. 1997. "A Challenge to Change." *Newsweek*. October 6.

Muwakkil, Salim. 1995. "Down by Law." *In These Times*. July 24.

"Stevenson, Robert Louis." 2013. The Free Dictionary website. Last modification unknown. http://forum.thefreedictionary.com/postst5550_To-hold-the-same-views-at-forty-as-we-held-at-twenty-is-to-have-been-stupefied-for-a-score-of-years--and-take-rank--not-as-a---.aspx.

Will, George F. 1996. "Decisiveness of Message Rather than Race." *Santa Barbara News-Press*. November 11.

Will, George F. 1997. "A GI Bill for Mothers." *Newsweek*. December 22.

Will, George F. 1998. "Official Negligence." *Newsweek*. February 16.

Chapter Five
Spring 2000—Fall 2013
Risk Taking

Introduction

As the year 2000 rolled around and civilization survived Y2K, Deb and I began a decade dominated at crucial points by risk taking. Risk taking is not to be confused with thrill seekers or adrenaline junkies. Those are the fight or flee chemical response which quickly dissipates. Risk underlies any journey into the unknown—sailing a ship into unchartered waters, running for political office, an entrepreneur's investment in a new venture, or changing a career. It is more long-term than an adrenaline rush (Gwin 2013). Our risk taking was based on prior experience and guesstimates as to the probable future if the risk was or was not taken.

My first large risk of the decade was to actively search for a new job. Sure, my company was struggling, but it had been my home for 18 years. In 2000 I turned 48, sort of old to begin a new career. But the risk taking paid off; by spring I found a new job, generally satisfying and well paying, which had nothing to do with my previous career as an editor of a political science journal. I greatly increased my skill set and learned about the working of local government from the inside.

On the heels of a new career, Deb and I began a series of risk taking entrepreneurial investments. In May 2000 we bought our first investment condo. By 2005 we owned three rental condos. It sounds like a sure thing, but there is always the potential of extended periods without a renter and positive cash flow turning negative for months at a time. We ended, for now, our real estate acquisitions with our fourth rental condo in St. George, Utah which we purchased in March 2010.

Our last perilous decision was to uproot ourselves from Santa Barbara and move to St. George, Utah in October 2009. No big deal, right? Maybe a big deal. I lived in Santa Barbara for 33 years, and Deb even longer. I gave up a well-paying job with great benefits (of course, a government job) to move more than 450 miles to no job. In fact, we moved without knowing a soul, other than a real estate agent, in our new community and neither of us had a job waiting. I was 57 years old, Deb a bit older. We left friends and family. As the senior years quickly approached, we made a huge life change.

Was it really a risk? You bet. Did it work out? Neither of us would move back to California. Deb has a part-time job she enjoys and I have a new career as a writer. We go hiking at least once a month and have new friends. Although we have about one-third of the income we had in Santa Barbara, our quality of life is much better. Don't be afraid of change.

References

Gwin, Peter. 2013. "The Mystery of Risk." *National Geographic*. June.

Me? I Work for the Government

During the last couple of years in the 1990s it became clear that the International Academy at Santa Barbara was dying. Sales and renewals of the three main publications (all serials) including my baby *Current World Leaders* were slow. The company never fully recovered from the early 1990s recession and the Internet was beginning to take a bite. Of course, we put our publications online. But we were late into the game, and much of the information we offered could be found at other websites for free. The last few years of the decade my hours were cut to much less than fulltime. It was time to move on.

I updated my resume, shaved my beard (Deb said I looked younger sans beard), and began an active search for a new job. Surely many Santa Barbara employers were dying to hire a middle aged overeducated white guy. Well, maybe not.

The search went on for more than a year. I concentrated on government jobs. Why not? The pay was as good as or better than comparable private sector positions, the benefits great, and government employees had every imaginable holiday off. I applied for every government job for which I was remotely qualified. I took the written exams for three county government jobs and must have done well because I interviewed for each. Included were two interviews for positions at the Santa Barbara County Assessor's Office. Sandra Petersen, supervisor of the Title Transfer Division, hired me as a Clerk III for her division. She was a good boss and we became friends.

I began my new job on May 1, 2000. Within a little over three weeks a real property appraiser position opened and I was offered that job. From clerk to appraiser in less than a month—not bad and a huge salary increase. (I tested and interviewed for both the clerk and appraiser positions.) On June 12 I formally began work as an Appraiser I in the Title Transfer Division.

The Assessor's Office is located downtown, about three miles from home. Just about every day for 9 ½ years I rode my bike to work. Like Post Office letter carriers, I delivered myself to work through good and inclement weather (rain, it never snows in Santa Barbara). On rainy days my backpack was full with a change of clothes. It was at times inconvenient, but my annual carbon footprint was infinitely smaller than Mr. Environmentalist Al Gore's daily carbon footprint.

Since I was computer savvy and rather organized, Sandra gave me a huge project to familiarize me with operations in our division—organize all the Title Transfer's disparate rules and guidelines into one procedures manual. This was in addition to my regular work and ended up taking several months. To complete this project, or to even understand what was needed, I had to immerse myself in our office procedures and the California Revenue and Taxation Code (R&T Code). The R&T Code was a three volume set with hundreds of pages of legalese, most dedicated to every conceivable aspect of the multitude of property taxes in California ("Property Taxes Law Guide" 2013). Sure, the land and improvement of your residence is taxable; but so are racehorses, aircraft, and "floating homes." (Not to mention some of the highest state income and sales tax rates in the nation.)

Beside tourism, Santa Barbara County has a fair amount of agriculture including many vineyards in the north county. Does the state tax grapevines? You bet. Let me give just a taste of the relatively straightforward, compared to some sections of the R&T Code, relevant laws governing the taxation of grapevines.

"ORCHARD" OR "VINEYARD" DEFINED. An orchard or a vineyard is a systematic planting of fruit and nutbearing trees or grapevines as opposed to individual plantings for ornamental purposes. The exemption under Section 3 (i), Article XIII, California Constitution, applies to such fruit and nut-bearing trees or grapevines planted in orchard or vineyard form. The fruit, nuts, or grapes, until harvested, are growing crops exempt from taxation under Section 3 (h), Article XIII, California Constitution.

(b) LENGTH OF EXEMPTION. The exemption applies to those trees in an orchard until four years after the season of planting in orchard form, and those vines in a vineyard until three years after the season of planting in vineyard form. The exemption ceases on the fifth lien date after the season of planting trees in orchard form, and on the fourth lien date after the season of planting vines in vineyard form. For example, fruit trees planted in orchard form in the 1995 planting season become assessable on the 2000 lien date ("Fruit and Nut Tree" 2004).

Pretty clear, huh? Remember this is a rather simple explanation of a tiny part of the law. The truly fun part is chasing down a definition or explanation. If you want to understand "X" then see R&T Code section "Y." Sometimes to understand section "Y" you had to visit R&T Code section "Z." And perhaps along the way you have to consult with the country attorney to get their take on court cases that may affect the law. It can, and does, take years for an appraiser to be conversant with relevant laws. Don't forget that the taxpayer is supposed to know about and understand these tax laws.

Each appraiser was expected to be an expert in his or her area—residential, commercial, agricultural, etc. While the county had staff attorneys to untangle particularly nasty laws and regulations, the appraiser was ultimately responsible for each valuation. Spend a few hours with the California R&T Code to understand the case for tax code simplification.

I was a good employee. Since the R&T Code was the basis for most everything we did, I made a concerted effort to learn the relevant portions. For a while a joke around the office was that I took a volume of the Code with me to the restroom. Sadly it was true. (I know, I needed a life.)

Within five years (June 2005), as quickly as can be achieved given office requirements, I was promoted to Appraiser III—the highest possible rank. My last three years I was the office appraiser for the Montecito area. I appraised the value of home purchases, additions, and remodels. You might know that Montecito is the home (or vacation home) of a fair number of rich and/or famous people—Oprah Winfrey, Michael Douglas, and their ilk.

Montecito was a particularly difficult area mainly due to the lack of housing tracts. In an area with many housing tracts, the houses in any one tract are pretty much the same—they are comparable. The appraiser does not have to make many value adjustments to the comparable properties to determine the value of the subject property (e.g. add value to a comparable since it has fewer habitable square feet than does the subject). Adjustments to comparable properties are the slippery slope of an appraisal—they can always be questioned by the taxpayer or your supervisor.

A basic appraisal to discover the market value of a house becomes difficult, sometimes very difficult, in an area dominated by unique large houses such as Montecito. The difficulty stems from the lack of comparable properties that are truly comparable. Because this area was so hard to do, the appraiser for Montecito had fewer cases to handle than did an appraiser who worked a tract house dominated area. That was fair—fewer, harder cases versus more, easy work items.

Upon being hired, I immediately became a member, dues were automatically deducted from my paycheck, of the local union that represented county workers—the Service Employees International Union (SEIU) Local 620. Unions can be useful, and certainly were in the past. But there are a few problems with this.

I wasn't happy with union membership being a condition of employment. Don't want to join the union and pay union dues? Then don't work here. That was the situation. I have no problem with employees voluntarily banding together to negotiate with employers, but I was not happy being forced into union membership.

I could go into a long discussion of the free rider concern in open shops where union membership is not mandatory. Suffice to say, state and federal laws protect employees in a myriad of ways—safety concerns, overtime, grievance procedures, and so on. These may have been initiated by unions, but are now firmly entrenched in law. Where unions "earn" their pay is negotiating wages and benefits.

How did I benefit from being a union member? No discernible way, and I probably suffered from being in a closed shop. I was a great employee, always completed my work in a timely manner and often helped others finish their work. By the time I became an Appraiser III (while many appraisers who had been in the office years longer than I never attained Appraiser III status) I was handling the toughest area in the county (and arguably in the state), Montecito, and finishing my annual work weeks before appraisers in easier areas completed their work. I was also frequently playing the role of temporary supervisor (without concomitant pay increase) when my group's supervisor was out of the office (a fairly frequent occurrence). Finally, I have a file of testimonial letters from taxpayers I assisted. A couple of months prior to my quitting and moving to St. George, Utah my supervisor and the County Assessor received the following letter:

July 15, 2009
Gentlemen:

I wanted to let you know that as a new homeowner in Santa Barbara, I had an exceptional experience that was so unique I had to share it with you.

Having bought a home in July 2008, I am certain you can imagine the stress of the economic downturn and how distressing its effects are on all of us. I had been informed by every significant broker that my home had lost 30% of its value.

I called the Assessor's Office and was directed to Tom Garrison who displayed such patience and guidance of various potential processes available to me, that I immediately felt better and renewed my faith in the "system."

He was so patient and clear minded, and most of all pleasant and kind, that I knew I had to share it with you. It is very rare to find that type of person and I hope he is appreciated. He clearly has a wonderful sense of humor too! When I mentioned to him he would get my vote for Governor, he burst out laughing followed by a robust "no thanks"!

He is very special and you are lucky to have him, as are we.

Yours very truly,

Robert Schnur
Santa Barbara Homeowner (Schnur 2009)

And no, I did not pay the taxpayer to write this letter. Many, perhaps most, Assessor Office employees never received a single testimonial letter after years on the job. (Because they were fairly rare, people tended to share testimonial letters.) Finally, I received this testimonial after more than nine years on the job—by that time many (most?) public employees are somewhat surly and just barely tolerate taxpayer questions.

I have no doubt that in an open shop I could have negotiated a better contract than what I was stuck with due to the union bargaining on my behalf. I was denied that opportunity. On the other hand, the Assessor's Office employees who never finished their work in a timely manner; were often late to work and early to leave; chatted 15 to 30 minutes each morning before beginning work (I don't begrudge employees talking a few minutes to settle in, but some folks went on and on just about every day); and surfed the Internet while on work time certainly benefitted from the union presence. They kept their jobs. And they earned a decent salary which they never could have negotiated on their own.

As many critics note, a union shop protects the lazy and unmotivated. As government employees (almost impossible to fire after the probationary period), some of my co-workers developed an entitlement mentality. They were entitled—too often with minimal effort—to a well-paying job with great benefits. In our office, at least one employee was a practicing alcoholic at work and it was years before she was eased out of her job. Another was stoned (smoking ganja) most days. He was simply transferred to another office.

Any half-way bright employee would keep these complaints to himself, or share with a few select friends. I wasn't that bright. In late May 2006 I sent the infamous "No Carrots, No Sticks" email to all the top management. In it I detailed my complaints/concerns about the work environment. The email began:

> No carrots and no sticks = an unnecessarily stressful, unpleasant, and extremely unfair work environment. Pithy (perhaps), yet true.

> In the four years I have worked in the residential division, the end of the year mess never goes away. Even after Pam's early year exhortations to "get your work done" (with an implied "or else") nothing changed. I believe the problem stems from weak supervision and management toward some appraisers and a dysfunctional work environment. Also, the fact that rewards for good work and repercussions for poor work are virtually nonexistent....

199

Did my challenging the system change anything? In the long run, no. The problems I detailed continued until I left in October 2009. And some management folks were extremely unhappy with me for years. To counter the office problems I tried to develop an "I don't give a shit attitude." That did not work. When I'm on the job I should do the best possible work, especially since taxpayers were footing the bill for my salary and benefits. Anything else was unacceptable.

The Assessor's Office was my "home" for 9 ½ years. It was a stressful job—the appraiser had to know extensive portions of the R&T Code, know the local office procedures, learn the three major methods of valuing a property, keep detailed records, work with the public who come to the office and during field checks, defend a dozen to several dozen assessment appeals each year, keep up with state-mandated ongoing education, and finish their work in a timely manner.

One might think my tenure in the Assessor's Office was one long nightmare. Not at all. Most taxpayers, probably 95%, were decent folks simply trying to understand the law or how an appraiser determined the value of their property. I got along well with almost all co-workers and many were self-motivated and wanted to do a good job—Sandra, Chris, a couple of Lindas, Elvia, Raul, Suzanne, and Mark among others. Sandra was my mentor concerning title transfer issues and her husband, Chris, filled the same role regarding the valuation of property. In the final analysis the job paid well and it is true that, "Rich or poor, it's always nice to have money."

References

"Fruit and Nut Tree and Grapevine Exemption." 2004. State of California Board of Equalization website. Last amended June 30, 2004. http://www.boe.ca.gov/proptaxes/pdf/r131.pdf.

Garrison, Tom. 2006. "No Carrots, No Sticks email." Email by Tom Garrison to the top management of the Santa Barbara County Assessor's Office. May 24.

"Property Taxes Law Guide." 2013. California State Board of Equalization website. Last revised 2013. http://www.boe.ca.gov/lawguides/property/current/ptlg/rt/reven ue-and-taxation-code-property-taxation.html.

Schnur, Robert. 2009. "Testimonial Letter about Tom Garrison." July 15.

Look Out Donald Trump, Here Comes Tom and Deb

Don Ho (2013) sang about tiny bubbles. Tiny bubbles are for sissies—Deb and I decided to ride the real estate big bubble in the first decade of the 21st century. Like everyone else, we did not know when the bubble would burst. By spring of 2000 I had a new full-time, fairly well paying job with the Santa Barbara County Assessor's Office (See "Me? I Work for the Government" story in this chapter.) While not exactly deep pockets, our financial situation looked bright. In addition, since Deb and I were officially capitalist pigs as a function of our membership in the Libertarian Party, we figured it was time to kick that recessive capitalist gene into gear.

My mom still lived in Bakersfield, California as a renter and rents kept increasing (till about 2008). Her rent was getting to the point where it was more than 50% of her Social Security check. Being a good son (sort of) and Deb a good daughter-in-law, we decided to act. On May 26, 2000 we bought an 816 square foot, two bedroom, one bath condo about a half mile from where mom lived—a nice, well maintained 18 unit complex. We struck a deal—mom could live there forever at the rent she was paying at her current apartment. Deb and I would ensure her new home was well maintained. It would have been nice to let her live rent-free, but we needed to pay the mortgage. This was acceptable and we helped her move in June.

As noted in other stories (See especially "Desert Rats" in Chapter Four), Deb and I became desert rats starting in the mid-1990s. We are the sort to hike around during the day, but appreciate a decent bed at night. Our sleeping in a bag on the ground while camping days were long gone. We took a few vacations to Laughlin, Nevada. In the daylight, we explored the area around Laughlin and went on several hikes. At night, it was buffet dinners and, usually, losing money playing video poker.

We like Laughlin, people gamble even in bad times, so why not buy another investment condo? On October 20, 2003 we added a second jewel—a two bedroom, one bath condo—to our real estate crown. Our condo in Laughlin might get lonely, thus in February 2005 we bought a second two bedroom, one bath condo unit in Laughlin.

Deb and I bought our last pre-Great Recession condo more than three years prior to the subprime mortgage meltdown. We did not buy at, or even near, the height of the value run-up. Were we really that smart? Kinda. I worked in the Assessor's Office and it was obvious way too many, often unqualified, buyers were chasing too few houses. Every week I saw sales of 1970s average condition tract houses go for 700 to $800,000 or more. Even given this was Santa Barbara, those same houses were selling for 400 to $500,000 just a few years earlier. It did not take a rocket scientist to understand that this could not continue indefinitely.

Any objective observer could see this coming. The Community Reinvestment Act (CRA), first enacted in 1977, required banks to report the distribution of their mortgage loans. By the mid-1990s CRA had become a powerful tool in the hands of ACORN (Association of Community Organizers for Reform Now) and allied activist organizations (many of which were subsidized by the Fannie Mae Foundation). These organizations, with the backing of politicians from both major parties, demanded increasingly more mortgage loans be made to marginal, at best, potential home buyers—buyers whose credit history, income, or down payments were inadequate by traditional home loan standards (these became known as "subprime loans"). The ostensible reason was to increase affordable housing. Bank regulators imposed lower mortgage lending standards. Members of Congress, particularly Democrat Representative Barney Frank of Massachusetts and Democrat Chris Dodd of Connecticut, pushed Fannie Mae and Freddie Mac (the purchasers of government-insured mortgages) to buy these high risk loans.

Until 1997, banks balked at lowering lending standards—what banker makes loans to people who almost assuredly can't repay the loan? That year the Clinton Administration ordered Freddie Mac and Fannie Mae to buy subprime loans, and told the banks to go ahead with the potentially bad loans since they now had a market where they could be sold.

In addition, the Federal Reserve Bank, beginning in the early 2000s, began a policy of making money very cheap—hence banks were awash with cash for questionable loans that the government forced them to make. In January 2001, the federal funds rate, the key benchmark for all interest rates in the country, was 6.5%. By August 2001 it was 3.75% and by the summer of 2002 it stood at 1%.

As American Enterprise Institute scholar Peter Wallison notes:

In the end, by 2008 there were 28 million subprime or very weak mortgages. ... That's half, incidentally, of all mortgages in the financial system. Of that 28 million, 20.4 million were on the books of government agencies like Fannie Mae and Freddie Mac and the FHA (Federal Housing Administration) and other government agencies and banks that were holding them as a requirement of the Community Reinvestment Act, which applied to banks. So that's why I say that the government's housing policy was responsible for creating these mortgages. They never would have been created without the government demanding that they be created and providing the funds to buy them.

My point was [that] without the government's housing policy, there never would have been a financial crisis (Randazzo 2012).

Thus a number of factors converged to ultimately create the subprime lending crisis that led to the financial meltdown of 2008. In each case it was government intervention that distorted markets and created a breeding ground for financial ruin (Allison 2012; Brittain 2009; Flynn 2009; McClaughry 2011; Sowell 2011)

As usual, Thomas Sowell (2009) puts in all in perspective along with some well-earned criticisms of Representative Barney Frank.

When the housing boom was going along merrily, Rep. Barney Frank was proud to be one of those who were pushing Fannie Mae and Freddie Mac into more adventurous financial practices in the name of "affordable housing."

In 2003 he said: "I believe that we, as the federal government, have probably done too little rather than too much to push them [financial institutions] to meet the goals of affordable housing and to set reasonable goals."

He added: "I want to roll the dice a little bit more in this situation towards subsidized housing."

In other words, when things were looking good, he was happy to acknowledge the role of the federal government in pushing the housing market in a direction it would have not have taken on its own.

Ultimately, those pushing for "affordable housing" through government interference in the housing market got what they wanted. In the aftermath of the 2008 Great Recession housing prices plunged for years across the nation. Too bad millions of people did not have jobs in which to earn money to buy these cheaper houses.

It was clear to me this was a bubble situation and it had to end, probably with a big crash in not too many years. For that reason, Deb and I quite buying real estate in 2005.

After moving to St. George in October 2009, we purchased our last, as of now, investment condo with cash left over from buying our house. The deal closed on March 23, 2010. Since this was well after the housing market crash, we got a good deal on the two bedroom, one bath unit in an eight unit complex.

You may think that in a small way we are rivaling Donald Trump in our real estate empire. I wish. What non-investors don't realize is the risk factor in any investment. Sure, in good economic times when all four condos are rented, we have a positive cash flow. But for several years beginning in 2008, one and sometimes two of the units were not occupied for months (occasionally many months) at a time. The Home Owners Association (HOA) did not say, "Your unit is not rented now, so you don't need to pay the monthly HOA fee." The utility companies were similarly unsympathetic. And don't even mention the local governments who demanded property taxes and other fees whether or not the unit was rented. Positive cash flows can easily go south.

Unfortunately the real estate empire Deb and I put together was not large enough to petition (via our voices and campaign contributions) the government and plead that we were "too large to fail" and request a taxpayer bailout. Or at least a government guaranteed (once again the taxpayer ultimately foots the bill) loan. Too bad for us crony capitalism (not to be confused with true free markets) exists only for those "too big to fail" or companies with friends in high places.

References

Allison, John A. 2012. "The Real Causes of the Financial Crisis." *Cato's Letter*. Winter.

Brittain, Dean. 2009. "Buyer Bust." *Liberty*. October.

Flynn, Mike. 2009. "Anatomy of a Breakdown." *Reason*. January.

Ho, Don. 2013. Wikipedia. Last modified September 18, 2013. http://en.wikipedia.org/wiki/Don_Ho.

McClaughry, John. 2011. "The Affordable Housing Scam." Book review of *Reckless Endangerment: How Outsized Ambition, Greed, and Corruption Led to Economic Armageddon* by Gretchen Morgenson and Joshua Rosner (2011). *Reason*. December.

Randazzo, Anthony. 2012. "The Financial Crisis Was the Result of Government Housing Policy." Interview with Peter Wallison. *Reason*. June.

Sowell, Thomas. 2009. "Blame Game." *Santa Barbara News-Press*. May 20.

Sowell, Thomas. 2011. "Liberal Land' lacks real logic." *The Spectrum*. November 27.

Is There Anything More Annoying Than a Family Christmas Letter?

Even being an agnostic for my adult life, I enjoy the Christmas holiday. I was raised as some sort of Christian. Most Sunday's mom and dad dragged me and the rest of the brood to the Congregational Church in Shafter. (Mom was raised as a Methodist, but there wasn't a Methodist Church in town. The Congregational Church made do in a pinch.) Later on I sporadically attended the local Southern Baptist Church with a neighborhood friend. As a teenager the Unitarian Universalist congregation held my spiritual attention for a while. The belief in God did not stick, although Christian ethics have served me well.

The holidays were fun as a kid, lots of presents, and everyone generally happy. No snow in Shafter but the Christmas spirit existed.

As an adult, I always got into the spirit of the season. For several years I served, along with Deb, as an usher at the Christmas services of the Santa Barbara Methodist Church to which Deb was a member. She was also the usher coordinator. You might wonder why an avowed agnostic would attend Christmas services and partake in the holiday. Two reasons. First, I was raised in a sort-of Christian household and Christmas was an important tradition. It was also important for wife number one and for Deb. I have nothing against positive traditions.

The second reason is tied to agnosticism. For me, agnosticism indicates the difference between belief and knowledge, rather than any specific claim to knowledge. In every, yes every, discussion I had with religious leaders (pastors, ministers, lay leaders) about God, the bottom line for them is *belief* in God. No one can empirically prove, or disprove, the existence of God. Basically, I don't much care. I, or anyone, can, and do, lead ethical lives without a belief in a supreme being. That's good enough for me.

However, there is the problem of Pascal's wager ("Pascal's Wager" 2013). Blaise Pascal, a 17th century mathematician, formulated his famous pragmatic argument for a belief in God. The argument goes as follows:

If you erroneously believe in God, and God does not exist, you lose nothing (assuming death is the absolute end). If you correctly believe in God, and God does exist, you gain everything (eternal bliss). However, if you correctly disbelieve in God, and God does not exist, you gain nothing (death ends all). Finally, if you erroneously disbelieve in God, and God does exist, you lose everything (eternal damnation).

So how should you bet? Regardless of any evidence for or against the existence of God, Pascal argued that failure to accept God's existence risks losing everything with no payoff for any of the four possible outcomes. The obvious best bet is to accept the existence of God. A big problem is that a person cannot simply will oneself to believe in something that is false for them.

Thus, I gain nothing in terms of eternal life by disbelieving, or refusing to believe due to lack of evidence, in a supreme being. But I stand to lose a great deal if God exists and I don't believe. Celebrating Christmas with good cheer is my little way of hedging my bet. I can envision part of a conversation at the pearly gates. "God, I know I repeatedly said I didn't have enough evidence to believe in you, but remember I enjoyed celebrating the birthday of your son. Maybe that counts for something? Come on, I was just joking about the lack of evidence part."

As much as I enjoy the Christmas holiday, there is one part that creates irritation like an itch you cannot scratch. No, I'm not referring to fruitcakes, although they are irritating. I'm talking about the family Christmas letter, tucked inside a nice card, extolling the wonders of family X during the past year. Yuck! I barely know family X and don't care that little Sally won an attendance award for sometimes showing up at her preschool.

As the Christmas holiday approached in 2005, Deb and I talked it over and decided to join the growing tsunami of Christmas letter senders. You know, a little something extra to annoy our family and friends. Being the family rebel, I wrote our Christmas missives and Deb edited and made suggestions. Unlike any Christmas letter we've had the misfortune to read, we decided that ours would have a different theme each year. In 2005 the theme was mystery stories. Here it is:

A Christmas Mystery
(2005)
by Tom & Deb

Louise, lounging atop her favorite armchair, was doing her super cat imitation with front legs outstretched. The fire crackled in the fireplace and nowhere was a hint of the approaching turn our lives would take. Suddenly came a knock at the door. Sonya began her awful howling. I yelled at the cat to "turn it down" and looked at Deb and said "your turn."

She answered the door. "Can I help you?"

"Ma'am, my name is Friday, Detective Sgt. Joe Friday. This is my partner Detective Bill Gannon. May we come in?"

"What's this about?"

"Ma'am, if you let us in we'll explain."

"Then come in."

"Deb, who's at the door?"

"Two detectives."

"Okay."

"Good evening ma'am, sir. We're here because we believe you may have information that could help us solve a horrendous crime. Someone, perhaps a thin man, stole a falcon."

"From Malta?"

"Yes, a Maltese falcon."

"We think you may have knowledge about this crime. Perhaps even in your subconscious. If you lead us through the major events of the past year, you might come up with something that could shed light upon this crime. That being said could you folks tell us where you were in January 2005?"

"Well," I began "we took a trip to Laughlin, Nevada with a friend, Jim Rockford. That guy sure has a lot of files. Anyway, we gambled, visited Nipton, and I came down with a cold. We also bought another investment condo in Laughlin."

"Did you see anything unusual on your trip?" asked Detective Gannon.

"Other than a lot of strange birds, not much. Deb, remember when those birds smashed into that telephone booth with a woman inside? Very strange."

Sgt Friday interrupted my rambling "Any other trips?"

"We went to Anza-Borrego State Park in March," Deb replied. "Some great hikes to Hellhole Canyon and Maidenhair Falls. And that one part where we walked up the 39 steps."

"Yeah, and that fellow we met who was really smart. He was a man who knew too much."

"That's interesting folks. How about other activities where you might have garnered some evidence about the crime?" Gannon wanted to know.

"Our coed softball team played a couple of seasons, spring and summer, last year. Deb and I played well and the team finished first and second respectively. I played third base and pitched a couple of games and Deb played the outfield. It was a lot of fun, but being about two decades older that just about everyone on the team we were pooped after the games. We would come home and take the big sleep."

"Any other trips?"

"Let's see. In July," Deb said "we visited Santa Cruz. We went on one hike in Big Basin Redwoods that went in a peculiar north by northwest direction. And, of course, we had to see the Mystery Spot."

"And then in September was our big Nevada, Arizona, and Utah trip. Wow! Of course the Grand Canyon was one stop. Amazing. I remember driving to our next destination and looking out the rear window and telling Deb that it was too bad we couldn't stay longer."

"Remember, sweetie, we then traveled through desert Navajo lands. When we stopped it was so quiet you could hear nothing but the silence of the lambs." Deb noted.

"You're right, if any lambs were there it was as if someone had murdered then in cold blood. Next was the spectacular slot canyon, called Antelope Canyon, in Navajo land near Page, Arizona. The color and lighting was unbelievable. It was as if we were in a star chamber."

"Anything else?" prompted Sgt Friday.

"A couple of days in Zion National Park. A very steep hike to Hidden Canyon above the Virgin River Valley. The hike was so steep I felt vertigo at some places. Walking along those cliff faces was scary and exciting, almost a fatal attraction. If you fell you would hit the ground with magnum force. One night we ate at the great little restaurant in Chinatown. Not many waiters, but the ones working were a few good men."

"Gosh, looking back the last year is almost like pulp fiction."

"You two have been extremely helpful," concluded Sgt. Friday. "From what you tell us it is clear that the Maltese Falcon can be found near water. I think where a point of land juts out into the ocean. And the only place that fits all the clues is Cape Fear. Detective Gannon and I will check it out. We will let you know if our hunch, based on your information, produces more than a seven percent solution."

And that, friends, is our 2005 Christmas Mystery.

As you can see, we made liberal use of references to mystery/cop books, movies, and TV series. We challenged each letter recipient to count the references. The correct answer is 22.

Putting aside all false modesty, that is a clever way to convey information about our activities for the year. Can you stand one more? Sure.

A Christmas Science Fiction Story
(2006)
by Tom & Deb

"Look out, look out. Sheesh, we barely missed the black hole."

"Not even close, I handled it like a starship trooper," Deb replied.

"Yeah, yeah, woman driver. We'll probably end up in the land that time forgot. We are truly lost in space. Speaking of forgot, did you remember to pack the soylent green for snacks?" said Tom. "I made sure that HAL had it on the list of supplies, so I'm sure it is here somewhere."

Leaning back in his custom fitted space chair Tom reminisces "Remember our January trip earlier this year to the Mojave Desert. That star cluster to our left reminds me of Zzyzx, the forgotten utopian town on the road to Primm. I'm glad we stopped there and walked the town and around the small lakes. Then the next day we did that nice hike up Caruthers Canyon to the abandoned mine."

"And the following day we braved very cold weather to hike up Teutonia Peak," says Deb. "Great views. And before that hike we made a stop at Kelso Depot. It was a beautifully restored railroad depot in the middle of the desert."

No one spoke for a while, we were on silent running. Then Louise, the cat, broke the silence (through her mind meld link with HAL) "Well, I certainly recall your leaving me alone in March to go jaunting off to Joshua Tree National Park. You guys came back with stories about how some rock formation looked like an alien. And how it was so quiet while hiking Hidden

Valley you could hear the flapping wings of a bird in flight. And the view from Mastodon Peak Trail. You two were so sickening with your stories, I thought there was some sort of invasion of the body snatchers and you guys were replicants. And besides, HAL tried to use the time machine to clean my litter box and made a mess of things. That stupid artificial intelligence couldn't figure out that poop, once out, does not return home."

"Hey, that's an idea. We can use the time machine to get out of this quadrant. I hear there a bunch of star wars in this area."

"No, that won't work. The timecop will arrest us," mumbled Tom.

HAL notes "the constellations to your left resemble ancient Indian petroglyphs, similar to some of those found in Inscription Canyon near Barstow. That is, as you humans described your June visit to said canyon to me."

Tom said, "Yeah, there were animal drawings, some abstract figures, and some that looked like little aliens. The weather was great and the petroglyphs were quite visible in that off-the-beaten path canyon."

"Speaking of paths, recall the harrowing experiences at Zion National Park in September? Yikes, water torture and vertigo. Hiking the Virgin River, in the river most of the way, what a cool experience. The narrow canyon with walls of rock several hundred feet high."

"It was fun," chimed in Deb. "Kind of a water world experience. And the next day we tackled Angel's Landing trail. Boy, that last half mile, a five foot wide trail with drop offs on either side of hundreds of feet. Scary."

"Walking that part as fast as I could felt like being a blade runner, albeit a very slow one since I was so scared, at the outer limits of fear. We must have been at least 2001 feet high," Tom noted. "The following day at Bryce Canyon was incredible. Remember our brief stay on forbidden planet? Bryce Canyon, with dozens of red spires reaching into the sky, reminds me of the forbidden planet."

"Unfortunately, September also saw the loss of Sonya the cat. She had more than 18 good years on the planet. That strange-eared veterinarian Dr. Spock assured us the force will be with her in cat heaven," Deb pointed out.

"Speaking of strange, recall that guy in our Monday evening yoga class. What is his name? Kirk, that's it James T. Kirk. Him and his hairy friend, Chewbacon. No, Chewbaca, always making weird noises at each class."

"Yeah, yoga is supposed to quiet the mind. Like our hike in Death Valley's Willow Creek Canyon in November. That was quiet. The day the earth stood still type of quiet. You could hear them, the bugs, crawling around."

"With all that hiking, we still managed to play two seasons of coed softball. Finished second in the summer season and first (or second, still to be decided as of press time) in the fall league. We played pretty well for two old folks."

"People," Louise the cat mused "none of this helps find our way home. It doesn't matter what you say, we are lost. Perhaps it is time to try plan 9 from outer space."

Tom said, "Don't get your fur balls in a tizzy. All we need to do is make a right turn at planet of the apes and then it's a clear shot to good old sol and earth. We'll be there quicker than a stepford wife can mix a cocktail. Overall, I'd say the past year has been a fantastic voyage. And that, friends, is our 2006 Christmas Science Fiction Story."

We once again included a little quiz in the story. How many references to science fiction books, movies, and TV series can you find? The correct answer is 29.

Each year since 2005 we have included a theme letter with our Christmas cards. Due to their overwhelmingly popularity, we now have a waiting list of people who want to be our friends just so they can receive our Christmas letter.

References

"Agnosticism." 2013. Wikipedia. Last modified October 22, 2013. http://en.wikipedia.org/wiki/Agnosticism

Garrison, Tom and Deb Looker. 2005. "A Christmas Mystery." December.

Garrison, Tom and Deb Looker. 2006 "A Christmas Science Fiction Story." December.

"Pascal's Wager." 2013. The Secular Web website. Last modified July 30, 2013. http://www.infidels.org/library/modern/theism/wager.html.

Sonya Deserved Better

One of the many interests Deb and I share is a love of animals. We were both raised with cats and dogs. I have never lived more than a few months in my entire life without a four-legged animal companion.

I believe we have an unwritten, but very real, contract with our animal companions. For their part, the animal simply lives its life and just be itself. The owner has much more responsibility. In a real sense I am the nanny state providing food, shelter, health care, exercise, discipline, and affection. It sounds unequal, but both parties benefit. Many studies clearly indicate animal companions benefit humans. For example, pet owners tend to have lower blood pressure and cholesterol levels, reduced stress, decreased mental fatigue, increased immune activity, and a sense of wellbeing ("Health Benefits of Pets" 2013). The animals benefit from the nanny state, companionship and affection, plus a safe environment—a truly win-win situation.

Kitten Sonya, 1988.

215

For most of our marriage, Deb and I owned two cats. We adopted Lucy as a kitten in March 1986. (See "Lucy the Vibes Monitoring Cat" in Chapter Four.) She was beautiful, smart, and an accomplished hunter. Approximately two years later a stray cat gave birth to a litter of kittens at Deb's workplace. She fell in love with one of the kittens and Sonya, a cute grey tabby, joined our household in April 1988.

Sonya was not the best hunter, nor an Einstein. However, she must have had dog genes somewhere in her DNA for she was extremely loyal. Deb and I would be working in the garden and ninja-like Sonya would appear to help.

Sonya brought us joy in the more than 18 years she was a member of our family. In mid-2006 she became seriously ill. The veterinarian gave us medicine to administer, and indicated she was quickly going through her nine lives. It was the beginning of the end. Deb and I knew we should end Sonya's life when the pain became obvious and expert's clearly state death is near.

Adult Sonya, 1990s.

At this point, I was 54 years old and Sonya had shared a full one-third of my life. By September, Sonya was in great pain and could barely move. It was time, I bundled her into the car—Deb could not bear to go—and Sonya and I took our last car ride to the vet's for her humane death. The vet asked if I wanted to be with Sonya as he administered the death cocktail. Thinking only of myself, I declined the offer through copious tears. I forgot the essence of loyalty is reciprocity. If you are loyal to me, I'll be loyal to you.

Upon arriving home, the impact of my action blossomed. I betrayed Sonya by not being with her at her death—I was cowardly. Sure, it would be ugly to see her put to death, but how ugly was it for her to die with a stranger?

Prior to this, all the cats with which Deb and I shared our life died suddenly when we were not there. We had no choice about being with them as they passed over to cat nirvana. Since Sonya's death only one cat, Louise, has been euthanized. Learning my lesson, I was there. Does it really make a difference? I convinced it does. The animal companion certainly knows its "parents." The last thing it sees should be the owner's face and the last feeling a soft pet.

I have been an agnostic for decades. But, if there is an afterlife, maybe a heaven, and animal companions are there, one of my first tasks after I die will be to find Sonya and apologize for abandoning her at her death.

Mahatma Gandhi ("Gandhi" 2013) noted that, "The greatness of a nation and its moral progress can be judged by the way its animals are treated." He was right and his judgment holds equally for individuals.

References

"Gandhi, Mahatma." 2013. Animal quote. Thinkexist.com website. Last modification unknown. http://thinkexist.com/quotations/animals/.

"Health Benefits of Pets." 2013. Centers for Disease Control and Prevention. Last updated July 28, 2010. http://www.cdc.gov/healthypets/health_benefits.htm.

Can I Make Up My Incompletes?

In college, a student can request, and usually receive, an "incomplete" for a course in which they have a decent excuse for not completing. I seldom did that, and when I did the incomplete was finished in record time.

Maybe there should be an incomplete grade for life projects in general. You know, that urge to learn Sanskrit in your Zen Buddhist period when you were 21. You rigorously studied the archaic language for at least two weeks, but somehow life got in the way and you never mastered Sanskrit. Would you like to have a chance to complete the project? I would like to complete some projects, others not so much.

In December 1980 I took a leave of absence from the UC Santa Barbara Political Science Department and from writing my PhD dissertation. In hindsight, I should have focused what energy I possessed and finished the damn thing. I had completed all my coursework, taken and passed my PhD exams, and written about two-thirds of the chapters for my dissertation. What happened? 1981 turned out to be a chaotic year: I got divorced (see "Divorce and the Great Santa Barbara Man Shortage of 1981" in Chapter Three for divorce details); had to move out of the UC Santa Barbara-subsidized married student housing since I was no longer married and no longer an active student; and had to find a job (see "Defeat the Devil: Diablo Canyon Nuclear Power Plant" and "New Job, New Love, New Life" stories in Chapter Three for details on finding employment.) Even given these challenges, I knew I would get back to it once things settled down—magical thinking on my part.

For the next decade, I occasionally dug out the dissertation and seriously thought about how great it would feel to be finished; but not great enough to actually do the work. Besides I was totally involved in leftist political activity in the 1980s. (See almost all stories in Chapter Three for details of my decade of political work).

Would I finish it now? Nope, too much work for very little gain. Having "Dr." in front of my name means little and at this point in my life I don't care.

By the mid-1990s our local Socialist Party group was dead and Deb and I were winding down our political work. We needed a new challenge. Sometime in March 1995, we chose to support the increasingly prominent idea in leftist circles—diversity. But being miscreants, we had a slightly different take on the meaning of diversity. For us it meant diversity in drinking. We bought a *Mr. Boston Official Bartender's and Party Guide* (64th edition, 1994) and decided to try each drink in the book. That's diversity. How long could that take? There are more than 1,200 drinks in the book. At one different drink a day that is about 3 ½ years. We could do that.

We enthusiastically embraced our task and on March 31, 1995 tried three different drinks. Great start. Each time we slurped a new drink, we would note the date and place of the drinking in the book so as to not duplicate our efforts. Unfortunately, we lagged a bit over the next few years. The last notation in *Mr. Boston* was January 2, 2003— a little less than eight years from the start. So what do you think? Six, seven hundred different drinks in eight years? Not quite, we sampled 40 different drinks. I'm embarrassed. We are not big drinkers, but that is a pitiful total.

This incomplete project needs closure. Deb and I decided to revisit this endeavor and do our best to complete it. Here is a toast from William Butler Yeats we both like.

> "The problem with some people is that when they aren't drunk, they're sober"

("Tulleeho Drinking Toasts" 2013).

Given the above, I complete most every project I begin. My family and friends will regale you with stories of my obsession with completing projects. I prefer to think of myself as focused.

References

Mr. Boston Official Bartender's and Party Guide. 1994. 64th edition. New York: Warner Books.

"Tulleeho Drinking Toasts." 2013. Tulleeho.com website. Last modification unknown. http://tulleeho.com/cb/toasts/.

Hell in the 'Hood

Why would anyone leave Santa Barbara? The Mediterranean climate means it never gets too hot or too cold (although it is fairly humid). Of course, there is not much in way of seasonal changes—boring. The white beaches set against the verdant Santa Ynez Mountains creates a soothing environment. All true. But, how about the narrow streets with crazy drivers? Or the lack of diversity with uber and more normal liberals dominating the political landscape locally and statewide during the past decade. And certainly don't overlook the extremely expensive cost of living. Depending upon which index is used, the cost of living in Santa Barbara is between 150 and 200 with the national average being 100 ("Cost of living in Santa Barbara, California" 2013A; "Cost of Living in Santa Barbara, California" 2013B). Up to twice the national average—yikes!

Even given the negatives Deb and I probably would have stayed in Santa Barbara if two things had not happened—neither over which we had any control. The first was a long-term trend. In March 1984 we bought a duplex on the eastside of Santa Barbara, a Spanish style, red tile roof charmer with hardwood floors, internal arches, and built-in cabinets. We loved the house and spent many weekends refinishing the floors, replacing the windows, and general upkeep on a house built in the 1920s. Up until the late 1990s we rented out the back portion and all was good at Casa Garrison/Looker.

Our Santa Barbara house, 2008.

Our neighborhood was mixed ethnicity, middle and working class—for a while. Everyone got along and we were friends with several neighbors. By 2000 or so, it began to radically change. Many people died or left, and were replaced by youngish working class, non-English speaking Hispanic families. It is difficult to know your neighbors if they do not speak the dominant language of the county—English. In addition, the toddlers were now teenagers. On both sides and in back of our house were large, loud Hispanic families. The parents on one side totally abdicated parental responsibility. That house was party central for years. Wanna-be gang bangers partied several times a week into the wee hours. Understand the lots were small; one house was only a few feet from the other. In addition, because of the temperate climate we did not have air conditioning; just open the windows for a nice evening breeze and the noise next door.

So why not politely ask the neighbors to cool it, especially late at night during the work week? We did, repeatedly, and were almost always met with stony looks and a mumbled "fuck you." Why didn't we call the cops about the noise and almost daily underage drinking? (As an aside, being libertarians Deb and I did not care if our neighbors drank and smoked pot almost every day. But we cared very much when the noise and shouting disrupted our lives.) We did, repeatedly. The police would show up 30 minutes later, joke around with the miscreants, and leave. No arrests—ever—for underage drinking or disturbing the peace. The police and parents did not care.

I must mention the public art that blossomed in our neighborhood around this time. No, not interesting statues or well-drawn murals on walls donated for that purpose. What our 'hood received was gang graffiti on most signposts, telephone poles, and vacant walls in the area. Deb and I had enough and took action. We bought spray paint that matched as closely as possible the background on which the graffiti appeared and painted over the thuggish "artwork." On silver poles, we painted over the graffiti with silver paint. We did this for months, often while the people we believed were the "artists" looked on. It was a bit tense, but the thug wannabes were not taking over our territory that easily. Did we receive any help from our neighbors? Not once. I imagine they were too afraid to challenge the gangs or simply did not care.

It was also pleasant to shop at the corner supermarket and most days not a single patron in the store spoke English. I'm all for bilingualism, but it behooves an immigrant to learn the dominant language of their new home. Why didn't I learn Spanish? I would if I lived in Latin America or Spain.

Deb and I began to stay longer than necessary at work because we dreaded coming home.

During the last few years we lived in Santa Barbara, to some degree I became what I detest—an angry person. Not all the time, but way too often while at home. I was not happy about this and neither was Deb. We both had stressful and jobs and instead of relaxing at home, we encountered a buzz saw of noise and obnoxious neighbors.

Hell—even we agnostics don't much like the sound of that. For many, hell is the idea of being immersed in burning oil for eternity. Others may see hell as being forced to watch an endless soccer game. My version of hell is having hellish neighbors forever—hell in the 'hood.

We seriously looked into moving to another neighborhood. Then things got worse. On July 31, 2009, Deb, the senior manager, and her entire Serials Division (approximately 35 people) at ABC-Clio were permanently laid off. Deb had been employed at ABC-Clio since 1979. She started as a production typist/proofreader and worked her way up to a division senior manager.

Now we were trapped in hell. It was very unlikely that Deb would find another job in Santa Barbara that paid anywhere near her previous salary. We had a large mortgage payment. If we relocated in the area we would be in the same financial bind. We could sell our house for a ton of money, but a replacement in the Santa Barbara area would cost a ton of money. No change except that we now had only one income. What to do?

The Chinese use two brush strokes to write the word "crisis." One brush stroke stands for danger; the other for opportunity. We were in a crisis and while there was no danger, we certainly had an opportunity. Never overly cautious, we decided to move to St. George, Utah. Life without adventure is boring. Deb had not found a new job and October 2, 2009 was my last day at work.

Moving made sense in many ways. The past fifteen years we had become desert rats. When we took time off from work, we almost always visited some desert location in California, Arizona, and Nevada. Since 2005 we spent considerable vacation time exploring southern Utah's red rock country—Zion National Park, Bryce Canyon, and many less crowded areas. Let's go.

Our St. George house, 2013.

In addition, the cost of living in St. George was below the national average ("Cost of living in St. George, Utah" 2013A; "Cost of living in St. George, Utah" 2013B), not 50 to 100% above as was Santa Barbara. We sold our Santa Barbara house and bought a new house, without a mortgage, in St. George. We were approaching early Social Security retirement age (62) and that coupled with the income from our rental properties and my measly pension from Santa Barbara County would be sufficient.

The question of us non-Mormons moving to the mother ship of the Church of Jesus Christ of Latter-day Saints (LDS) was a concern. But our experience with LDS and non-LDS neighbors and in daily encounters dispelled any worries. Our new 'hood was multi-ethnic with LDS and, surprisingly, many former LDS members. In four years in St. George, we have yet to experience the obnoxious neighbor syndrome.

References

"Cost of living in Santa Barbara, California." 2013A. Areavibes website. Last modification unknown. http://www.areavibes.com/santa+barbara-ca/cost-of-living/.

"Cost of living in Santa Barbara, California." 2013B. Sperling's Best Places website. Last modification unknown. http://www.bestplaces.net/cost_of_living/city/california/santa_ barbara.

"Cost of living in St. George, Utah." 2013A. Areavibes website. 2013. Last modification unknown. http://www.areavibes.com/st.+george-ut/cost-of-living/.

"Cost of living in St. George, Utah. 2013B." Sperling's Best Places website. Last modification unknown. http://www.bestplaces.net/cost_of_living/city/utah/st._george.

Those Who Can Do, Those Who Can't Write

Upon arriving in St. George in October 2009, Deb and I spent a few months learning the area and its wonders. We were amazed the county landfill was free for a reasonable amount of residential trash.

Or consider shopping carts. In Santa Barbara (at least at the Scolaris food store where we shopped most of the time) the stupid carts always had one wheel that was stuck or the bearings were shot and all you could do was push it in a circle around the periphery of the store. *All* the carts were dented and rusted and when you tried to pull one from the row, it never came out easily (if at all). By contrast, in St. George the shopping carts in *all* the stores are tricked out—polished chrome, wheels aligned and working properly, and they easily slide out of the row. It's a beautiful thing.

And while not yet mandatory, gun ownership in Utah is certainly not something to hide or be cautious about mentioning, as was the case in Santa Barbara. In Utah everybody owns guns. Yet Utah has a much lower murder rate per 100,000 residents, in most years twice as low, as gun control crazy California ("Death Penalty Information Center" 2013). The gun shop is great—mortars, RPGs (not really), everything a gun toting westerner could want. Yahoo!

On the down side, the streets of St. George were not solid gold, just gold plated. Since it was simple gold plating, we decided to look for fulfilling part-time jobs to supplement our income.

Early in 2010 I began applying for any position in which I was even remotely qualified: clerk at the county library; department assistant at Dixie State College (the local four-year college); junior appraiser in the county Assessor's Office; and private investigator with a nation-wide security and investigative company. (I always wanted to be a private investigator—sort of a Jim Rockford type of the "Rockford Files" fame). I interviewed for these and other positions. Alas, no one offered me a job. Was I overeducated? Too old? Smelled funny? Who knows? I was not deterred and by the end of 2010 began exploring other avenues.

Deb, on the other hand, interviewed for one job and was quickly hired in January 2010 as the Dixie State College library (soon to become Dixie State University) weekend circulation supervisor. It was the perfect job since she knew about libraries from her previous employment and it was part-time.

How about writing as a new career? I was an editor for 18 years, had published several articles, and liked to write. Why not since no one wanted to hire me.

In late 2010 I put together some essays. Within a two week span from the middle of December to the beginning of the New Year I had three opinion essays published—not a bad start.

My first essay "Limited government: Privatize liquor sales," was published (December 19, 2010) by *The Salt Lake Tribune*, a liberal-leaning important regional newspaper with a large circulation. In it I took the state government to task for being hypocritical. The state is dominated, and has been for decades, by conservative, limited government-loving Republicans. However, these politicians seem to think that limiting the sale of liquor and wine (other than in a restaurant or bar) to state-owned and operated liquor stores somehow coincides with limited government. Considerable evidence shows that contrary to what state politicians say, state-owned liquor stores do not alter the drinking habits of residents—a major blow to their argument. This is an example of politicians treating adults as children, not a very effective method to encourage and strengthen personal responsibility; a cornerstone of limited government thinking. This is a clear case of the nanny state gone wild, but it passes muster in a Mormon dominated state (Garrison 2010A).

My second essay, published December 26, 2010 in the local newspaper *The Spectrum*, compared Santa Barbara to St. George. The two cities are similar in population, orientation toward tourism, and have magnificent natural beauty. St. George does have a lower crime rate, much lower median gross rent, and very much lower cost of living. I concluded the essay with this passage:

> In St. George, like all small communities (and more so than Santa Barbara), what's available is what you make it. If you want to sit back and be entertained 100% of the time, you won't find it in St. George. The night life does not compare with Santa Barbara, no real bars here. But as you entered your fifth and sixth decades, night life fueled by alcohol is not much of a priority for most

folks. If you exert the effort, outdoor activities and many community events abound.

To my fellow St. George residents I say "You live in the real world equivalent of Disney's Fantasyland. Enjoy it" (Garrison 2010B).

My third essay, "Capitalism 101: Remember the Beanie Babies!" was published January 2, 2011 by *The Salt Lake Tribune*. It was a tribute to free markets as the engine of economic success using Ty Warner, the inventor of Beanie Babies, as an example. The importance of this message, often overlooked or distorted by today's politicians and media, deserves a lengthy look:

> Who, besides Warner, benefits from his entrepreneurship? Millions of Beanie Babies have been sold. That means cloth, tag, plastic bean, packaging, and plastic eye and nose manufacturers plus the assembly plants to put it all together made a profit. New workers were hired and current employees retained. Thus Beanie Babies ensured the employment of hundreds (thousands?) of employees not directly employed by Warner. With Warner's orders also came a need for more accountants, managers, janitors, secretaries, supervisors, lawyers to handle legal issues, etc. These companies prospered because of Warner's idea and because they all desired to make a profit.

> Truck drivers and shipping companies certainly profited from transporting the materials and finished product. And don't overlook the gas stations and refineries that sold fuel to the transportation companies. Again, jobs were created or, at least, maintained due to the silly little toys.

> How about Warner's employees? He began with two workers; now has approximately 300. How many of his employees have put their children through college due to Beanie Babies? Bought a new house?

> Beanie Babies did not simply appear in stores. Marketing was needed. How many jobs were created and/or maintained advertising Beanie Babies?

Taxes—Beanie Babies generated millions of dollars in sales tax, increased or maintained income taxes, corporate taxes, gasoline taxes (remember the transportation people), and others. Include tax preparers, bookkeepers, lawyers, and/or accountants. And government at all levels received increased tax revenue.

The simple fact that money circulated through the economic activity generated by the manufacture and selling of Beanie Babies helped the entire economy. The people who maintained their job, and new hires, spent money on food, housing, education, dentists, clothing, etc.—again stimulating the economy. All this due to a stuffed toy.

I imagine even the most liberal/left partisan gets the point by now. And I undoubtedly overlooked some of the connections generated by the manufacture and marketing of Beanie Babies. Ty Warner and Beanie Babies increased the world's wealth in absolute terms—wealth literally created out of nothing.

What motivates everyone involved in Beanie Baby economics? Altruism? No. The government told them to? No. Friendship? No. What motivated the thousands of people involved was self-interest. The individuals wanted a paycheck and the companies wanted a profit. Self interest in a free market equals increased wealth for everyone. Amazing. [Emphasis added.]

The Beanie Baby story is the quintessential free market story. Everyone gains through interlocking self-interest. Perhaps we should celebrate not denigrate the power of capitalism (Garrison 2011A).

All of a sudden I was a writer. To hell with a "regular" job. Only one problem, these essays were gratis. Reading the local newspaper gave me an idea. Deb and I went on at least one hike per month exploring southwest Utah and adjacent areas (southeastern Nevada and northern Arizona). I noticed that the staff outdoor/hiking writer for the local newspaper was a little weak. Since we went on a hike at least once a month, why not write-up our adventure and submit it to the local paper for a fee? That worked, and my first paid hiking story was published in *The Spectrum* on May 27, 2011 (Garrison 2011B). Since then my paid hiking stories appear once a month.

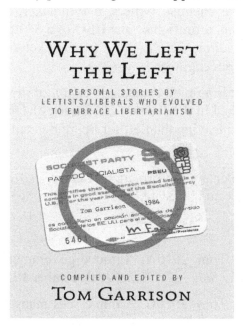

Why We Left the Left book cover.

I had other projects, in July 2012 I compiled, edited, and included my story in my published ebook, *Why We Left the Left: Personal Stories by Leftists/Liberals Who Evolved to Embrace Libertarianism*. (See "Why I Left the Left" in Chapter Four for my story.) The book examines a political question that intrigues almost everyone who studies, participates, or is interested in politics: "Why do people identify with a certain ideology and/or political party?" Numerous scholarly and popular books examine political ideology/party identification and why certain ideologies attract certain individuals. This book examines that question in two separate, yet joined phases. Why do people initially identify with the Left/liberalism and why do these same individuals abandon that ideology to evolve into libertarians? This inquiry is unique in its focus on 23 former liberals/leftists who become libertarians.

One popular conception of libertarians is that they are, for the most part, disgruntled old white guys. While that group is represented, more than 25 percent of the stories are from women and more than two-thirds are by people younger than 50. This gender and generational diversity extends to occupations—contributors include college students, law students, an attorney, a professional artist, public school teachers, a chemist, writers, a filmmaker, a law professor, a stay-at-home mom, a firefighter, the CEO of a $40 million company, a TV reporter, an editor, the CEO of a free market environmental think tank, and a research engineer.

The book is a much expanded version of my story "Why I Left the Left," published in the January 2000 issue of *Liberty*. I figured that I was not alone in leaving the Left for libertarianism—I was right.

References

"Death Penalty Information Center." 2013. Murder Rates Nationally and by State. http://www.deathpenaltyinfo.org/murder-rates-nationally-and-state#MRreg.

Garrison, Tom. 2010A. "Limited government: Privatize liquor sales." *The Sale Lake Tribune*. December 19.

Garrison, Tom. 2010B. "Couple sees many positives to living in St. George." *The Spectrum*. December 26.

Garrison, Tom. 2011A. "Capitalism 101: Remember the Beanie Babies!" *The Salt lake Tribune*. January 2.

Garrison, Tom. 2011B. "Expand your horizons." *The Spectrum*. May 27.

Garrison, Tom. 2000. "Why I Left the Left." *Liberty*. January.

Garrison, Tom. 2012. *Why We Left the Left: Personal Stories by Leftists/Liberals Who Evolved to Embrace Libertarianism.* Book Baby. July.

"The Rockford Files." 2013. Wikipedia. Last modified October 18, 2013. http://en.wikipedia.org/wiki/The_Rockford_Files.

Timeline:
Personal and Historical

[My age for almost the entire year is in parentheses next to the timeline year.]

1952

- January 18—I was born. Yahoo!

- November 4—Republican Dwight Eisenhower ("Ike") defeats Democrat Adali Stevenson 55.2% to 44.3 in the popular vote for president. This was the first presidential election since 1928 won by the Republicans.

1953 (1)

- April—James Watson and Francis Crick present their research indicating the double helix structure of the DNA molecule and opening the floodgates to genetic research. Little did I know at 15 months of age that this research would contribute greatly to the scope of science fiction books and movies which I have enjoyed since my late teens.

1955 (3)

- April 12—Jonas Salk announces his development of an effective polio vaccine. This injected vaccine, and the later oral vaccine developed by Albert Sabin, reduced polio to a seldom seen disease with only a few hundred cases each year worldwide. As recently as 1952 the US experienced an outbreak of 58,000 cases. Another boost to human longevity. Now we just need to figure out how to make those extra years productive and enjoyable.

- December 1—The Montgomery Bus Boycott began. This campaign, a seminal episode in the US Civil Rights Movement, started when a black woman, Rosa Parks, refused to surrender her bus seat to a white man. The boycott lasted more than a year and propelled the Civil Rights Movement into the forefront of America's conscience.

1956 (4)

- November 6—In a rematch of the 1952 presidential election, Republican Eisenhower defeated Democrat Adali Stevenson and increased his popular vote margin to 57.4% to 42%.

1960 (8)

- May 9—The US Food and Drug Administration announced pending approval of the first oral contraceptive, paving the way for the sexual revolution of the 1960s (yippee!). By 1965, 6.5 million women were using the pill. This number increased for decades. Questions about the safety of oral contraceptives began early and continue to this day.

- November 8—In one of the closest elections in US history, Democrat John Kennedy defeats Republican Richard Nixon. Kennedy received 49.7% of the popular vote to Nixon's 49.5%. In raw numbers this means Kennedy was elected with a lead of 112,827 out of more than 68 million votes cast.

1961 (9)

- May 5—Piloting *Freedom 7*, Alan Shepard become the first American, and second person behind soviet cosmonaut Yuri Gagarin on April 12, 1961, to enter outer space. Shepard's mission was a 15-minute suborbital flight. Ten years later, Shepard became the fifth person to walk on the moon during the Apollo 14 mission.

- Spring 1961—"The Space Traveler," my science fiction story was published in *Golden West Stories*, a Richland Elementary School mimeograph publication. While the style was a bit stilted, the tale contained the essential element of a space opera—a gallant hero fighting horrible space monsters.

- August 13—The German Democratic Republic (East Germany) begins construction of the Berlin Wall. The East German government claimed the Wall was erected to prevent western "fascist elements" from influencing East German. In reality, the Wall circumvented East Bloc emigration and defections to the West. Before the erection of the Wall approximately 3.5 million East Germans fled to the West. During the Wall's existence, from 1961 to 1989, the flood of eastern immigration was reduced to a trickle—about 5,000 people attempted to escape over or under the Wall. Between 100 and 200 were killed in the attempt.

1963 (11)

- November 22—President John F. Kennedy assassinated in Dallas, Texas. Vice president Lyndon Johnson becomes president. I am one of the few people who do not have an indelible memory of where I was (most likely in school) or my reaction to this tragedy.

1964 (12)

- February 7—The British invasion commences when the Beatles deplane at JFK Airport in New York City. They give several concerts and appeared on The Ed Sullivan Show producing a record TV audience. While I very much liked their music, my soul will always belong to the original bad boys of rock 'n roll—Mick Jagger and the Rolling Stones.

- August 7—Congress passes the Gulf of Tonkin Resolution (with only two dissenting votes in the Senate, it was unanimous in the House of Representatives) authorizing President Johnson, without a declaration of war, to use conventional military forces in Southeast Asia. In 1961 the US had about 2,000 military personnel in South Vietnam; by the end of 1964 the number was 16,500. This number grew to more than 535,000 in 1968. The US anti-war movement grows in proportion to the number of US troops deployed.

- November 3—In the fifth most lopsided presidential election (in terms of popular vote) Democrat Lyndon Johnson defeats Republican Barry Goldwater 61% to 39% of the popular vote.

1966 (14)

- June 1—I earned a "Future Scientist of America" Award in the 8th grade from the National Science Teachers Association.

- Summer—In my first foray into the adult work world I worked as a "jigger," and sometimes "sewer," in an onion packing shed in my hometown of Shafter, California. I earned $104.26 for a couple weeks work. I continued this summer work—later years in potato "sheds," moving irrigation pipes, and picking peaches—until 1969 when I topped out at $541.36.

- Fall—Begin my freshman year at Shafter High School. I earned an athletic letter in "C" football as a lean, mean 135 pound tackle. The team compiled a record of two wins and five loses.

1967 (15)

- Spring—I earned an athletic letter in "C" track and field for pole vault and discuss. In at least two cases I can document, I won 1st place in both events in one meet. I know, a strange combination.

- Fall—Begin my sophomore year at Shafter High School and earned an athletic letter in "B" football as a tackle. The team finished with a two (wins) and seven record—a long season.

1968 (16)

- Spring—I earned an athletic letter in "A" (varsity) track and field for pole vault. Thanks to my effort, and that of others, the varsity team won the league championship.

- April 4—Civil rights leader and nonviolence advocate Martin Luther King, Jr. is assassinated in Memphis, TN. A big blow to all Americans.

- August 14—The Final Judgment of Divorce is granted and my parents are no longer married. They had been squabbling for years and this was a good thing.

- Fall—Begin my junior year at Shafter High School. In mid-February 1969 my mom and I move to Bakersfield, California and I attend West High School (Bakersfield).

- November 5—In a close election, Republican Richard Nixon defeats Democrat Hubert Humphrey and American Independent candidate George Wallace. Nixon received 43.4% of the popular vote, Humphrey 42.7, and Wallace 13.5%.

1969 (17)

- February 18—I was suspended for two days from Shafter High School for smoking on campus. Luckily my mother and I were in the process of moving to Bakersfield, so I never had to tell her that I was suspended. I guess she knows now.

- Spring—I earned an "A" (varsity) athletic letter in track and field at West High School (Bakersfield) for pole vault.

- July 20—The American spacecraft *Eagle* lands on the moon with astronauts Edwin "Buzz" Aldrin and Neil Armstrong while Michael Collins orbits the moon in the command module. Armstrong becomes the first person to walk on the moon with the words "One small step for man, one giant leap for mankind."

- August 15-18—Woodstock Music and Art Fair in Bethel, New York. Largest gathering (300,000 people) for peace and love in the "hippy" era.

- Fall—Begin my senior year at West High School (Bakersfield).

- October 15—National Moratorium to End the War in Vietnam. I attended the march and rally in Los Angeles. While staunchly anti-war I was disturbed to see signs and hear chants ("Ho, Ho, Ho Chi Minh, the NLF is going to win") which were more pro-National Liberation Front (South Vietnamese communists) than anti-war. I was against the war, but not a communist sympathizer.

1970 (18)

- January 19—(Day after my 18th birthday) I began a 2 ½ year battle with the Selective Service System (The Draft) over my claimed conscientious objector status. At any point during this struggle I could have claimed a student deferment (2-S) or found to be unfit for military service (4-F) due to poor eyesight, but I chose to fight for conscientious objector status.

- March 11—I filed Form 150 (claiming conscientious objector status) with the local Selective Service System (The Draft).

- April 22—First Earth Day. This, now annual, event was founded by Senator Gaylord Nelson as an opportunity for environmental teach-ins.

- May 20—I received a $200 scholarship from the West (Bakersfield) High School Faculty Club.

- Spring—I earned a second "A" (varsity) athletic letter in track and field at West High School for pole vault.

- June—I received a $100 scholarship from the Bakersfield Unitarian Universalist Fellowship. This month I also began volunteer work as a draft counselor with the Kern County Draft Information Service.

- June 12—I graduated from West (Bakersfield) High School.

- September—I began the BA program in Political Science at California State College, Bakersfield. I financed my education with student loans, grants, work-study and my wife's employment (after our marriage on June 24, 1972). My parents could not afford to pay for my college education.

- October—I organized the Cal State Bakersfield Draft Information Service. I served as director and draft counselor until the draft ended on June 30, 1973.

1971 (19)

- January 8—I am classified 1-A (available for military service) by the Selective Service System (The Draft).

- March 4—I had a personal appearance before the local Selective Service System Board (The Draft) to discuss my conscientious objector (CO) status. CO status was denied and I was classified as 1-A (available for military service).

- August 5—The Draft lottery is held for my birth year. Men with my number, 51, will certainly be drafted (the lower the number out of 365, the better chance of being drafted).

- December 11—Libertarian Party founded in Colorado Springs, Colorado in the home of David Nolan.

1972 (20)

- 1972—I joined the War Resisters League, USA. I kept this membership until the mid-1990s.

- 1972—I received a scholarship from the Bakersfield Unitarian Universalist Fellowship.

- April 26—The Selective Service System (The Draft) local Appeal Board denied my appeal for conscientious objector status and continued my status as 1-A (available for military service).

- May 31—The State Director of the Selective Service System (The Draft) requests that the local Board reopen my classification, and reinstating my rights of personal appearance and appeal.

- June 13—I took a pre-induction physical for the Selective Service System (The Draft) in Fresno, California. This was a final step for men classified 1-A (available for military service) before being drafted. I was found to be unfit for military service (4-F) due to poor eyesight.

- June 24—I married my first wife, Lorraine Denise Irwin, at the California State College, Bakersfield campus. The campus opened in September 1970 and this was the first marriage there. I was 20 and Lori was 18. "They" said it wouldn't last. They were right.

- July 6—The Selective Service System (The Draft) reclassifies me as 4-F (not qualified for military service). I knew from the beginning of this struggle with the Selective Service System (The Draft) that once I took a physical I would be classified 4-F due to poor eyesight.

- August 18—I completed a short class and became a Registration Deputy County Clerk in Kern County, California. This means is that I could legally register voters in Kern County. I did so, and not once committed any form of fraud.

- November 7—National election day. After working diligently as a foot soldier for many months in the Bakersfield campaign for George McGovern, my candidate is on the wrong side of landslide in the presidential election against Richard Nixon. Nixon won 61% of the popular vote and McGovern garnered 38%. I was not a happy camper.

- December 20—I received a $300 Pelletier Foundation Scholarship.

1973 (21)

- January 22—The Supreme Court in a landmark decision, *Roe v. Wade*, ruled that the right to privacy under the due process clause of the 14th amendment extended to a woman's decision to have an abortion. While not an absolute right to obtain an abortion any point in a pregnancy, it struck down many state laws prohibiting all abortions. This decision prompted a national debate over the parameters of abortion that continues to this day.

- February—I served as campaign manager for Jim Leek in his first foray into local politics. Jim ran for Bakersfield City Council from the Seventh Ward. Election day was February 27 and the turnout was low, 30.4% or 1,359 voters. Jim, the most liberal candidate in the field, finished third out of three candidates and received 171 votes (12.6%). Later that year I conducted an extensive project using survey research to analyze the voting in that election for a Political Science class at California State College, Bakersfield.

- April 11—Lori and I wrote a protest letter to the Internal Revenue Service that we sent along with our (1972) federal tax return. The letter noted that we were law-abiding citizens and would pay our full federal tax, but did not want our money to fund military spending. This was the first of 11 consecutive years of including a protest letter and refusing to pay some of the federal taxes due for the 1981 to 1983 tax years.

- June 30—The last man is inducted into the Army through The Draft.

- August—Lori and I visited the Institute for the Study of Nonviolence in Palo Alto, California for two days. The Institute was founded by Joan Baez and Ira Sandperl. I had been interested in nonviolent direct action as a means of social change since my late teens. That interest continues today. My never completed PhD dissertation was titled "Nonviolence and Democracy: Exploring the Linkages."

- December—I received a $300 Pelletier Foundation Scholarship.

1974 (22)

- June 9—I graduated magna cum laude with a BA degree in Political Science and minor in Sociology from California State College (now University), Bakersfield (3.64 GPA).

- July 1—Lori and I began The Great Cross Country Trip in a borrowed van. In 39 days we traveled through 26 states and ended up at our starting point, Bakersfield, California. Our easternmost destination was Boston. Along the way we visited several friends and made some new friends. What a great country—friendly people everywhere and much natural beauty. Adventure in every state, the trip of a lifetime.

- August 9—Richard Nixon, the 37th president of the US, resigns from office in the wake of the two-year long Watergate break-in, cover-up, and investigation. He is the first president in American history to resign.

- September—I began the MA degree program in Political Science at the University of California, Davis. I financed my education with loans, grants, and a teaching assistant position for both years at UC Davis. My parents could not afford to pay for my college education.

1975 (23)

- 1975—I joined the American Political Science Association and kept this membership until the late 1990s.

- April 4—Microsoft is founded by Bill Gates and Paul Allen in Albuquerque, NM. Microsoft and many other companies made major contributions to the computer revolution that today provides almost instant access to people around the world and immense computing power in hand-held devices. Reality is now the stuff of science fiction only 30 or 40 years ago.

- April 30—The fall of Saigon, South Vietnam ends the Vietnam War and more than 20 years of almost non-stop fighting in Southeast Asia. The Communist Viet Cong and the North Vietnamese Army were victorious. However, within 20 years and the fall of the Soviet Union and its Eastern European allies many free market reforms and cutbacks of government controls were instituted in unified Vietnam. So who ultimately won?

1976 (24)

- June 18—I graduated with a MA degree in Political Science from the University of California, Davis (3.74 GPA).

- August 3—Under the provisions of the Freedom of Information Act, I requested copies of any and all files maintained by the Federal Bureau of Investigation (FBI) relating to me. (See September 2, 1976 for their reply.)

- August 20—I earned a Community College Instructor Credential for Government (Theory and Practice, Local and International) from the California Community Colleges (valid for life).

- September 2—The Federal Bureau of Investigation (FBI) replies to my August 3, 1976 Freedom of Information Act request by saying that "... a search of the index to our central records system revealed no information to indicate that you have been the subject of an investigation by the FBI."

- Fall—My Zen period begins. For the next few years I study Zen Buddhism and occasionally meditate. It is difficult to still the mind (well, mine anyway).

- September—I began the PhD program in Political Science at the University of California, Santa Barbara. I financed my education at UC Santa Barbara with loans, grants, various teaching and research positions, and my wife's employment. My parents could not afford to pay for my college education.

- November 2—Democrat Jimmy Carter wins a close presidential election over Republican Gerald Ford; 50% to 48%. The electoral vote was the closest since 1916.

1977 (25)

- Spring and summer—I taught an American Government class at Allan Hancock Community College (Lompoc campus) for the spring and summer semester.

- March—I won a $5.00 gift certificate award for my poem "Shoes" in *The Egocrat* poetry contest. *The Egocrat* was published by Merlin's Bookshop, Isla Vista, CA. Isla Vista is the student community adjacent to UC Santa Barbara.

- June—I won Honorable Mention for my poem "Paths" in *The Egocrat* poetry contest. *The Egocrat* was published by Merlin's Bookshop, Isla Vista, CA. Isla Vista is the student community adjacent to UC Santa Barbara.

- August 3—Lori and I are on our way to the 10th Annual War Resisters League (WRL) Conference in Olympia, Washington. A 13-day vacation highlighted by four days of meeting and getting to know the heavyweights in the peace movement. One of the highlights was meeting and having a couple of long discussion with Dave McReynolds, a long-time WRL and Socialist Party USA activist.

1978 (26)

- September—I received, with Professor J. Theodore Anagnoson, a University of California Instructional Development Grant for $2,700 for an evaluation of the Undergraduate Political Science Program at UC Santa Barbara. The result, published in September 1979, was a "Report on an Evaluation of the Undergraduate Political Science Program at the University of California, Santa Barbara."

- October 16—At the first Graduate Students Association (GSA) Council meeting of the school year I, the Political Science

Department's representative, proposed a motion opposing Proposition 6 (Briggs Initiative) that was appearing on the November ballot. The vote was unanimous. The Briggs Initiative required that any gay or lesbian teacher could be fired on those grounds alone. The Initiative lost in the November 7 general election 58% to 42 %. This was the first political stance ever taken by the GSA. But not its last.

- November 7—At the monthly GSA Council meeting I authored and ushered through (ten to nine vote) a resolution formally legitimizing the GSA Council to take positions on political issues. The resolution read "The GSA Council shall decide, on an ad hoc basis, which issues are suitable for consideration. This will include, but not be limited to, taking stands on particular political issues by a majority vote."

1979 (27)

- April 19—Elections for the GSA Executive Committee. I assembled a slate of candidates as the "People Opposed to Oppressive Politics" (POOP) Party that won all six offices. The POOP Party was organized a few months prior to the election. I was elected as Vice President for Academic Affairs—the only candidate to not win unanimously, even though I ran unopposed. Political rabble rouses are not loved by all.

- May 7—On my initiative the UC Santa Barbara Graduate Students Association (GSA) Executive Committee endorsed the nationwide boycott of Coors beer. A letter was written to the *Daily Nexus* (UC Santa Barbara student newspaper) explaining our position and encouraging all students to support the boycott.

- Fall—I was appointed as a Political Science Department Teaching Associate at UC Santa Barbara. I taught a class in Political Interest Groups at the Ventura, California extension campus of UC Santa Barbara.

- September—I received a University of California Academic Senate Patent Fund Grant for my dissertation research. The title was 'Nonviolence and Democracy: Exploring the Linkages."

- September—I was Co-Principal Investigator with Professor J. Theodore Anagnoson of "Report on an Evaluation of the Undergraduate Political Science Program at the University of California, Santa Barbara." This was a year-long research into the strengths and weaknesses of the undergraduate Political Science Program at UC Santa Barbara. Published and distributed by the Political Science Department.

- October—First issue of *The Monthly Planet*, UC Santa Barbara Graduate Students Association (GSA) bi-monthly newsletter is published. I was the driving force behind the newsletter and served as its co-editor. I also wrote an advice column (entirely fictional) titled "Ask Dr. Zhivago" and several articles over a one-year span.

- December 24—The Soviet Union sends regular military troops into Afghanistan at the request of the pro-Soviet Afghan government. This request for military assistance was in response to the stepped-up guerrilla campaign by anti-regime Mujahedeen rebels backed by the United States. This was the Soviet Union's Vietnam. The bloody civil war lasted until 1989 when the last Soviet troops departed the country.

1980 (28)

- Winter—I was appointed as a Political Science Department Teaching Fellow at UC Santa Barbara. In addition, my marriage, almost always shaky, deteriorates this year.

- January 23—On my initiative the UC Santa Barbara Graduate Students Association (GSA) Council unanimously endorsed the Nestle products boycott. The January 25, 1980 *Daily Nexus* (UC Santa Barbara's student newspaper) reported on this and quoted me as saying "They [Nestle] sell a powdered milk formula in parts of the world where clean water is unavailable, illiterate mothers can't read the instructions on the label, and family incomes may be so low that 20-80 percent of the entire family income is spent on the infant." Sounds like something I would say.

- January 31—I gave a major anti-draft speech at an Anti-Draft Rally before crowd of more than 500 people at UC Santa Barbara.

- November 4—Republican Ronald Reagan defeats incumbent Democrat President Jimmy Carter in a landslide, 51% to 41% (with independent John Anderson receiving 7%).

- December—I ended active participation in the PhD Political Science program at the University of California, Santa Barbara. Finished as ABD (All But Dissertation) (3.97 GPA) It was time to leave the ranks of career graduate students.

1981 (29)

- January 2—My wife, Lori, moved out. This led to a final divorce decree on October 29, 1981. During the year I fell in love with just about every woman I knew or new woman I met.

- February 13—I landed a job as Peace Action Coordinator of The Gathering Place, a peace resource center in Santa Barbara. During my tenure I organized and co-organized several local peace and political events.

- September 20—I was arrested with 1,959 other people (over a ten-day period) for blockading and unlawful assembly at Diablo Canyon Nuclear Power Plant. For months I had trained, and trained others, for this act of civil disobedience through the statewide Abalone Alliance and my Isla Vista affinity group, "Infinity." I spent three days in "jail" in the gym at Cuesta College, near San Luis Obispo, California.

- September 22—I appeared before Judge Wood of the San Luis Obispo Municipal Court and pled "no contest" to blockading and unlawful assembly at Diablo Canyon Nuclear Power Plant. I read a statement about civil disobedience and nuclear power plants, paid a $20 fine, and left.

- September 28—I quit my job at The Gathering Place. The governing board did not think it appropriate for a Peace Action Coordinator to practice civil disobedience at Diablo Canyon Nuclear Power Plant. (Isn't that exactly what a peace activist should do?)

- October 12—I began work at the International Academy at Santa Barbara as the Managing Editor of *Current World Leaders*. I stayed at the International Academy until April 2000.

- October 24—An "Untying the Knot Celebration" party celebrating our divorce is hosted by Lori and me. Great fun was had by all.

- October 29—The divorce with my first wife, Lorraine Denise Irwin, becomes final. When Lori and I got married "they" said we were too young and it would not last. "They" were right!

- November—I joined a newly purchased house collective (named TRACT HOUSE) with 5 other folks (including two kids) in the Santa Barbara suburb of Goleta. This was a collective ownership and living arrangement. We were going to make the ordinary revolutionary. Owning a home is ordinary, but a home owning political collective is revolutionary. Our long range plan was to use TRACT HOUSE as a nonviolent revolutionary base camp in Goleta. We were like a guerilla group in the countryside—getting to know the territory and people and building a solid base from which to spread the revolution. More specifically we were all going to get involved in Goleta politics.

1982 (30)

- January—Deb and I joined the Santa Barbara Tenants Union.

- March—I moved out of TRACT HOUSE for two reasons: Deb and I could save more money for a down payment on our own house by living in her apartment with a roommate; and seven people (including Deb and two kids) in a four bedroom tract house was a bit crowded.

- March 8—International Women's Day. Oh, I also married Deborah Ann Looker. Yea!

- Spring—I joined the Santa Barbara Chapter of the Gray Panthers. I kept the membership until the early 1990s.

- Spring—I joined the American Civil Liberties Union and kept this membership until the late 1990s.

- May 22—I participated in a debate on "Nonviolence as a Theory of Social Change—How Effective?" in the citadel of radicalism—Berkeley, California. I represented People for a Nuclear Free Future, Santa Barbara (the local group organizing against Diablo Canyon Nuclear Power Plant; it was part of the larger state-wide Abalone Alliance) and argued for the efficacy of nonviolent direct action. Howard Ryan representing the East Bay Anti-Nuclear Group argued against a purely nonviolent approach. I clearly won the debate, but I don't think Howard agreed.

- July—Deb, me, Scott and others organize a Santa Barbara Chapter of the War Resisters League. The Chapter is very active with considerable focus on organizing war tax resistance the next few years. I served in various offices over the next three years.

- October—The Santa Barbara Peace Fund Escrow Account is organized by the Santa Barbara War Resisters League chapter. I served as a member of the Board of Trustees of the Santa Barbara Peace Fund Escrow Account for 10 years. The Account was established as a repository for individuals to deposit phone tax and income tax money that was not being paid to the federal government—a form of war tax resistance.

1983 (31)

- January 7—Deb and I joined the Socialist Party, USA.

- April 15—A war tax resistance press conference/protest at the main Post Office was organized by the Santa Barbara War Resisters League. This was the culmination of months of organizing and public campaigning including several newspaper articles, three newspaper ads, radio interviews, outreach to other groups, a war tax resistance counseling service, and having information tables at several events. I, along with seven other war tax resisters, read a personal statement about my war tax resistance and gave it to the media. As of April 15 the Santa Barbara Peace Fund Escrow Account had 18 depositors and $3,156.27 in resisted taxes.

- June—The Santa Barbara Peace Fund Escrow Account had $4,382 and 23 depositors.

- July 4—Deb and I attended the annual California Socialist Party campout at Big Sur, California. A three-day event held each year on the July 4th weekend to gather, exchange ideas, and meet new comrades. This was our first campout. We attended each year through 1992 and often led discussion groups. We also encouraged many Santa Barbara comrades and friends, family members, and assorted fellow travelers to attend—and many did.

- Fall—Deb and I were two of the founding members of the Santa Barbara Chapter of the Socialist Party, USA. I served in various offices of the local chapter over the next 10+ years. For 11 years this group sponsored dozens of local and statewide events; worked with a variety of local progressive groups; actively participated in state and national socialist organizations; was the core for my two Santa Barbara City Council campaigns; worked tirelessly for local, state, and national progressive candidates and issues; published a bimonthly newsletter (*LEFT OUT*) for six years; and educated hundreds of folks about socialism (a good thing at the time—yes, still of value because education is always good).

1984 (32)

- March 16—Deb and I buy our first house, a duplex in Santa Barbara.

- March 19—Last day as tenants—yea!

- Spring—I began serving on the Board of Directors of the South Coast Information Project. My Board membership ended in 1986 and I remained an organization member until 1990.

- Spring—I was appointed by the Santa Barbara City Council to serve on the Rental Housing Mediation Task Force. This group gathered information about landlords and tenants and mediated disputes between tenants and landlords (but only for landlords and tenants who voluntarily used the service).

- June 22—After months of unreasonable demands and two illegal retaliatory rent increases by our (last) landlord, "Icky", Deb and I sue him in Santa Barbara Small Claims Court for recovery of our cleaning deposit and other charges (e.g., $200 for bad faith actions on his part). We bested him and on this date received a judgment in our favor of $593.54 plus $9 court costs—we had requested $626.19.

- November 2—Our last landlord, "Icky," appealed his loss in Small Claims Court (June 22, 1984) to Superior Court. He hired an attorney and I acted as our attorney. On this date Deb and I again won and received a judgment of $365.27 for damages, $10 for bad faith by the defendant, plus $9 for court costs.

- .November 6—Capping off the year, on November 6 Republican President Ronald Reagan defeated Democrat Walter Mondale 59% to 41% in a second landslide victory. Mondale did manage to win his home state, Minnesota, and Washington, DC. While, as socialists, we did not support those slightly to the left Democrats, the scope of Reagan's victory gave pause to those who thought the nonviolent democratic socialist revolution was imminent.

- December 4—"Icky", our last landlord and twice loser in court, did not pay the judgment against him and we had to take further legal action to receive our money. On this date he finally paid what he owed.

1985 (33)

- January—My campaign committee began serious organizing for the Santa Barbara City Council election in November. My first foray as a candidate into "adult" electoral politics. During the campaign I attended 8-10 public candidate forums, appeared on TV and radio, and met with hundreds of people individually and in groups/organizations.

- January—Deb begins serving on the Santa Barbara Gay & Lesbian Resource Center Board of Directors (the first heterosexual or "breeder"). She served until 1988.

- January—By January I (Deb and I for the 1982 tax year) had paid all back federal taxes plus interest and penalties that were not paid due to war tax resistance.

- January 17—My City Council campaign's first fundraising letter mailed.

- January—I was elected Secretary of the Rental Housing Mediation Task Force.

- March 11—Soon after being elected as General Secretary of the Communist Party of the Soviet Union on March 11, Mikhail Gorbachev began a series of reforms attempting to save the tottering Soviet economy. Included were Glasnost, or increased openness and transparency in government institutions and some degree of freedom of speech; and Perestroika, a restructuring of and decentralizing the economy. While Gorbachev had no intention of undermining the fundamental control of the

247

economy and politics by the Communist Party, the reform movement took on an independent life and within six years the Soviet Union had dissolved. The mother ship of worldwide communism was dead.

- May 16—I formally announce my candidacy for Santa Barbara City Council on the steps of City Hall.

- July 15—I registered to vote with the socialist-feminist California Peace and Freedom Party—the only socialist party with ballot status in California.

- November 5—Election day for my first run for Santa Barbara City Council. I finished sixth out of six candidates; received 3,736 votes (I certainly don't have that many friends), and raised $5,447. 17.7% of the voters chose me as one of their three choices (three open seats)—almost 1 in 5. Not bad for a first time openly socialist candidate at the height of the Reagan Presidency and in his adopted home town.

1986 (34)

- January—I was elected Vice Chairperson of the Rental Housing Mediation Task Force by other Task Force members.

- February 11—I was elected to the Santa Barbara Tenants Union Steering Committee and Chair of the Office and Tenants Rights Information Committee.

- Spring—1st Annual Santa Barbara Socialist Sports Festival and Bar-B-Que sponsored by the Socialist Party/Solidarity, Santa Barbara Chapter. The sports festival, held at our house, was clearly the highlight of the spring season for Santa Barbara area socialists and fellow travelers. It featured six events (table tennis, checkers, darts, basketball, cube building, and water balloon toss) and top three finishers each won a prize. As a nod to political correctness, all participants received a certificate suitable for framing. It was great fun to observe the underlying competitive nature of many local socialists. This annual event lasted for five years.

- Spring—Deb and I join and spend months and much effort working with the Central Coast Citizens Against LaRouche (No on Proposition 64) campaign. This statewide proposition was designed to attack AIDS patients by allowing health officials to quarantine them. It was defeated by a margin of 71% to 29% in the November 4 election.

- May 17—Deb and I were award presenters and helped organize at 3rd annual "The Prom That Dare Not Speak Its Name" sponsored by the Santa Barbara Gay & Lesbian Resource Center. Deb and I were one of the first heterosexual couples (aka "breeders") to attend this event. Deb served on the Santa Barbara Gay & Lesbian Resource Center Board of Directors (the first heterosexual and first socialist) from 1985 through 1988.

- October—I gave a talk about rent control and the No on Prop 64 Campaign to the Socialist Society at the University of California, Santa Barbara. About 20 people attended.

- November 4—Rent control loses in Santa Barbara election 58% to 42%. This is the 3rd loss at the polls for rent control in eight years. Through our membership in the Santa Barbara Tenants Union, Deb and I worked diligently for months for rent control. Proposition 64 (the LaRouche initiative), a statewide proposition designed to attack AIDS patients by allowing health officials to quarantine them was defeated by a margin of 71% to 29%. Deb and I spent considerable time and effort on this campaign.

- November—I had a book review titled "An Independent Socialist Ticket or Support of Liberal Democrats?" published in *The Socialist* (newsletter of the California Socialist Party). The book by Eric T. Chester was titled *Socialists and the Ballot Box: A Historical Analysis* (Praeger: 1985).

- December 16—Twenty-nine applicants, including me, vie for one Santa Barbara City Council vacant seat. (The seat was vacated when a sitting Council member won election to the Santa Barbara County Board of Supervisors.) The "campaigning" for the seat had begun election night, November 4. I filed an application and spoke before the Council, but, surprise, was not appointed.

1987 (35)

- January—My campaign committee began serious organizing for the Santa Barbara City Council election in November. My second run for the City Council. During the campaign I attended

6-8 public candidate forums, appeared on TV and radio, and met with hundreds of people individually and in groups/organizations.

- February—My City Council campaign's first fundraising letter is sent out

- April 10—Formal announcement of my candidacy for Santa Barbara City Council on the steps of City Hall.

- May—The first issue of *LEFT OUT*, bimonthly newsletter of the Santa Barbara Socialist Party/Solidarity Chapter is published. The newsletter emphasized the "news behind the news" with an analysis of prevailing institutions, issues, and events from a democratic socialist viewpoint. While focused on local issues, it often published articles of a wider interest. Deb and/or I served on the editorial board and/or production staff for every issue. Under the pseudonym of The Cat I wrote a column "Scratching in the Dirt" which appeared in almost every issue. I also wrote approximately 25% of the articles over the lifetime of *LEFT OUT*. At its height we had almost 200 subscribers, about a third were paid subscribers. After six years of continuous publication, *LEFT OUT* died of natural causes with the May/June 1993 issue.

- June 12—President Ronald Reagan makes his famous speech at the Berlin Wall wherein he challenges Soviet leader Gorbachev to "… tear down this wall."

- November 3—Election day for my second run for Santa Barbara City Council. I finished eighth out of 12 candidates and received 1,887 votes—10.2% of the voters chose me as one of their three choices. My campaign raised $5,525.

1988 (36)

- January—I gave a talk in San Luis Obispo, California on "Running Openly as a Socialist in Local Elections." Twelve hundred, I mean 12, people attended.

- May 28—Deb and I received "Special Thanks" for our work on the 5th annual "The Prom That Dare Not Speak Its Name," sponsored by the Santa Barbara Gay & Lesbian Resource Center. Deb served on the Santa Barbara Gay & Lesbian Resource Center Board of Directors from 1985 through 1988.

- June 7—I was elected to the Santa Barbara County Peace and Freedom Party Central Committee and served as Chairperson of the Committee.

- November 8—Rent control loses in Santa Barbara election 60% to 40%. This is the 4th loss at the polls for rent control in ten years. Through our membership in the Santa Barbara Tenants Union, Deb and I worked for months for rent control.

1989 (37)

- March—Using concepts from his earlier hypertext systems, British engineer and computer scientist Tim Berners-Lee wrote a proposal for what would eventually become the World Wide Web. His breakthrough was to marry hypertext to the Internet. From this humble beginning less than 25 years ago, the majority of the planet's population at least knows of, if not utilizes, the Web.

- November 9, 1989—Fall of the Berlin wall and the beginning of the end of political divisions between East and West Europe. The German Democratic Republic (East Germany) constructed the Wall in 1961. The East German government claimed the Wall was erected to prevent western "fascist elements" from influencing East German. In reality, the Wall circumvented East Bloc emigration and defections to the West. Before the erection of the Wall approximately 3.5 million East Germans fled to the West. During the Wall's existence the flood of eastern immigration was reduced to a trickle—about 5,000 people attempted to escape over or under the Wall. Between 100 and 200 were killed in the attempt.

1990 (38)

- 1990—From this year to the present, Deb and I spend most vacation time exploring the desert areas of California, Arizona, Nevada, and Utah. Very part-time desert rats.

- January—I was promoted to Editorial Director of *Current World Leaders* at the International Academy at Santa Barbara.

- Spring—5th (and last) Annual Santa Barbara Socialist Sports Festival and Awards Ceremony sponsored by the Socialist Party/Solidarity, Santa Barbara Chapter. Deb and I hosted the festivities at our house and which was clearly the highlight of the spring season for Santa Barbara area socialists and fellow travelers. We featured six events (table tennis, checkers, darts, basketball, cube building, and water balloon toss) and top three finishers won a prize. As a nod to political correctness, all participants received a certificate suitable for framing. It was great fun to observe the underlying competitive Socialist nature.

- June 5—I was elected to the Santa Barbara County Peace and Freedom Party Central Committee and served as Chairperson of the Committee.

- June 8—Under the provisions of the Freedom of Information Act, I requested copies of any and all files maintained by the Federal Bureau of Investigation (FBI) relating to me. (See July 24, 1990 for their reply.)

- July 24—The Federal Bureau of Investigation (FBI) replies to my June 8, 1990 Freedom of Information Act request by saying that "A search at FBI Headquarters of our electronic surveillance indices, as well as the indices to our central records system files, revealed no record responsive to your Freedom of Information-Privacy Acts request other than your previous request and our response to you dated September 2, 1976." What does a guy have to do to get noticed by the FBI? Ten years of solid radical political work means nothing to them?

1991 (39)

- December 26—The formal dissolution of the Soviet Union. Marxism-Leninism had a short run in the overall scheme of human history.

1992 (40)

- 1992—I was listed in the 4th edition of *Who's Who in Writers, Editors & Poets: United States and Canada 1992-1993.*

- February 29—Representing the Peace and Freedom Party, I spoke at a meeting of the Santa Barbara Junior Statesmen of America. Also speaking were representatives of the Libertarian Party and the Green Party. About 25 people attended.

- May 2—May Day picnic at a local park organized by the Santa Barbara Socialist Party/Solidarity Chapter. About 40 people attended. I spoke along with a Green Party representative and a labor union official.

- June 2—I was elected to the Santa Barbara County Peace and Freedom Party Central Committee and served as Chairperson of the Committee.

- July—I self-published *The New Alliance Party: A Media Analysis* as the Chairperson of the Santa Barbara County Peace and Freedom Party Central Committee. The New Alliance Party (NAP) was an undemocratic, hierarchical organization (many labeled a cult) that for several years attempted to take control of the Peace and Freedom Party. This analysis consisted of a collection of 17 independent left newspaper and journal articles discussing and criticizing NAP.

- October—The Santa Barbara Peace Fund Escrow Account ceases to exist due to lack of interest. War tax resistance deposits are returned to their owners.

- November 3—Democrat Bill Clinton wins the presidential election in a three-way race against Republican George Bush and Independent H. Ross Perot. Clinton captures 43% of the popular vote with Bush at 37% and Perot at 19%.

1993 (41)

- January—I began serving as an Advisory Board member of *ABC Poli Sci*; published by Santa Barbara-based ABC-Clio. I served as an Advisory Board member until 1998.

- March—Deb and I founded Pacifica Communications—our own company to publish *Guide to Political Videos*. The *Guide*, published bi-annually, included descriptions/reviews of political (broadly defined) videos; distributor/producer, title, price, and advertiser indexes; and full bibliographic and ordering information. We did all the work—contacting video distributor/producers; data entry; editing; layout and graphics; marketing; and fulfillment.

- May/June—Last issue of *LEFT OUT* published. It died of natural causes.

- May/June—After playing in tournaments for a couple of years, Deb and I achieved United States Table Tennis Association national rankings. We played doubles and singles and my highest ranking was #885; Deb topped out at #1,209. That

253

doesn't sound very good, but hundreds of players were ranked below us (*Table Tennis Today*. May/June 1993).

1994 (42)

- January—Deb begins serving on the Board of Directors of the Santa Barbara Metropolitan Transit District. She served until 2002 and was chairperson from March 1997 to March 1998 and March 2001 to March 2002.

- December 31—I let my membership in the Socialist Party, USA expire.

1995 (43)

- Spring—I was listed in the 25th edition of *Who's Who in the West*.

- June 7—The local daily newspaper, the *Santa Barbara News-Press*, published my essay titled "Rational discourse in discussing immigration," that strongly criticized a previous article supporting massive open door illegal immigration. This and two letters to the editor also dealing with illegal immigration published over the next 10 months leads to numerous discussions with my friends, acquaintances, socialist "comrades," and strangers concerning illegal immigration. Overwhelmingly (70-80%) people agreed with my analysis—including three or four socialist friends.

- July 27—The weekly local newspaper, *The Santa Barbara Independent*, published my letter to the editor titled "No Victims Allowed," which criticizes a previously published essay supporting illegal immigration.

- October 23—Thomas Smith Garrison (my father) died.

1996 (44)

- January 25—Pacifica Communications wins the *Business Digest* (Santa Barbara) magazine's Best of Business Award in the category of Communications.

- April 13—The local daily newspaper, the *Santa Barbara News-Press*, published my letter to the editor titled "Let's have reasoned debate on immigration issue."

- November 5—Democrat Bill Clinton wins re-election with 49% of the popular vote. Republican Bob Dole receives 41% and Independent H. Ross Perot gathers 8% of the popular vote.

- December—Pacifica Communications dies. We never made more than a couple of thousand dollar profit in any year and it was killing us to work full-time jobs and then come home and do Pacifica Communications work part-time for years.

1997 (45)

- Spring—I was listed in the 1st edition of *Who's Who in the Media and Communications*.

- August 27—I joined the national Libertarian Party. Around this time I also registered to vote in California as a Libertarian Party member.

1998 (46)

- Spring—I had a part-time job as editor of Santa Barbara Electric Transportation Institute (SBETI) magazine. I edited one issue of *SBETI Currents* (Spring 1998; Volume 3, Number 1).

- Spring—I was listed in the 27th edition of *Who's Who in California* (1998-1999).

2000 (48)

- January 1—Y2K and the world did not end.

- January—My essay, "Why I Left the Left," was published in *Liberty* magazine (a libertarian publication). This sparked many discussions with friends and "comrades" (some, after this article was published became former—they wanted nothing to do with a leftist traitor).

- May 1—I quit my position at the International Academy at Santa Barbara (the company had been slowly dying for years) and was hired as a Clerk III at the Santa Barbara County Assessor's Office.

- May 26—Deb and I purchase our 1st investment condo in Bakersfield, California. It is an 816 square foot, two bedroom, one bath unit in a small complex into which my mom moved and lives there today.

- June 12—I was promoted to Real Property Appraiser I at the Santa Barbara County Assessor's Office.

- July 9—I earned a Real Estate Salesperson License from the California Department of Real Estate.

- August 11—I earned a Certified Property Tax Appraiser certification from the California State Board of Equalization.

- November 7—In only the fourth presidential election in which the popular vote winner did not win a majority of the electoral votes, Republican George W. Bush defeated Democrat Al Gore 271 electoral votes to 266 electoral votes. In the popular vote Gore received 48.4% and Bush 47.9, with Green Party candidate Ralph Nader at 2.7%.

2001 (49)
- June 12—I was promoted to Appraiser II at the Santa Barbara County Assessor's Office.

2003 (51)
- October 20—Deb and I purchase our 2nd investment condo, a two bedroom, one bath unit in Laughlin, Nevada.

2004 (52)
- January 9—My sister, Kathy Stearman (nee Garrison) died at the age of 53. She suffered a massive stroke more than a year before and steadily deteriorated. She was a good person and good sister.

- Spring—The co-ed softball team on which Deb and I played, The Untouchables, wins the championship of the Santa Barbara Recreation League.

- November 2—In a second close election, Republican George W. Bush is re-elected and defeats Democrat John Kerry 51% to 48%.

2005 (53)
- January 31—Bill Hanson, good friend and one of my professors at California State College, Bakersfield, died.

- February 16—Deb and I purchased our 3rd investment condo and the 2nd one in Laughlin, Nevada. It is an 810 square foot, two bedroom, and one bath unit.

- June 28—I was promoted to Real Property Appraiser III, the highest level and appraiser can attain, at the Santa Barbara County Assessor's Office.

- Summer—The co-ed softball team on which Deb and I played, The Snot Rockets, (we did not chose the name) finishes in 2nd place in the Santa Barbara Recreation League.

- Fall—The co-ed softball team on which Deb and I played, The Snot Rockets, wins the championship of the Santa Barbara Recreation League.

- December—Deb and I sent our first "theme" Christmas letter— "A Christmas Mystery." Pretty clever if I say so myself. We have continued this, now tradition, to the present.

2006 (54)

- March 7—I earned an Advanced Certified Property Tax Appraiser certification from the California State Board of Equalization.

- May 24—I sent my infamous "No Carrots, No Sticks" email to all the top management in the Santa Barbara County Assessor's Office. In it I detailed my complaints/concerns about the work environment. Did my challenging the system change anything? In the long run, no. The problems I detailed continued until I left in October 2009.

2008 (56)

- November 4—The first black (actually half black) person, Democrat Barak Obama, is elected president with 53% of the popular vote. He defeated Republican John McCain who received 46% of the vote. The Republican Party nominated a woman, Sarah Palin, for vice president. The Obama and McCain campaigns combined spent more than $1 billion.

2009 (57)

- July 31—The Serials Division of ABC-Clio, of which Deb was the senior manager, disappears. No, not abducted by aliens, but shut down by a decision of the owner and top management. Approximately 35 people, including Deb, lost their jobs. Deb had been employed at ABC-Clio since 1979. She started as a production typist/proofreader and worked her way up to a division senior manager.

- October 2—My last day of work at the Santa Barbara County Assessor's Office. I quit, moving to St. George, Utah. Also escrow closed and the appropriate documents were recorded for the sale of our Santa Barbara house. We were very happy to leave the old 'hood behind.

- October 19—Deb and I bought a new house in St. George, Utah. We paid cash and are totally debt free.

- November—We send out our first "what we are thankful for on Thanksgiving" list. A nice mixture of humor and seriousness. It has become an annual tradition.

2010

- January—Deb was hired as the Dixie State College library (soon to become Dixie State University) weekend circulation supervisor—a perfect job since she knew about libraries from her previous employment and it was part-time.

- March 23—Deb and I purchase our 4th investment condo; this one in St. George, Utah. It is a 923 square foot, two bedroom, one bath unit in an eight unit complex. We paid cash and are totally debt free.

- December 19—My essay "Limited government: Privatize liquor sales" is published by *The Salt Lake Tribune*. This is the first of 40 essays (as of November 2013) I have published in the *Tribune* or the local daily newspaper, *The Spectrum*, over the next three years.

2012 (60)

- April 20—We received a letter from St. George Mayor Daniel McArthur that read in part "I would like to take this opportunity to let you know how much we as a city appreciate the care you have taken to maintain your beautiful landscaping. … It is truly a pleasure to walk by your home." Deb and I have spent considerable time and energy (plus a bunch of money) to create an attractive and semi-xeriscape landscape.

- June 13—My essay "Connections" wins first prize in the River Work Writing Contest adult non-fiction category. While winning a few other contests for writing, this is the first one that was accompanied by serious monetary award—$250. The essay described the Virgin River as the nexus for many connections, and how exploring the river and riparian environment brings these connections to life.

- July—My ebook *Why We Left the Left: Personal Stories by Leftists/Liberals Who Evolved to Embrace Libertarianism* was published. I was the compiler, editor, and essay contributor. I worked on this project for about a year. The book examines a political question that intrigues almost everyone who studies, participates, or is interested in politics: "Why do people identify with a certain ideology and/or political party?" Numerous scholarly and popular books examine political ideology/party identification and why certain ideologies attract certain individuals. This book examines that question in two separate, yet joined phases. Why do people initially identify with the Left/liberalism and why do these same individuals abandon that ideology to evolve into libertarians? This inquiry is unique in its focus on 23 former liberals/leftists who become libertarians.

- November 6—Democrat President Barak Obama is reelected with 50.6% of the popular vote. He defeats Republican Mitt Romney who receives 47.9% of the vote. Combined the two major party campaigns spent more than $2 billion. Libertarian Party candidate Gary Johnson, former two-term governor of New Mexico, received approximately 1% of the vote, or 1.2 million votes.

2013 (61)

- April 10—Dr. Charles McCall died. He was first my teacher and then a friend since my undergraduate days at California State College, Bakersfield.

- September—I begin volunteering once a week at PAWS (Providing Animals With Support), a nonprofit, nongovernmental, no kill animal shelter.

Another Book by Tom Garrison

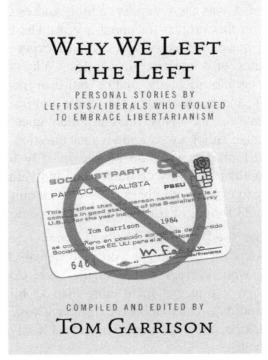

Why We Left the Left: Personal Stories by Leftists/Liberals Who Evolved to Embrace Libertarianism is available in ebook and paperback formats. The book examines a political question that intrigues almost everyone who studies, participates, or is interested in politics: "Why do people identify with a certain ideology and/or political party?" Numerous scholarly and popular books examine political ideology/party identification and why certain ideologies attract certain individuals. This book examines that question in two separate, yet joined phases. Why do people initially identify with the Left/liberalism and why do these same individuals abandon that ideology to evolve into libertarians? This inquiry is unique in its focus on 23 former liberals/leftists who become libertarians.

One popular conception of libertarians is that they are, for the most part, disgruntled old white guys. While that group is represented, more than 25 percent of the stories are from women and more than two-thirds are by people younger than 50. This gender and generational diversity extends to occupations—contributors include college students, law students, an attorney, a professional artist, public school teachers, a chemist, writers, a filmmaker, a law professor, a stay-at-home mom, a firefighter, the CEO of a $40 million company, a TV reporter, an editor, the CEO of a free market environmental think tank, and a research engineer.

The print and ebook versions of ***Why We Left the Left*** can be found in most estores.

Address all inquiries to Tom Garrison at: whywelefttheleft@yahoo.com. Consider visiting the ***Why We Left the Left*** Facebook page. Your comments are welcome.

Made in the USA
Las Vegas, NV
09 May 2021